Representations of Black Womanhood on Television

Representations of Black Womanhood on Television

Being Mara Brock Akil

Edited by
Shauntae Brown White and
Kandace L. Harris

LEXINGTON BOOKS
Lanham • Boulder • New York • London

Published by Lexington Books
An imprint of The Rowman & Littlefield Publishing Group, Inc.
4501 Forbes Boulevard, Suite 200, Lanham, Maryland 20706
www.rowman.com

6 Tinworth Street, London SE11 5AL, United Kingdom

Copyright © 2019 by The Rowman & Littlefield Publishing Group, Inc.

All rights reserved. No part of this book may be reproduced in any form or by any electronic or mechanical means, including information storage and retrieval systems, without written permission from the publisher, except by a reviewer who may quote passages in a review.

British Library Cataloguing in Publication Information Available

Library of Congress Cataloging-in-Publication Data

Names: White, Shauntae Brown, editor. | Harris, Kandace L.
Title: Representations of black womanhood on television : being Mara Brock Akil / edited by Shauntae Brown White and Kandace L. Harris.
Description: Lanham : Lexington Books, 2019. | Includes bibliographical references and index.
Identifiers: LCCN 2019019932 (print) | LCCN 2019021930 (ebook) | ISBN 9781498592673 (Electronic) | ISBN 9781498592666 (cloth : alk. paper) ISBN 9781498592680 (pbk: alk. paper)
Subjects: LCSH: Akil, Mara Brock, 1970– Criticism and interpretation. | Women television producers and directors—United States. | African American television producers and directors. | African American women screenwriters. | African American women on television.
Classification: LCC PN1992.4.A338 (ebook) | LCC PN1992.4.A338 R47 2019 (print) | DDC 791.4302/32092—dc23
LC record available at https://lccn.loc.gov/2019019932

∞™ The paper used in this publication meets the minimum requirements of American National Standard for Information Sciences—Permanence of Paper for Printed Library Materials, ANSI/NISO Z39.48-1992.

Printed in the United States of America

For all black women everywhere . . . stay true to yourself. For authenticity is not only magical, but infinite.
—*SBW and KLH*

For Nia and Kai, your authentic voice matters. In loving memory of the Rev. Dr. Kathryn G. Brown, your voice inspired many in their quests for true womanhood.
—*SBW*

For my parents—my late father, James and my mother, Cherry. Thank you for seeing me, listening, and encouraging me to never be silent.
—*KLH*

Contents

Foreword ix
Imani M. Cheers

Introduction: Being Mara 1
Kandace L. Harris

PART I: REPRESENTATIONS OF BLACK WOMANHOOD 11

1 "*Girlfriends*—There, Through Thick and Thin!": African American Female Sisterhood and the Quest for Happiness 13
  Tina M. Harris and Katie D. Scott

2 The Complex Girlfriend: Toni Childs as a Hybrid Controlling Image on *Girlfriends* 33
  Shavonne R. Shorter

3 Real, Respectable, or Both: Respectability on *Being Mary Jane* through the Words of Mara Brock Akil 47
  Natasha R. Howard

4 "Girl, You Know I Got You": The Ideology of Sisterhood on *Being Mary Jane* 67
  Shauntae Brown White

5 What *Love Is* ___ and Is Not: A Critical Discourse Analysis 87
  Roslyn M. Satchel

PART II: AUDIENCE RECEPTION/SOCIAL MEDIA INTERACTION   109

6   Relating to *The Game*: Meaning Making Among Fans   111
Lisa M. Paulin

7   Race, Gender, and Participatory Dynamics: Facebook Representations of *Being Mary Jane*   133
Mia Moody-Ramirez

8   Social TV and Stereotypes: The Social Construction of #BeingMaryJane on Twitter   153
Morgan W. Smalls

9   @MaraAkil: An Analysis of Mara's Balance of Life, Family, and Production on Instagram   177
Candace P. Parrish

Afterword: What Representations and Racial Messages Television Teaches Our Children   191
Ronald L. Jackson II

Index   195

About the Contributors   199

Foreword
Imani M. Cheers

For the first time in close to three decades, Black women are starring in leading roles not only in films, sitcoms, and dramas but also as showrunners, directors, writers, and executive producers of some of the most successful programs across viewing platforms. Along with the increase in media ownership, think Oprah's OWN and Cathy Hughes' Radio One, a surge in visual representation and ownership is directly related to the political, social, educational, and economic progress made by Black women in the United States in the last half a century. From Michelle Obama, Kamala Harris, and Stacey Abrams to Oprah Winfrey, Issa Rae, and Regina King to Johnnetta B. Cole and Angela Davis, Black women are the leading cultural, political, and social influencers.

Mara Brock Akil is a creative connoisseur and a sensational storyteller. Her ability to create rich, complex, and engaging characters is unparalleled. She began her career writing on shows such as the critically acclaimed yet short lived *South Central*, and then moved into a producer role on fan favorites *The Jamie Foxx Show* and *Moesha*. Brock Akil knew the power in ownership and creative control of her work and started her first production company Happy Camper Productions in the late 1990s. Her first project, the beloved *Girlfriends*, effectively challenged stereotypes and pushed boundaries in the wake of predecessor *Living Single* and at the height *Sex and the City*.

Brock Akil didn't need to compete. Her almost cult-like following was immediate due to the familial characters she introduced to an audience eager to see themselves on the small screen and embrace their fictional besties. Black women are magical. Literally, noire pixy dust in tangible form and Brock Akil knows how to celebrate our triumphs and tribulations. From Joan and Toni to Melanie and Tasha and Mary Jane Paul, these characters embodied the struggles and success that Black women face on a daily basis both personally and professionally. At a time when Black women's voices are too often marginalized and silenced, Brock Akil has been at the forefront of empowering unity and solidarity, through her visual representations of #BlackGirlMagic.

It is no coincidence that in September 1968 Diahann Carroll debuted in the TV series *Julia* and became the first Black woman to portray a professional, while across the country in New York, Shirley Chisholm became the first Black woman elected to the U.S. Congress. The social, political, and economic parallels of the last fifty years are connected to Black women's control of their visual representation. When Black women own their creative television representation specifically, their unique lived experiences create dynamic stories that cross racial and cultural boundaries.

I grew up immersed in Black culture and history; my father was a photojournalist for *Jet/Ebony Magazine*; so the first images of Black people I saw where in a publication created by Black people for Black people. That distinction is imperative; representation *matters* but the *ownership* of that representation is critical. Brock Akil has given a generation of Black women creatives a blueprint of Hollywood endurance and perseverance. From media ownership (she is co-owner of Akil Productions with her husband Salim Akil) to television representation (*The Game, Being Mary Jane, Love Is___, Black Lightening*) Brock Akil is an industry powerhouse, a beacon of creative energy #rootingforeverybodyblack.

Being Mara is timely, yet overdue. There has not been a comprehensive analysis of Brock Akil's body of work and contributions to the field. It's necessary that Black women are at the forefront of this television scholarship. Congratulations to the editors and contributors, this is a rewarding homage to one of the greatest television creatives in the industry.

In solidarity and respect,
Imani M. Cheers, PhD.

Introduction

Being Mara

Kandace L. Harris

This edited volume came to fruition from a 2016 National Communication Association convention panel in Philadelphia. Following our panel, *"Being Mary Jane/Being Raced and Gendered": Civic Callings for a Responsible Media in Representing African American Women on the Small Screen*, we could not help but acknowledge the interwoven theme of authenticity in representation in each presentation on the popular Black Entertainment Television (BET) series. In its third season at that time, *Being Mary Jane*, starring Gabrielle Union, was a ratings success, averaging 2.6 million weekly viewers since its premiere in July 2013. The series followed Mary Jane Paul, a successful television news anchor who is balancing her career, family, and a love life. Paul continues to soar professionally; however, she is unable to find the perfect mate. With the working title of *Single Black Female*, the show was based on the heavily reported statistic that "42 percent of African-American women have never been married." Mara Brock Akil, *Being Mary Jane's* showrunner and executive producer, said in a *Vanity Fair* interview that Mary Jane's semi-singledom over the course of three seasons was intentional (Mercer 2015). "It's one woman's story of looking inward and defining her own idea of happiness when confronted with a crumbling white picket fence" (par 7). This challenge to what defines happiness for women who may choose their careers over conventional relationships resonated with viewers, and particularly Black women. In her article, *In Defense of Being Mary Jane and Flawed Fictional Black Women*, Harris (2014) applauded Brock Akil for proving time and time again that she knows how to tell a good story about Black women. Harris characterizes Brock Akil's *Being Mary Jane* as "an unapologetic look at a flawed protagonist whose interior drastically conflicts with the perfectly manicured exterior" (par 5). She described the series as relatable, obsessively entertaining, and necessary for Black women longing to unleash their vulnerability.

For over twenty-five years, Mara Brock Akil has explored Black women's and Black men's experiences with purpose. As a writer for television sitcoms *The Jamie Foxx Show* and *Moesha*, and the creator and executive producer of *Girlfriends* and *The Game*, she has collaborated on and chose projects that feature majority Black casts and make a concerted effort to empower and uplift Black voices (Pearson 2018). Yet, despite her successful track record for creating one of BET's highest rated shows, some critics have questioned Brock Akil's name not being mentioned in the same sentence as *Scandal* and *How to Get Away with Murder*'s Shonda Rhimes (Williams 2015). However, for Brock Akil notoriety is not the measure of her success.

> There aren't a lot of lights or big marquees around my name or my work, yet my core audience knows exactly where I am. We've been having a conversation through the work for years. We've been here, we are here, and we'll always continue to be here. . . . I used to want to make sure that the powers that be could see value in us. Now I'm over it because that ain't my problem anymore. . . . It's really not my job anymore to make people see our value. (Kameir 2016)

While Brock Akil praises the work of Rhimes and her larger-than-life characters like Olivia Pope, she tries to deliver portrayals of Black women that are subtle and complex, stories that hit a little closer to home (Smith 2015).

In the forward of a 2017 study by Darnell Hunt, *Race in the Writer's Room*, Brock Akil noted that not seeing her herself, her mother, sisters, friends, and men in her life on television has influenced her scripted work to be "a documentary of Black people's existence" stretching out the distorted depictions, and shading in the Black people's complex humanity. In her book, *Representations of Black Women in the Media: The Damnation of Black Womanhood*, Gammage (2015) argues that Blacks in media production, like Brock Akil, must take special interest in inserting the real voices and perspectives of everyday Black women, and not reproduce the same manufactured images:

> Black women must play a key role in defining authentic Black womanhood. The Black woman's perspective must guide all attempts to represent her life in the media. Failure to do so will result in the same stereotyped imagery that currently corrodes popular media. Black women's voices are unique and diverse and deserve appropriate attention. They can no longer serve as the objects of sexual fascination, symbols of immorality, and cheap labor. (152)

She asserts that contemporary media provide a venue to promote an anti-Black woman agenda that constantly assaults African American humanity through stereotypical portrayals of Black women in current popular representation and perceptions of Black womanhood. Yet, she also notes that networks rely on Black viewership, and it is imperative that for Black viewers who are not satisfied with the images produced, to demand shows and programs that more accurately speak to their needs as consumers. This is especially pertinent to Black women as they, and their spending power, play a vital role in influencing mainstream culture in fashion, beauty, television, music, and civic engagement for women of all races (Finley 2017).

Cheryl Grace, senior vice president of U.S. strategic community alliances and consumer engagement at Nielsen, believes it is important to understand how Black women's strong life-affirming values affect what they buy, watch, and listen to. "Marketers must recognize the intercultural influence of Black women on the general market as an increasingly vital part of how all women see themselves, their families and the rest of the world" (Grace as cited by Estrada 2017). Brock Akil has "actively worked to tear down stereotypes of black women, whereas most shows would continue to portray black women as angry, bitter, and vindictive" (Pearson 2018, par 4). In a 2016 interview, Brock Akil explained:

> I approached *Girlfriends* almost like a documentary of our existence, what we were thinking about at the time. What we were thinking about not only our friendships, but what we were thinking about our dreams, whether that included marriage or not, what we thought about sexuality, what we thought about the workplace, what we thought about being sometimes the only black person in the workplace, or because you were the only two black people in the workplace, you decided to be friends. . . . That friendship was born out of that experience. Those were the things I wanted to talk about. I wanted to put us at the table. (Bierly 2016, par 5)

On-screen representation serves as an important way to glean information about the world (Boboltz and Yam 2017). In that, representation matters.

As one of the several Black women showrunners on television today, Brock Akil gives viewers authentic and relatable viewpoints that could only come from a Black woman, and the television industry as a whole seems to recognize that African American women are capable of running and delivering a show (Toby 2016). During the 2015–16 television season, broadcast network programs became more racially and ethnically diverse, resulting in Black female characters increasing from 17 percent in 2015–2016 to 21 percent (Lauzen 2017). A 2017 Nielsen analysis of television viewership found that several programs with a predominantly black cast or a main storyline focusing on a black character were drawing substantial non-black viewership, crossing cultural boundaries to grab diverse audiences and start conversations (Nielsen 2017). Notably, in 2016–2017, television shows and characters on ensemble series seemed to be more "unapologetically Black." Yet, while

Brock Akil's *Being Mary Jane*, Ava DuVernay's *Queen Sugar*, and Issa Rae's *Insecure*, are recent examples of progress, the industry is failing as a whole (Kilkenny 2017). There still needs to be stronger pipelines to onboard more African American women, and men, as showrunners and executive producers (Toby 2016).

According to the Center for the Study of Women in Television & Film, women only accounted for 27 percent of all creators, directors, writers, producers, executive producers, editors, and directors of photography working on broadcast network programs in 2016–2017 (Lauzen 2017). This becomes even more problematic when race is examined. In Hunt's *Race in the Writer's Room*, a study by Color of Change, it was found that over 90 percent of showrunners were white with either no women or no people of color working as showrunners on eleven of the study's eighteen broadcast, cable, and digital networks in 2017 (Hunt 2017). In addition, the study also found that Blacks only represented 5.1 percent of television showrunners, and 4.8 percent of writers in 2016–17 television season. Rashad Robinson, the executive director of Color of Change, the civil rights advocacy non-profit that commissioned the study, believes "the outrageous level of exclusion in writers' rooms has real-life consequences for Black people, people of color and women" (Kilkenny 2017). This exclusion contributes to the lack of diversity as Black, and women, showrunners tend to hire more Black, and women, writers. In recent years, social media has been instrumental in taking to task the failures of showrunners, networks, and the industry as a whole—a pressure that can help reinforce the achievements of Rhimes, DuVernay, Rae, Glover, and their peers (Bastien 2017). In the book, *Voices of Labor: Creativity, Craft, and Conflict in Global Hollywood*, Brock Akil says industry diversity is a key issue for her and supposes the need for storytellers, creatives, and executives to be more inclusive or audiences will find it somewhere else:

> People are no longer interested in seeing themselves excluded. They want to be included. If you include them, they will come to the party. I think we're starting to see that through the shows that are becoming successful. If you look at the core of why they're successful, it's that they're telling different stories. (Curtin and Sanson 2017, 27)

Brock Akil also states that technology has made it possible for people who do not find themselves on any of the traditional media seeking out their own stories on newer platforms, a trend that television executives should consider in drawing diverse audiences.

Brock Akil's goal of "creating dynamic characters that look and feel like people [she] knows" (Williams 2015) has her ranked as one of Hollywood's top television showrunners in which her company, Akil Productions, with her husband Salim recently received a three-production deal with Warner Bros. The first project, *Love Is___* premiered on June 19, 2018, on the Oprah Winfrey Network (OWN). Created, executive produced, and inspired by the Akils, the series, a romantic drama, followed a power couple in Black Hollywood. The series was renewed six weeks later, as it ranked as the number one show on cable in its time period with women viewers from the age of twenty-five to fifty-four, according to OWN and Nielsen (Petski 2018). However, *Love Is___* was canceled by OWN in December 2018 amid domestic abuse and copyright infringement allegations from an alleged former mistress against Salim Akil. Brock Akil would post on Instagram the same day as the announcement:

> I am saddened that this great group of #artists and #storytellers will no longer get to create together on this project in this way. This was a special tribe—assembling teams like this is by the grace of God—and I will miss not being on set with them to make more magic. And though I know we will all go on to create more amazing work, I'm grateful there was a moment in time that we came together and had the courage to give our best to try and tell a story about love with love. #InTheLandOf #LoveIs. (Akil 2018)

Followers and fans of the show posted comments on Brock Akil's Instagram page expressing their disappointment and requests for the show to continue. Viewer Tambia Harris (2018) posted, "Please bring this show back!!" while @_herrbeauty (2018) posted, "I have been waiting for THIS show WHY.?!?!. . . .We were getting real TV with substance again. What about what we want as viewers." Although the series was cut short, it did accomplish Brock Akil's goal of "sharing the story of black love with a wider audience" (Turchiano 2018, par 1):

> I don't really think we've really seen the humanity of black love deep enough. I treated the direction of this almost like an independent film or a foreign film because . . . that is how I feel our existence is in this country is. We're foreigners, so we have to tell our stories in ways that celebrate our own beauty and even our own flaws. And we invite the audience into that conversation so it will then open them up and the conversation will evolve.

As editors of the volume, we too were disappointed by the cancellation of *Love Is__*. Brock Akil wanted viewers not only to see the beauty in the flaws of her characters' love story but more importantly embrace the humanity of those characters.

The second project, based on the DC Comics superhero series *Black Lightning*, premiered on The CW on January 16, 2018. *Black Lightning* follows a high school principal challenged with using his superpowers to save his community. Renewed for a second season, Brock Akil, who serves as executive producer, felt it was important for the series to portray a positive narrative for Black men (N'Duka 2018). "Outside in the world, we're talking a lot about black men, and a lot of times the images don't see him as not just a father, but a man loving his women and as a principal, having to be a father to other children" (Brock Akil as cited in N'Duka 2018, par 3). Devereaux (2018) contends that *Black Lightning* deserves all of the praise and attention it has gotten for its dedication to diversity and excellent storytelling. "The show touches on pivotal issues such as racism, political and governmental corruption, police brutality, the inequality of the criminal justice system, the school to prison pipeline, as well as drug and gang issues within groups of lower socioeconomic status" (par 9). She argues that it is evident that the authenticity and intensity of the show are, in fact, intentional.

With twenty-five years of work behind her, it's simple: Mara Brock Akil's body of work explores humanity. With each character creation there is this sensibility of authenticity. "Within our beautiful frailties and flaws is where our humanity exists—between those extremes. No one is perfect. . . . The journey of humanity is to get back up again and keep trying, and I think that is what is beautiful" (Brock Akil as cited Penn 2015). The works in *Being Mara* are theoretically anchored in Patricia Hill Collin's *Black Feminist Thought* highlighting Mara Brock Akil's body of work as trailblazing as it intentionally addresses Black humanity for audiences and specifically provides context for Black women's lived experiences and empathy for their womanhood. The works also critically analyze representations of Black womanhood and explore themes found in audience reception and social interaction online.

REPRESENTATIONS OF BLACK WOMANHOOD

Part I uses Black feminism scholarship to examine representations of Black women, identity, voice, respectability, and friendship. In chapter 1, Tina M. Harris and Katie D. Scott offer a rich analysis of the show *Girlfriends* and its depiction of African American female identity and sisterhood through the characters of Joan, Maya, Lynne, and Toni. Their chapter outlines characters who are very complex with diverse experiences that prevent them from being pigeonholed into troubling tropes that continue to stigmatize African American women. Shavonne Shorter examines a hybrid of the Black Lady controlling images in chapter 2 using thematic analysis of Jill Marie Jones's real estate broker character, Toni, on *Girlfriends*. Natasha R. Howard provides a thematic analysis that interrogates episodes of *Being Mary Jane* for the themes pertaining to Black women's sexuality, relationships, and respectability in chapter 3. In chapter 4, Shauntae Brown White discusses the construction of friendships between women of color on *Being Mary Jane*. White contends that the women on *Being Mary Jane* demonstrate the ethic of caring which includes both holding one another accountable, but also loving each other through each other's flaws and faults. Methodologically driven by critical theories and autoethnography, Roslyn Satchel examines race and gender representations in *Love Is___* in chapter 5. Satchel asserts that while *Love Is___* is a counter-hegmonic narrative that challenges dominant cultural ideologies, she questions the hegemonic treatment of femininity and masculinity with main characters of the series, Nuri and Yasir.

AUDIENCE RECEPTION/SOCIAL MEDIA INTERACTION

Part II of *Being Mara* analyzes audience reception to gain a deeper understanding of audience experience, identification, and engagement. Lisa M. Paulin explores viewership of *The Game* and their navigation of the show's themes in chapter 6. She found that focus group participants believed that *The Game*'s depictions of Black women with varying personalities, ambitions, strengths, and weaknesses were significant and made it distinctive from other shows that had mainly white casts. Chapter 7 investigates the participatory dynamics of online audiences on Facebook during the fourth season of BET's *Being Mary Jane*. Using a Black feminist lens, Mia Moody-Ramirez assesses patterns of social media audience interaction on Facebook. Chapter 7 specifically offers background and context for audience response to Mary Jane's work, family, and personal drama—a critical reflection on the show's characters and an analysis of the comments posted to the popular Facebook page. Morgan W. Smalls, in chapter 8, uses textual and thematic analysis of Twitter to explore the contemporary Jezebel stereotype in *Being Mary Jane*. Smalls argues that despite Mary Jane's relatable characteristics, the treatment of her sexuality brings to mind a modern-day Jezebel, which has the potential to negatively impact the lived expectations of Black women on television, Twitter, and beyond. Finally, in chapter 9 Candace P. Parrish analyzes Brock Akil's use of her personal Instagram account to provide more insight on how she balances and presents her career, motherhood, and life in general to followers. This chapter seeks to help shape not only the narrative of self-representation and performance but also find connections between the creator and producer of the dominant and recurring themes in her shows.

Mara Brock Akil's success is unprecedented for an African American showrunner in television. Her work represents Black women's authentic voices, their humanity, and experiences in negotiating their professional lives, their interpersonal relationships, and their place in the world. Brock

Akil's characters are complex who possess positive traits while also being deeply flawed. More specifically, she creatively speaks to and for Black women, raising the requisite question, "Can she have it all? And, at what cost?" Despite her longevity and success, she remains under the radar in not only name recognition, but also critical analysis. *Being Mara* collectively works to provide a contemporary text that not only highlights her rise to showrunner but also her commitment to diversity on the screen and behind the scenes. More importantly, *Being Mara* is an effort to critically resource Brock Akil's work as a collection that deliberately exhibits the complexities and intricacies of Black women's experiences.

BIBLIOGRAPHY

Akil, Mara. *Instagram post*, December 19, 2018. https://www.instagram.com/p/BrlWr46hLK9/.
Bastien, Angelica Jade. "Claiming the Future of Black TV." *The Atlantic*, January 29, 2017. www.theatlantic.com.
Bierly, Mandi. "Girlfriends' Creator Mara Brock Akil Talks the Real Secret of Black Women on TV". *Yahoo*, October 5, 2016. www.yahoo.com.
Boboltz, Sara, and Kimberly Yam. "Why On-Screen Representation Actually Matters." *Huffington Post*, February 2017. www.huffingtonpost.com.
Collins, Patricia Hill. *Black Feminist Thought: Knowledge, Consciousness, and the Politics of Empowerment.* New York: Routledge, 2000.
Curtin, Michael, and Kevin Sanson. "Mara Brock Akil, showrunner." In *Voices of Labor: Creativity, Craft, and Conflict in Global Hollywood*, by Michael Curtin and Kevin Sanson. Oakland: University of California Press, 2017.
Devereaux, Marielle. "Why Black Lightning Matters". *Affinity*, April 14, 2018. http://culture.affinitymagazine.us/.
Estrada, Sheryl. "Black Girl Magic to Propel Black Spending Power Toward $1.5 Trillion by 2021: Nielsen Report." *DiversityInc*, September 22, 2017. www.diversityinc.com.
Finley, Taryn. "Black Women's Buying Power Is Helping To Define Mainstream Culture." *Huffington Post*, November 22, 2017. www.huffingtonpost.com.
Gammage, Marquita Marie. *Representations of Black Women in the Media: The Damnation of Black Womanhood.* New York, NY: Routledge, 2016.
Harris, Chevonne. "In Defense of Being Mary Jane and Flawed Fictional Black Women." *Huffington Post*, January 10, 2014. www.huffingtonpost.com.
Harris, Tambia. *Instagram post*, December 19, 2018. https://www.instagram.com/p/BrlWr46hLK9/.
_herrbeauty. *Instagram post*, December 19, 2018. https://www.instagram.com/p/BrlWr46hLK9/.
Hunt, Darnell. *Race in the Writers' Room.* Los Angeles: University of California, 2017.

Kameir, Rawiya. "How Mara Brock Akil Plans To Save TV." *The Fader*, April 22, 2016. www.thefader.com.

Kilkenny, Katie. *The Number of TV Episodes Directed by Women and Minorities has Hit an All Time High*. November 2017. www.psmag.com.

Lauzen, Martha M. *Boxed In 2016–17: Women On Screen and Behind the Scenes in Television*. Center for the Study of Women in Television & Film, San Diego State University, 2017.

Mercer, Amirah. "BET's Hit Drama Being Mary Jane Is Redefining Single Womanhood." *Vanity Fair*, November 24, 2015. www.vanityfair.com.

N'Duka, Amanda. "'Black Lightning' EPs On Telling The Superhero's Rebirth Story & Season 2." *Deadline*, April 15, 2018. www.deadline.com.

Nielsen. *For Us by Us? The Mainstream Appeal of Black Content*. February 8, 2017. nielsen.com.

Pearson, Jaylen. "Get to Know the Couple behind The CW's Black Lightning." *Medium*, January 15, 2018. www.medium.com.

Penn, Charli. "Mara Brock Akil: 'Our Truth Is Beautiful, We Are Enough.'" *Essence*, February 19, 2015. www.essence.com.

Petski, Denise. "'Love Is ___' Renewed By OWN For Season 2". *Deadline*, July 31, 2018. www.deadline.com.

Smith, Jada F. "With 'Being Mary Jane,' Mara Brock Akil Specializes in Portraits of Black Women." *New York Times*, October 20, 2015. www.nytimes.com.

Toby, Mekeisha Madden. "Who Run The World? Black Women Showrunners, of Course." *Essence*, November 15, 2016. www.essence.com.

Turchiano, Danielle. "Mara Brock Akil on Celebrating the 'Humanity of Black Love' in 'Love Is___'". *Variety*, June 19, 2018. www.variety.com.

Wiiliams, Brennan. "Why The 'Being Mary Jane' Creator Is About To Become A Household Name." *Huffington Post*, November 6, 2015. www.huffington.com.

Part I

REPRESENTATIONS OF BLACK WOMANHOOD

Chapter 1

"*Girlfriends*—There, Through Thick and Thin!"

African American Female Sisterhood and the Quest for Happiness

Tina M. Harris and Katie D. Scott

As the "embodiment of #BlackGirlMagic" (Bonner 2016), Mara Brock Akil has breathed life into creative works in television that celebrate the diversity, beauty, and richness that reside within African American women. Her career has been driven by an undying commitment to create and develop characters that are "unapologetically black," or as Brock Akil prefers "black on purpose" (Smith 2015). Brock Akil has used her power to create a space where narratives about raced, gendered, and classed experiences are foregrounded in ways that have been all too rare (Vejnoska 2016). She has gained "a tremendous amount of power in the industry" over the course of her career, which is "almost unprecedented for a woman in Hollywood" (Vejnoska 2016), let alone an African American woman. Her career began in 1994, where she quickly rose through the ranks in the television industry. Brock Akil has been an assistant, producer, writer, and executive producer on television shows such as *The Sinbad Show* (1993–1994), *South Central* (1999), *Moesha* (1996–2001), *The Jamie Foxx Show* (1996–2001), *Girlfriends* (2000–2008), *The Game* (2006–2009; 2011–2015), *Being Mary Jane* (2013–2017), and *Black Lightning* (2016–present). Despite not having reached mainstream appeal to the same extent as the amazingly successful and talented Shonda Rhimes, Brock Akil has carved out a much-needed niche in television. A critique of her different shows offers further evidence that she is an underappreciated writer and producer (Johnson 2018) whose work should be valued and recognized for the important role it has played in redefining depictions of African American identity and culture in television.

Brock Akil's creative energies as executive producer have been primarily focused on highlighting the intersectionality of African American women, while also showcasing an ensemble of strong, vulnerable, flawed, and beautifully complex African American characters (Siegel 2004)—mostly women—who are relatable and markedly different from early mass media depictions. Granted, there have been other television shows, such as *The Cosby Show* (1984–1992) *A Different World* (1987–1993), *Living Single* (1993–1998), *Martin* (1992–1997), and *The Fresh Prince of Bel-Air* (1990–1996), that featured a predominantly African American ensemble cast (Smith 2015); however, there were few that specifically explored the inner workings of African American[1] female friendship and sisterhood in the way that *Girlfriends* did. Mainstream audiences had *Friends* (1994–2004) and *Sex and the City* (1998–2004) as visual texts that, in many ways, reflected their experiences as heterosexual Caucasian American young professionals negotiating their professional and personal lives in very entertaining and insightful ways. Unfortunately, their realities lacked the racial coding of blackness (or "otherness") that was so important to African American audiences. The characters' experiences were mostly relatable for their Caucasian American fan base.

According to Smith (2015), "[th]e pictures Akil paints depict fabulous, upwardly mobile women having the same kinds of conversations that Carrie Bradshaw would have with her 'Sex and the City' friends—if any of them were black." In an interview, Brock Akil stated that *Sex and the City* failed among African American audiences because its depictions of African American women were wrong. Brock Akil expressed concerns about these representations and narratives, noting that "there wasn't even an attempt to be inclusive. It was almost like we were invisible" (Bierly 2016). She further explained that Black women become visible "when you are with your own, you are allowed a safe place to be, and your girlfriend is a really rich relationship for you, and nuanced. It was meaningful on a very deep level, and I wanted to express that." Such is the case with Brock Akil's *Girlfriends*. It had a particular appeal for Black[2] millennial women (Johnson 2018), despite Hollywood's failure to bring those experiences from the margins to the center. While the now-defunct UPN network was the leading television network offering viewers diverse television programming, it was commended for providing a space and platform for narratives from African Americans to be heard (Downey 2005). It was a champion in efforts to deconstruct the long-held controlling images of African Americans that became all too common. Audiences were offered a variety of characters that reflected the diversity that exist within this systemically oppressed community.

As previously noted, Brock Akil's *Girlfriends* is a show that reflected UPN's support of diverse programming for African Americans (Downey 2005). In fact, she explained that she was given "carte blanche" "to do something that I had been longing to do" and that she "poured all my passion into" (Siegel 2004). The success of the show is partially due to UPN's and the CW's commitment to diversity; however, it is the artistry, dedication, and commitment of Brock Akil that birthed an historic television show that is groundbreaking in its reflection and celebration of African American intersectionality. *Girlfriends* has characters and storylines that resonate specifically with young African American women who saw themselves reflected in these four diverse characters. As Masters (2012) noted, "Mara knew something about writing strong female characters." This was also evidenced by the subsequent success of her spinoff *The Game*. The thirst for relatable programming was so strong for fans that, when the show was cancelled, they launched a petition that ultimately resulted in the decision by Black Entertainment Television (BET) programming chief Loretha Jones to resurrect the show. This aided the network in garnering "a record-breaking 77 million viewers, the highest basic cable sitcom premiere at that time, and it averaged a 1.79 rating in its fifth season" (Masters 2012). This post-*Girlfriends* success offered further evidence that Brock Akil is an undervalued storyteller whose many stories have yet to be told, and there is a thirsty audience ready to listen and watch (Downey 2005).

THE CASE FOR APPLYING BLACK FEMINIST THOUGHT TO *GIRLFRIENDS*

In an interview about the significance of *Girlfriends* in the fight for accurate media portrayals of African American women, Brock Akil stressed the importance of having programs that showcase the complex and rich nuances of African American sisterhood (Bierly 2016). She further explained:

> Achieving this goal involved approaching the show almost like a documentary of our existence, what we were thinking about at the time. What we were thinking about not only our friendships, but what we were thinking about our dreams, whether that included marriage or not, what we thought about sexuality, what we thought about the workplace, what we thought about being sometimes the only Black person in the workplace, or because you were the only two Black people in the workplace, you decided to be friends, meaning Joan and William [played by Reginald C. Hayes]. That friendship was born out of that experience. Those were the things I wanted to talk about. I wanted to put us at the table. (Bierly 2016)

Brock Akil saw the value of community and relationship within African American sisterhood and chose to reflect and celebrate that in *Girlfriends*. She provided an in-depth and textured understanding of the intricacies and nuances of this close-knit community created by women who were connected to each other for nearly half of their lives.

It is our position that *Girlfriends* offered aspiring, young African American women counterimages that resisted and challenged the longstanding controlling images of African Americans as a whole that have become all too familiar. These tropes have played a critical role in shaping societal and self-perceptions about what it means to be raced and gendered in the United States. This is very troubling given that many of these gendered images (i.e., Mammy, Jezebel, Sapphire, tragic mulatto) can be traced back to colonialism and slavery (Collins 1986, 1989). While many modern depictions of these stereotypes are not as overtly racist as they originally were, they have set the foundation for how society is to perceive and respond to African Americans. In order to destigmatize this community and celebrate its inherent beauty and value, it is imperative that the African American community remains critically engaged in dialogue and scholarship exploring these very important tensions. Thus, it is the goal of our essay to offer an analysis and critique of *Girlfriends* and its depiction of African American female identity, sisterhood, and intersectionality through the characters of Joan, Maya, Lynn, and Toni. We argue that the characters individually and collectively reflect the complexity and richness of humanity that exists within the African American community. Each woman was designed to offer counterimages that resist conformity to the images of Jezebel, Mammy, and Sapphire, among others, that have come to inaccurately represent African American female identity.

We use Patricia Hill Collins' *Black Feminist Thought* (1986) to analyze *Girlfriends* and the ever-evolving sisterhood of these very complex characters who Brock Akil has used as a vehicle for social justice and empowerment in mass media on behalf of African American women who see themselves wholly or partially represented in this very powerful television show. Black Feminist Thought is a framework we use to demonstrate how, as a self-identified feminist, Brock Akil uses mass media to advance the three assumptions of Black Feminist Thought. As a theory, it "affirms the importance of Black women's self-definition and self-valuation," draws "attention to the interlocking nature of race, gender, and class oppression," and "involves efforts to redefine and explain the importance of Black women's culture" (Collins 1986, S16, S19, and S21). Our critique will demonstrate how Brock Akil's positionality as a Black feminist (Montford 2014) informed her creation of *Girlfriends*, which is a narrative that has given voice to the many ways that African American women are subjected to systemic racial and gender oppression. Each character contributes to the interwoven relationships that define who they are as beautifully flawed and incredibly multifaceted women. Individually and collectively, the sisterhood serves as an exemplar of what

African American sisterhood means for women who rarely see themselves affirmed in or validated by the media. To that end, Brock Akil has created a space where African American women can attest to the reality of "triple jeopardy" (i.e., racism, sexism, and classism) in relatable and authentic ways. The end result is a plethora of narratives about intersectionality attesting to the rich intellectual and cultural capital that reside within the African American community. It is our hope that this will inspire others to carry on Brock Akil's tradition of recognizing the shared vision and many voices (Akil 2017) that function to bring African American women together for change in how they are represented in popular culture and society as a whole.

Black Feminist Thought as a Framework

Due to space limitations, we offer a basic definition of Black feminist thought and an argument for its utility in celebrating the work of Brock Akil, specifically the television show *Girlfriends*. Black Feminist Thought "consists of ideas produced by Black women that clarify a standpoint of and for Black women" (Collins 1986, S16). Collins argues that African American women have a unique standpoint, which is oftentimes ignored in feminism as a social movement and in other standpoint theories. Thus, Black feminist thought offers insight into and gives voice to the unique, varied, and underrepresented experiences of a historically marginalized group subjected to double (i.e., race and gender) and triple (i.e., race, gender, and class) jeopardy in all aspects of life (Collins 1989). At its very foundation, Black feminist thought articulates the ways in which "Black women's everyday acts of resistance challenge two prevailing approaches to studying the consciousness of oppressed groups" (Collins 1989, 746), the first being that the less powerful identify with the more powerful and have "no valid interpretation of their oppression." The second assumption is that the oppressed are "less human than their rulers and, therefore, are less capable of articulating their own standpoint" (Collins 1989, 747). These assumptions are inherently flawed, as they negate the personhood of oppressed groups and deny their very existence. Moreover, the oppressor denies and suppresses the very existence of the oppressed because it can lead to the oppressed choosing ways to resist all forms of domination (Collins 1989). This resistance also leads to the oppressor losing its power, which is something the oppressor will avoid at all costs. Given these very troubling dynamics, it is imperative that the standpoints of Black women be included in our theorizing of systemic oppression in our professional and private lives.

Collins identified three key themes of Black feminist thought: (1) the inextricable relationship between "structure and thematic content of thought" regarding "historical and material conditions shaping the lives of its producers"; (2) "Black women possess a unique perception shared by Black women as a group"; and (3) diversity among Black women (i.e., class, region, age, sexual orientation) "has resulted in different expressions of these common themes" (1986, S16). In essence, Black feminist thought is a lens that allows people to better understand that the way we, as members of multiply oppressed groups, think and understand our realities is directly related to our socially constructed identities (i.e., race, gender, sexual, religious). We understand who we are because of the messages received from society, and respond to our realities through those various lenses of oppression. According to Black feminist thought, there are universal themes within the standpoint of Black women that manifest themselves in different ways for these women, thus speaking to the in-group diversity that remains unrepresented in scholarship. Collins argued that it is the role of Black female intellectuals "to produce facts and theories about the Black female experience that will clarify a Black woman's standpoint for Black women" (1986, S16). This includes personal observations and interpretations of those experiences with Black womanhood that surpass essentializing claims and evolve into "different expressions of common themes" to which Black women can relate.

Black feminist thought is critical to scholarship because it provides a platform for articulating the experiences with systemic oppression that are common to African American women. More importantly, it recognizes the value of self-definition and its role in empowering women against systemic oppression in all its forms. As Amoah noted, it is "the practice of narrative" that provides disempowered groups the opportunity to "reclaim their voices" (1997, 85), which is directly related to scholarship on Black feminist thought. Narrative is defined as "the telling of one's own story" (Amoah 1997, 85), and in the case of Black feminist thought scholars they are using their personal experiences as "outsiders within" (Collins 1986) to create a story about the interlocking nature of oppression to which they are subjected as marginalized beings within academe, which is typically white and male dominated. According to Collins, Black feminist thought was and continues to be concerned with the creation of self-generated standings by which to evaluate "Afro-American womanhood" across "a wide range of literary and social science works" (1986, S18).

Similar to communication scholars Bell et al. (2000) and Hill (2016), we accept the call to centralize the resistant communicative experiences of African American women specifically through the use of mass media. We argue that *Girlfriends* is a visual text that Brock Akil created in order to document experiences with oppression that African American women have endured and continue to endure on a regular basis. The four lead characters and their interlocking journeys provide viewers with a safe and affirming space (Bierly 2016) that affords them the opportunity to reflect on and embrace their intersectionality in their journey toward empowerment.

GIRLFRIENDS AS A VISUAL TEXT

Girlfriends tells the story of "four accomplished and yet refreshingly imperfect African-American women in their 20s" (Smith 2015). Over the show's eight seasons, the audience witnesses their individual and collective growth and maturity when faced with such issues as singleness, sexuality, financial crisis, colorism, fibroids, pregnancy scares, marriage, and divorce, among many others. An overarching theme and arc in their story is the sisterly bond that connects the women and inspires them to be a better version of themselves for themselves and each other (Vejnoska 2016). While they clearly have familial networks that are pivotal to their identity development in varying degrees, it is their sisterhood that becomes the most important form of social support for these women that seemingly lasts a lifetime. It is in their "sister circle" where these women allow themselves to be vulnerable and gain perspective on how to best deal with life in a patriarchal and racist society. The women are "fabulous" and "upwardly mobile" as they remain "in a perpetual state of getting their lives together" (Smith 2015).

The central character, Joan Clayton, is the mother-figure of sisterhood. She is an up-and-coming lawyer in her late twenties who is preoccupied with being married. Joan is fairly confident in her abilities as a professional, but she is initially very uncertain about her desire for a "happily ever after." As the group's glue, her home serves as a safe space for women where they socialize, commiserate with, and counsel each other. Toni Childs is an aspiring realtor to the rich and famous and Joan's childhood friend. She is self-admittedly preoccupied with materialism and superficiality and boldly owns this part of her identity. Maya Wilkes is, in her words, an "authoress" (i.e., author) who begins the show married and the mother of one child. She and Joan meet when she is working as Joan's assistant at the law firm. Maya became a teenage mother and wife, and she vacillates between confidence and insecurity as she establishes her identity as an adult. The least "predictable" and conforming of the group is Lynn Searcy, who happens to be a biracial adoptee in a white family. She is a bohemian of sorts who, though highly educated, mooches off of her friends and appears to shirk her responsibilities as an adult. Joan and Lynn met in college. Lynn is known for her sexual fluidity and creative personality, which oftentimes clashes with the beliefs and values of the other girlfriends. Initially, jealousy strains their various relationships as they all vie for Joan's attention and a stronger bond with her; however, they become more comfortable with each other once they recognize their commonalities as African American women. The women eventually forge a sisterhood and bond that affirms their intersectionality as African American women with shared and differing standpoints.

Each of the 172 episodes contributes to the dominant narrative of intersectionality as articulated through the women's sisterhood. While their closeness predates the first episode, it is further forged as they connect over the ongoing evaluations of their communicative experiences with systemic oppression as raced, gendered, classed, and sexual beings. Additionally, it is their deliberate commitment to sisterhood and the African American community that supports our contention that *Girlfriends* is a narrative that embodies the three basic assumptions of BFT (Collins 1986). The characters individually and as a collective stress "Black women's self-definition and self-valuation," direct "attention to the interlocking nature of race, gender, and class oppression," and reflect efforts by Brock Akil and the characters themselves "to redefine and explain the importance of Black women's culture" (Collins 1986, S16, S19, and S21).

CLUSTER ANALYSIS: CRITICAL MOMENTS OF SISTERHOOD AND INTERSECTIONALITY

The focus of our analysis of *Girlfriends* was on sisterhood, and our goal throughout the process was to identify the communicative processes that the characters engaged in with each other that spanned across all eight seasons. The methodology used was cluster analysis. It involved identifying recurring clusters and subterms that emerged from analysis of the data, which in this case was 172 episodes of the show. Our analysis subsequently focused on the intensity of terms (Foss 1989), and the terms were reflective of overarching themes embedded in either a specific episode or in the overall arc of the series. Several clusters were identified that established a general category descriptive of a common theme (i.e., subterm) (Foss 1996) that connoted an affirming and/or empowering message reflective of a worldview of sisterhood as per Brock Akil. This methodology afforded us the opportunity to offer an interpretation and understanding of an artifact we argue is valuable to many African American women. Thus, cluster analysis involved a four-step process: "(1) formulating a research question and selecting an artifact; (2) selecting a unit of analysis; (3) analyzing the artifact; and (4) writing the critical essay" (Foss 1996, 65). According to Foss, "the critic may create a method from a concept or concepts related to the artifact and the question. The question may be a theoretical construct from communication or another field" (1989, 18). Thus, our critique is the result of our question regarding the function of the show *Girlfriends* in reflecting messages of sisterhood and intersectionality. To achieve this goal, the following question was asked in this study: "In what ways do the African American female characters engage in communicative practices that reflect sisterhood and Black feminist thought? And how does this sisterhood contribute to understandings of intersectionality?"

Our analysis resulted in the identification of one dominant cluster, which is support. As with any relationship, there are incidents where the support and connection between the women is strained. The women are usually able to resolve the issue and move forward; however, there are times where they reach an impasse that threatens their bond. Our analysis found that, in general, the women are supportive of each other and work to overcome relationship-threatening differences. There is an element of realism in the individual characters, their sisterhood, and how they manage their relationships. This finding supports our contention that Brock Akil's approach as a storyteller and rhetor has successfully given voice to relatable narratives that portray the qualities of sisterhood and intersectionality unique to African American women. The supportive cluster yielded two categories of subterms reflecting positive messages the women communicated to each other that were indicative of their investment of emotional, relational, and sometimes financial resources into the relationship. Three subterms identify "sites" or contexts of support, and four subterms reference actual types of support the women provide each other. The three sites of support are (1) relational conflict and tensions, (2) relational rules and boundary management, and (3) identity performance. The four types of support (House 1981) are (4) emotional, (5) instrumental, (6) informational, and (7) appraisal/affirmation.

Sites of Social Support

Relational Conflict and Tensions

As a sisterhood and community, the women generally espoused a collectivistic ideology that informed their approach to their individual and collective problems. The women consulted with each other about relationship problems, with men or each other, they believed needed to be either discussed or resolved. There were also unpleasant and difficult confrontations when a girlfriend's behavior was deemed problematic. Three events occurred in Season 6 and episodes 12, 13, and 17. In Season 6 and episode 12 (S6:12), Maya has a difficult yet direct conversation about Lynn's failure to show "follow through." Before this exchange, Lynn expresses concern about being excluded from the panel at Maya's seminar for her self-help book, "Oh Hell Yes." Maya explains that Lynn, as a bohemian and carefree spirit, lacks commitment to her professional goals and other important life decisions. This episode illustrates how the women trust and invest in each other to speak truthfully, even if it may hurt; similar conversations take place with each girlfriend throughout the seasons. They recognize that they only want the best for each other, and though it may be painful to hear, the standpoint of the other girlfriend can only help in the process of self-actualization and empowerment.

Episodes 13 and 17 of Season 6 involve the girlfriends having several conversations with Joan and among themselves about the "new" Joan who is evolving into a shallow, materialistic socialite. Joan has quit her prestigious law firm career and opened her restaurant bar, the J-Spot. The J-Spot's success leads to Joan becoming an "it girl" among Hollywood celebrities and the rich. Her social circle is broadening, which also means she has more dating options, both of which are new for her. The women observe these changes in the "matriarch" of the sisterhood and become increasingly frustrated. Her relational priorities shift from them to her new associates and her multiple dating partners, revealing a struggle Joan faces throughout the show: when she thinks her "happily ever after" is nearby, her focus on the sisterhood wanes. Joan's integrity is compromised, and the girlfriends choose to address their concerns by limiting their contact with her. Eventually, there are direct individual confrontations by Toni and Maya that ultimately result in Joan addressing her lack of loyalty to and investment in the sisterhood. Her absence from the sisterhood and preoccupation with her new status cause a considerable strain for her relationship with a struggling Toni, which Joan regrets albeit too late.

Overall, these patterns of communication that occur within these various sites reflect the women's commitment to the theme of BFT regarding self-definition and self-valuation (Collins 1986). They treat these difficult conflict situations as opportunities for personal growth and increased self-awareness. This is particularly important for them as African American women since they recognize their sisterhood as a safe space for trust and connection. Their interpersonal network is also a place where they can escape from the systemic oppression they regularly face in their professional and personal lives.

Relational Rules and Boundary Management

This second subterm involves communicative exchanges about the need for rules to help them manage their interactions and relationships with each other. In Season 1, there is discussion of the "black girl code" (S1:1) about the women not dating each other's ex-boyfriends. S1:2 involves Joan explaining her three-month rule for dating. She believes that abstaining from sex for three months with a new partner helps determine the quality of the relationship. S1:3 is an episode where Toni becomes angry with Joan for choosing not to join her in a fight when Toni is jumped by a woman at the club. Toni explains that there is an expectation of unconditional support for African American women (i.e., collectivism) that includes physical altercations.

While the scenario was atypical for the women, it allows them to have an explicit communicative exchange about the kind of support they expect from each other that is understood and does not necessarily have to be explicitly expressed; it is just understood.

In S2:3, Joan expresses frustration with the women about how they do not respect the spatial boundaries she has for her home. While her home is deemed the hub of the sisterhood, Maya, Lynn, and Toni arrive unannounced at all hours of the day and night and oftentimes catch Joan off-guard. Joan is disappointed that they assume that they have unlimited accessibility to her regardless of her need for privacy. Season 6 has three episodes (3, 5, and 19) where the women discuss the boundaries that have been crossed and are causing problems in their relationship. S6:3 involves Joan confronting Maya and Lynn about how they take advantage of her financially at the J-Spot when they choose to never pay for their food and drink. It becomes a test of their relationship.

In S6:5, Maya and Lynn discuss the boundaries they have set in order to manage their individual relationships with Joan and Toni. Because Joan and Toni are having trust issues, Maya and Lynn create a rule that forces them to be secretive about the time they spend with Toni (S7:5). Toni is dealing with a pending divorce and a custody battle, and Joan proves to not be dependable, as she is focused on her status as a socialite. The women's relational commitment to each other and the sisterhood is strained, hence the introduction of rules for boundary management. Joan and Toni discuss this one-on-one in S6:19 in relation to Joan's decision to simultaneously date three men. Joan states that "being there" to offer support for each other is at the heart of their friendship.

Season 7 is a tumultuous one for the sisterhood. Joan faces the hard truth about her nearly nonexistent relationship with Toni, while also confiding in Maya and Lynn that "My girlfriends are my family." (At this point, Toni has moved to New York with baby daughter Morgan.) Maya confronts Joan (S7:2) about her covert efforts to reclaim her identity and role as the hub of their friend group. She pointedly accuses Joan of trying "to suck everything back into your great room" and complains about the "the cult of Joan's house." It leads to a genuine conversation about Maya's new role as hub hostess since moving to the suburbs (S7:3). Maya admits it is finally a way to reciprocate the hospitality that Joan has shown her through the years. It is later in the season that Joan (S7:5) has an emotional breakdown over her "breakup" with Toni. Upon learning about Maya and Lynn's secret meetings, Joan feels betrayed and hurt. She eventually admits the depth of the pain she is experiencing over losing her closest friend.

A relational rule the women eventually try to introduce into their sisterhood is whether or not to use the word "bitch" among themselves (S8:3).

Joan and Maya discuss the history of the word and the parallels between it and the n-word. They address how important it is to understand each other's perspectives about the impact that sexism and racism in language choices have on their identities as African American women. Although they do not resolve the issue, the internal conflict Joan and Maya have about whether the word is a slur or term of endearment demonstrates the real-life controversy surrounding words many believe oppress and/or empower historically marginalized groups.

As these exemplars demonstrate, the women are making diligent efforts to adapt their relationship in ways that ultimately serve as a form of empowerment. They recognize that, in order to have healthy relationships with each other, it is imperative that they create and implement rules that provide protection from relational and life stressors, while also affirming who they are as African American women with distinctly different personalities and life goals. The problems that emerge within these episodes demonstrate that there are "historical and material conditions shaping the lives of" these African American women (Collins 1986, S16), thus illuminating for audiences how complex these characters are as well as African American women in real life.

Identity Performance

The third subterm, identity performance, reflects the pressure felt to perform their raced and/or gendered identities within and outside of the sister circle. In episodes 3 and 5 of Season 1, the women communicate about societal expectations that they behave (S1:3) and look (1:5) a certain way in relation to whites. Episode 3 centers on the women's behavior at a club. They discuss the external pressure they feel to conform to societal expectations regarding "performances" of Blackness in the presence and absence of whites. A similar discussion is had about colorism and beauty standards (1:5). Joan and Toni share their heartfelt thoughts on these issues when they call out each other's decision to not date two different men because Toni's friend is "too black" and Joan's friend has very feminine hips. They discuss the superficiality of their reasonings, but then become even more honest about the rejection they feel from the Black community and society at large due to colorism. They describe to each other the hurt they have experienced as a result of this rejection, and immediately affirm one another as a show of support, love, and acceptance.

Maya and Lynn are pressured to perform their racial identities in professional settings, which causes them stress that they try to manage and reconcile. Maya has experiences that reflect the idea of an "outsider within." She is an upwardly mobile woman who moves from working-class to middle-class status as a result of her best-selling novel. It is written from the standpoint of a working-class woman, which made her relatable to her immediate community and other African American women. She feels her writing style and advice are "too black" (S6:6), so she assimilates to dominant culture by adopting a more Eurocentric voice in her writing. She and her family also move to the suburbs in an effort to have a better life. Maya eventually abandons assimilationist ideas and embraces her Blackness as well as her experiences with working- and middle-class cultures. In the next season, Maya revisits these issues (S7:11) when she returns to her old neighborhood. She immediately feels disconnected and out of place. Maya and her husband Darnell eventually decide to move back to the city, which is largely motivated by her need to be physically closer to the sister circle and for her son Jabari to be more connected to Black culture and his old friends (S7:6).

Conversely, Lynn experiences systemic racism when she discovers that the real reason her recording label is not promoting her folksy music is because she does not "sound black" and is not "black enough" (S7:11). She vents her frustrations to Joan and Maya about being forced by society to "check a box" or to clearly identify with either her Blackness or whiteness and not both. This proves troubling for Lynn who is biracial, embraces both parts of her identity, but identifies primarily as a Black woman because of her phenotypic features and cultural experiences. Lynn eventually decides to collaborate with another African American female artist (S7:12) on the label to fight systemic racism and colorism from the ground up. (While the woman is not a part of the sisterhood, her relationship with Lynn speaks to the power of collaboration and social activism relative to Black feminism.)

This theme speaks to the fact that African American women "possess a unique perception shared by Black women as a group" (Collins 1986, S16). They are responding to specific instances of racism and colorism and feel empowered through their sisterhood to directly confront these issues as they arise. Their connection and community provides them with opportunities to engage in perspective-taking as they make sense of their marginalized status in society.

Specific Types of Support

Emotional

Emotional support is a dominant quality of the sisterhood, and nearly every episode of the series offers evidence of how important it is to each of them to give and receive from each other empathy, love, and care. Explicit mentions of the importance of and need for emotional support are present in fifty plus episodes. Because space limitations do not permit a discussion of each, we will provide an overview of some of the issues women deal with that prompt the need for emotional support from the sisterhood.

During Season 1, the women offer support for Joan as she struggles with singleness (S1:1). (This is a recurring issue throughout the series.) They are there when Joan has a pregnancy scare (S1:8) and Maya has a procedure to have fibroids removed (S1:18). As an escape from the stressors of life, Joan initiates a girls trip to Jamaica for Toni (S1:22). Toni also receives support after a setback at work (S2:1) and her subsequent breakup with Greg (S2:7). Joan attempts to offer support to Toni in the form of protection when she has a failed business launch. Joan vows to support Toni as she (S3:24 and 25) begins to plan for her wedding to Todd, who happens to be Jewish. Toni tries to cheer up Joan (S4:13) who is a hopeless romantic spending Valentine's Day alone. During that same season, the women express concern (S4:23) for Toni's well-being when husband Todd leaves her. There is also concern about Lynn (S5:4) when she starts street performing. Regardless of what joys and pains they experience, the women also find time to bond and share secrets (S5:14) and support each other's professional endeavors (S5:15), while also being willing to evaluate whether or not they are providing Joan (S5:16), for example, with the support she needs from their network.

Season 6 begins with Toni/Todd and Maya/Darnell (S6:1) dealing with marital problems (S6:9). Toni asks Todd for a divorce, and, although already married, Maya and Darnell agree to date each other to establish renewed relational intimacy. Joan and Lynn bond as they commiserate about their relationship problems (S6:02). Toni is a new mother and is frustrated and anxious about this new role (S6:03) as well as her impending divorce. She sees herself as a failure, but she finds comfort and support when Maya discloses that she had the same fears when she was a young mother.

In S6:4, Maya defends her loyalty to the sisterhood when Darnell accuses her of spending too much time with them. This episode also involves Maya and Lynn apologizing to Joan for failing to reciprocate her constant support as she works hard to make the J-Spot successful. Later, they have an intervention to save the restaurant (S6:6) and then pool their money together (S6:10), which they present to Joan as a gift and a show of instrumental and emotional support. The season also shows Toni struggle with identity politics (S6:11) as she contemplates whether to raise Morgan as Christian, Jewish, or both. Similarly, Lynn experience identity politics regarding her sexuality (S6:12) when she spontaneously enters into a lesbian relationship with a stranger whom (Jennifer) she saves from suicide. The next few episodes involve the women's growing concern for Lynn's codependency on Jennifer and then them cheering her up over the breakup.

The need for emotional support reflects the diversity of the needs of women. Moreover, this is indicative of the diversity that exists among this group of African American women and those women in the real world. While they do have some commonalities, they have differences relative to class, age, sexuality, and relational needs that supports the theme of BFT that Black women are not monolithic (Collins, 1986); rather, they are a diverse group who express their intersectional identities in very important and powerful ways.

Instrumental Support

The fifth theme of instrumental support refers the provision of financial and tangible resources to each other to fulfill a specific need. They are done out of love and are unconditional. Joan is the most financially stable of them all; therefore, she offers each of them constant financial support. Examples include hosting Maya's vow renewal ceremony (S1:10), allowing Lynn to live with her rent free (the majority of the series), and taking Maya on a shopping spree to distract her from her miscarriage (S8:6). Toni provides similar support to Lynn when she hires Lynn as her personal assistant. Lynn and Maya also provide financial support to Joan (S6:10) when she is unable to continue investing in the J-Spot. These gestures reflect the women's literal and figurative investment in each other's lives.

Instrumental support also involves aiding with specific tasks, such as Joan and Lynn developing and implementing a plan to help get Joan a man (S1:00; S2:9; S6:9) and then break up (S1:5), Toni helping Maya get medical help for her fertility issues (S1:15), and all of them helping Lynn prepare for interviews (S3:5). Maya also hires Toni as a realtor when she and Darnell are house hunting. The women seem to view this as an unwritten rule in their relationship. While offering this assistance sometimes comes as a sacrifice, they do it because they are fulfilling a need for a member of their family.

This theme reflects the ways in which the women reflect on how their intersectionality informs their needs at specific moments in their lives. Moreover, it demonstrates that, as raced, classed, and gendered beings, they have identities that are fluid, which ultimately speaks to the inextricable relationship between "structure and thematic content of thought" (Collins 1986, S16). Thus, the societal structures shaping their realities as African American women empower them as producers of knowledge that ultimately benefits the group and them as women seeking counsel from within their community of sisterhood.

Informational Support

The women also tend to need informational support when they are trying to resolve myriad issues that require assistance from others. Maya, Toni, and Lynn regularly attempt to provide Joan with relationship advice (S1:12, S1:21). Lynn provides Toni will sex advice when she is preparing for her wedding night with Todd (S3:21). There are issues involving ethics and morals that prompt the women to intervene. Examples include Joan revealing Toni's affair to her then-boyfriend Stan (S1:22), advising her about opening her own real estate office, and warning Lynn about becoming "friends with benefits" with their mutual friend William.

Lynn offers Maya informational support (S7:6) when Jabari is acting out and she suspects he is having difficulty adjusting to life in the suburbs and being a Black boy in a predominantly white school and neighborhood. Joan and Maya confront Lynn about her decision to sing karaoke (S7:8) instead of pursuing her music career. A contentious argument ensues, with Lynn accusing Joan of being disappointed that Lynn didn't follow Joan's "master plan" for Lynn's life. Joan says, "You are a grown ass woman down here in Korea Town singing karaoke and calling it a gig, okay. You were . . . stalling. You need to get over your . . . fear of failure or success and get out there and do it for real this time." The trio collectively brainstorms ways for Lynn to launch her music career.

As with instrumental support, informational support is directly related to the intersectional identities of the women. They confide in each other about their problems and end up receiving advice on how to best manage certain aspects of their lives. The advice is coming from a place of love and genuine concern. It is borne from the lived experiences of the girlfriends, which are related to their interconnected identities (Collins 1986, S16). As such, they are able to trust that the advice is sound, appropriate, and trustworthy.

Appraisal and Affirmation

The final subterm, appraisal and affirmation, is a form of support women seek from each other in order to validate who they are as African American professional women in their self-discovery. In Season 1 (S1:2), Maya, Lynn, and Toni encourage Joan to have a one-night stand in order to increase her self-confidence and self-esteem. This theme is also present in Season 3 (S3:19) when they all accompany Joan to a nude beach to support her desire to live what she believes is a "full life."

There is a theme that carries over into several episodes. It speaks to their need for acceptance from each other, and when it is threatened, they allow their jealousy to take over. This is evident when relational tensions reveal Toni's jealousy of Joan's relationships with Lynn and Maya (S1:3). Toni discloses her feelings to Maya in the middle of a conflict, which leads the women to reconciling their differences and realizing it is okay for them to have relationships with each other and Joan.

Another example of this theme is the multiple times the women (S6:12, S7:8, 8:11) encourage Lynn to follow her passion and pursue her music career. They support her by affirming her musical talent and offering advice when she appears afraid to risk being rejected by recording labels. Nevertheless, Maya and Joan go to clubs and karaoke bars when Lynn has a set to validate her identity as a singer. It is with their support and encouragement that Lynn eventually musters the strength and courage to put herself out there, which eventually pays off and leads to her big break.

This theme reflects the need for the women to be accepted and valued by each other, which is primarily supported by their communicative experiences (Bell et al. 2000) and are central to understanding how African American women cope with their subjection to multiple forms of systemic oppression. It is within this private space where they have the unique opportunity to be empowered and affirmed as the complex beings that they are.

DISCUSSION AND CONCLUSION

Currently, there are very few television shows or scripted programs that offer African American women narratives affirming who they are as raced, classed, and gendered beings. Historically, they have been the brunt of racist caricatures, such as the Mammy, Jezebel, Sapphire, and tragic mulatto (Orbe and Harris 2015), and have had to fight against these stereotypes both in mass media and their personal lives. They have been held to an unreasonable standard of conformity that propels them into spaces where they must actively resist the negative tropes that have been ascribed to them (Davis 2015). As we have demonstrated, Brock Akil has done an impressive and very important job in contributing to this movement of resistance by creating the television show *Girlfriends*. She has explained in numerous interviews that it has always been her goal to present narratives that give voice to the diverse and powerful experiences of African Americans in general and African American women specifically that are oftentimes excluded from mainstream media outlets. Nevertheless, Brock Akil has used her Hollywood clout to present audiences with counterimages that showcase the complex and rich nuances of African American sisterhood (Bierly 2016).

Our critique of *Girlfriends* offers evidence that the existence of powerful images in the media serve a greater purpose in society beyond entertainment. These images not only address the issue of inclusivity in programming but they also educate audiences about the social activism that occurs behind the scenes to get these narratives on the small (and big) screen. To support this argument, we used Collins' (1986, 1989, 2000) BFT to demonstrate how Brock Akil used this specific program as a vehicle for social justice and empowerment. Social justice was achieved by Brock Akil using her power to create narratives reflecting intersectional experiences typically marginalized by dominant society. Her characters were inspired by her own lived experiences and observations as an African American woman. Collins' BFT (1986) as a critical lens has demonstrated how a self-identified feminist, Brock Akil, who is also African American, uses mass media to advance the three assumptions of the theory. More specifically, the show "affirms the importance of Black women's self-definition and self-valuation," draws "attention to the interlocking nature of race, gender, and class oppression," and "involves efforts to redefine and explain the importance of Black women's culture" (Collins 1986, S16, S19, and S21). This was evidenced in the themes that emerged from our critique.

Although every episode was not dedicated to race, the characters were faced with situations and circumstances requiring them to use their gender, class, sexual orientation, education, and/or religion, among other identities, as a lens through which to understand and respond. The women sought various types of support from their sister circle that they could get from their other interpersonal networks. An analysis of all 172 episodes lead to an identification of the following types of support: (1) relational conflict and tensions, (2) relational rules and boundary management, (3) identity performance, (4) emotional, (5) instrumental, (6) informational, and (7) appraisal/affirmation. These findings are critical because they demonstrate that Brock Akil purposely and effectively used her positionality as a Black feminist (Montford 2014) to create a very important narrative about African American women and intersectionality. She has provided a platform for stories inspired by the experiences of real African American women seeking representation in mass media. The characters reflect the diversity of these women and how, as Collins (1989) noted, their intersectionality speaks to a rich and diverse culture that thrives in spite of systemic oppression. The sisterhood itself also demonstrates how the collective—as a cultural community—is essential to the knowledge women gain as a result of sharing and learning from each other's lived experiences.

Our critique, along with the other works in this book, provides considerable evidence regarding the importance of both television programs and scholarship that promote an ideology of inclusivity. Systemic oppression in the form of racism, classism, and sexism has attempted to silence those who have been rendered less powerful, as their voices have tremendous potential to societal change profoundly impacting those who have historically benefitted from this power differential. The works of women like Brock Akil offer further evidence that there is a need for producers of knowledge (Collins 1986) in mass media who are dedicated to centering historically marginalized voices (Bonner 2016; Hill 2016). Moreover, there is an imperative for African American communication scholars to engage in scholarship highlighting (and celebrating) the ways that communicative practices of African American women serve the greater function of empowerment and affirmation (Bell et al. 2000; Davis 2015; Hill 2016). Our work will ultimately make an important contribution to the collection of narratives in mass media and academe showcasing the rich intellectual and cultural capital that reside within the African American community.

This goal has been achieved through our application of Collins' BFT (1986) to *Girlfriends*. The show tells the story of an ever-evolving sisterhood among very complex characters. Thanks to Mara Brock Akil, she used her power in the entertainment industry as a vehicle for social justice and empowerment on behalf of African American women who are rarely represented in such powerful and nuanced ways. The theory has allowed us to demonstrate how, as a self-identified feminist, Brock Akil uses mass media to advance the three assumptions of BFT. It is clear that Brock Akil's positionality as a Black feminist (Montford 2014) informed her creation of *Girlfriends* to serve as a narrative giving voice to the experiences of African American women that need to be heard.

NOTES

1. African American and Black are used interchangeably throughout this text. We alternate between the two terms to reflect the fluidity of these identity labels.
2. We have chosen to capitalize Black and use it as a proper noun within this chapter. It is a label that we argue has a positive connotation for many group members, thus affirming the importance of treating it as a proper noun.

REFERENCES

Akil, Mara Brock and Salim Akil. 2017. "TV's Top Producers Talk from the Trenches: 'Being Mary Jane.'" Interview by *Variety,* August 22, 2017. Print, 337 (6): 68–80.

Amoah, Jewel. 1997. "Narrative: The Road to Black Feminist Theory." *Berkeley Women's Journal of Gender, Law & Justice* 12 (1): 84–102.

Bell, Katrina E., Mark P. Orbe, Darlene K. Drummond, and Sakile Kai Camara. 2000. "Accepting the Challenge of Centralizing Without Essentializing: Black Feminist Thought and African American Women's Communicative Experiences." *Women's Studies in Communication* 23 (1): 41–62. doi: 10.1080/07491409.2000.11517689.

Bierly, Mandi. 2016. "Girlfriends" Creator Mara Brock Akil Talks the Real Secret of Black Women on TV." *Yahoo Entertainment,* October 5, 2016. https://www.yahoo.com/entertainment/girlfriends-creator-mara-brock-akil-talks-the-real-secret-of-black-women-on-tv-162849807.html.

Bonner, Lisa. February 2016. "Behind Black Hollywood." *Ebony* 71 (4): 26.

Collins, Patricia Hill. 1986. "Learning from the Outsider Within: The Sociological Significance of Black Feminist Thought." *Social Problems* 33 (6): S14–S32. doi: 10.2307/800672.

Collins, Patricia Hill. 1989. "The Social Construction of Black Feminist Thought." *Signs* 14 (4): 745–773. https://www.jstor.org/stable/3174683.

Collins, Patricia Hill. 2000. *Black Feminist Thought: Knowledge, Consciousness, and the Power of Empowerment, 2nd edition*. New York: Routledge.

Davis, Shardé M. 2015. "The 'Strong Black Woman Collective': A Developing Theoretical Framework for Understanding Collective Communication Practices of Black Women." *Women's Studies in Communication* 38 (1): 20–35. doi: 10.1080/07491409.2014.953714.

Downey, Kevin. February 7, 2005. "UPN's Year-Round Appeal: February is Not the Only Month for Black-Themed Programs." *Broadcasting & Cable* 135 (6): 23.

Foss, Sonja K. 1989. *Rhetorical Criticism: Exploration and Practice*. Illinois: Waveland Press.

Foss, Sonja K. 1996. *Rhetorical Criticism: Essays and Perspectives*. Illinois: Waveland Press.

Hill, Marcus A. 2016. "Do Black Women Still Come First? Examining Essence Magazine Post Time Warner." *Critical Studies in Media Communication* 33 (4): 366–80. doi: 10.1080/15295036.2016.1225968.

House, James S. 1981. *Work Stress and Social Support*. Massachusetts: Adison-Wesley.

Johnson, Victoria. 2018. "Mara Brock Akil on Love is _, Her Marriage, and Why She Isn't 'Begging' for a *Girlfriends* Movie." *Vulture,* June 19, 2018. https://www.yahoo.com/entertainment/mara-brock-akil-love-her-183806240.html.

Masters, Kim. August 17, 2012. "And the Hits Keep Coming: They're Black, Muslim and Gorgeous in an Industry Not Known for its Diverse Embrace. Yet Husband and Wife Salim and Mara Brock Akil Have Made One Hollywood Winner After Another, and Now Have Whitney Houston's Final Film, *Sparkle*, as Their Biggest Bet Yet." *Hollywood Reporter* 418 (28): 46.

Montford, Christina. 2014. "'Being Mary Jane' Producer Mara Brock Akil Urges Women to Use Their Voices, Be Heard." *Atlanta Black Star,* November 24, 2014. https://atlantablackstar.com/2014/11/24/mara-brock-akil-tells-women-use-voice/.

Orbe, Mark and Tina M. Harris. 2015. *Interracial Communication: Theory to Practice, 3rd ed.* California: Sage Publications.

Siegel, Tatiana. November 8, 2004. "Gal Pal: Creator-Executive Producer Mara Brock Akil is Passionate About Her Show's Portrayal of Black Women." *Hollywood Reporter* 386 (23): 18.

Smith, Jada. "Being Mara Brock Akil: Designer of Lifelike Women Has 'An Authentic Way of Writing Black Voices.'" *The Spectator*, November 2, 2015, G3.

Vejnoska, Jill. 2016. "WOMEN'S HISTORY MONTH: Mara Brock Akil Makes Great TV: TV Writer, Producer Enjoys Rare Success as Woman in Hollywood." *The Atlanta Journal-Constitution,* March 22, 2016, D1.

Chapter 2

The Complex Girlfriend

Toni Childs as a Hybrid Controlling Image on Girlfriends

Shavonne R. Shorter

Mara Brock Akil is one of the most well-known writers and producers of the 1990s and 2000s. Brock Akil began her career writing for the FOX series *South Central* and serving as supervising producer on *The Jamie Foxx Show*. But it was arguably her first stint as series creator and co-executive producer of the series *Girlfriends* that catapulted her success. Set in Los Angeles, *Girlfriends* chronicled the lives and interactions of four African American women in their late twenties and early thirties. The popular series ran for eight seasons, with 172 episodes on UPN—which later became the CW in 2006 (Variety 2008).

Series topics focused on their individual love lives, careers, families, and their navigation of all these aspects with the support of each other. Each character had their own unique personality that was meant to resonate with the show's viewership. Sharetv.com provides a detailed biography on each character. Joan Clayton (Tracee Ellis Ross) was the central figure of the show as the women's connections to each other came through her. A high-profile lawyer, Joan would give up her career which was fraught with stress to achieve her dream of opening up her own restaurant. She spent much of the show dating different men, both casually and as a part of more serious relationships, before eventually becoming engaged in its final season. Antoinette "Toni" Childs (Jill Marie Jones) was a childhood friend of Joan's and her college roommate. A real estate agent who eventually goes on to open her own agency, she dated different men but ultimately married, and divorced, Todd Garrett, a white plastic surgeon. Lynn Searcy (Persia White) was also the college roommate of Joan and Toni. She spent her time working odd jobs, never fully committing herself to anything until she decided to form a band.

She was the most free-spirited when it came to relationships as seen through her open talks about having casual sex and dating both men and women. Lastly, there was Maya Wilkes (Golden Brooks), Joan's one-time assistant at her law office. Maya went on to become an author of self-help literature. A divorcee she casually dated throughout the show before reconciling with her ex-husband Darnell. Most of the storylines surrounding Maya focused on her being a single mother to her son Jabari. But what viewers likely did not realize was that the show promulgated characters that represented "controlling images."

CONTROLLING IMAGES ON GIRLFRIENDS

Collins (2004) defines controlling images are stereotypical tropes that depict Black women in a number of degrading ways. Collins shares that controlling images are grounded in slavery and the control that white slave masters had over black female bodies. Indeed controlling images have taken on many forms such as the Mule (hard working field hand who was profitable), Jezebel (sex obsessed seductress), Breeder (woman who has many children that can be sold for profit), Welfare Mother (one who lives off the government and is a bad mother to her children), the Freak (a wild and crazy, sexually limitless woman), the Superstrong Black woman/Superwoman (a strong, independent, woman who manages all aspects of life with ease), and more (Collins 2004, 56). These images have become master tropes in terms of the ways in which the world perceives Black people, specifically women, by way of integrating these images into the medium that undoubtedly has a major impact upon everyday life, the television. Not surprising, some of this imagery would be woven into the personas of the *Girlfriends* characters. Joan represents the "Black Lady," a woman who is educated, successful, and respectable. Lynn with her wild sexual impulses represents the "Jezebel." Maya in her attempt to balance being a working single mother and career woman represents the "Super Strong Black Woman/Superwoman." Yet, upon a cursory analysis it appeared that Toni's character did not fit squarely into the definition of just one controlling image. Instead, Toni was a combination of a many controlling images, representing a hybrid of many of the images aforementioned.

Rhetor Kenneth Burke (1969) argued that the principle of identification is grounded in the need for one person to connect to another through shared experiences. He asserted that language provides the means through which identification takes place and that identification happens through using language as a persuasive force. "You persuade a (wo)man on insofar as you can talk his/(her) language by speech, gesture, tonality, order, image, attitude, idea, identifying your ways with his(hers)" (56). If art is said to imitate life, what shared or lived experience is Brock Akil as creator exhibiting through Toni Childs? The purpose of this chapter is to explore and examine the character Toni Childs, referencing Collins' Black feminist epistemology to analyze who she represents, and to provide commentary on Toni's lived experience.

THEMATIC ANALYSIS

Research examined each episode of the *Girlfriends* series that featured Toni Childs. Although *Girlfriends* aired for eight seasons, Jill Marie Jones, the actress who played Toni Childs, only appeared through the sixth season as she elected not to renew her contract (Pannell 2017). In total 137 episodes were analyzed. All relevant interactions between Toni Childs and the other characters on the show were transcribed for analysis. The typed transcriptions served as the documents of analysis. Data from the transcripts were analyzed via a thematic analysis.

In a thematic analysis, recurring patterns, also known as themes, are drawn out from a text to understand more about it (Braun and Clarke 2006). To complete the most thorough and in-depth analysis possible, the author must be extremely familiar with the text. Videos were watched multiple times and transcribed. After this, the next step was initial coding, in which the research looks for keywords that appear frequently within the text as an indication of a budding theme. It is also in this portion of the analysis that research looks for unique pieces of data that stand out or a part from the work. Completing these steps are the preliminary actions taken toward establishing solid themes.

Owen (1984) suggests that for a theme to exist it must have three characteristics. It must be repetitive, a concept that shows up over and over again in multiple ways throughout the course of the data set. It must be forceful, an unmistakable presence within the data. And lastly, it must be recurring, showing up frequently within the data set. After finding the themes, they were analyzed for a final time, and then given a name. Supporting context and quotes from relevant episodes were then matched up to a theme to give it sufficient support. Because the essay contrasts Toni Childs with that of other controlling images, themes were then also compared to research surrounding the controlling image as a means of further analysis. After examining her character, it is evident that she was a hybrid image of "the Black Lady", "Sapphire", and "the Gold Digger". She was also found to be the antithesis of the "Super Strong Black Woman/Superwoman."

THE PROFESSIONAL BLACK LADY

Lubiano (1992) best defines the Black Lady Overachiever controlling image in her analysis of how the world characterized Anita Hill during her testimony at then future supreme court justice Clarence Thomas' confirmation hearings. Hill, a law professor at the times of the hearings, previously worked with Thomas at the Department of Education and at the Equal Employment Opportunity Commission and testified that Thomas had made multiple comments of a sexual nature and sexually harassed not only her and but also his fellow coworkers. Hill was considered a threat to his confirmation—the second African American man to sit in the Supreme Court. The Black Lady's "disproportionate overachievement stands for black cultural strangeness and ensures the underachievement of 'the black male'" (335). Thus, by "achieving middle-class success via education, career and/or economic success, black women are responsible for the disadvantage status of African Americans" (335). The image of the Black Lady serves to show how professional Black women are considered a detrimental force in American culture. In applying the image to the Toni Childs character, it is important to note that she is highly educated. Early on in the show it was revealed that Toni Childs went to the University of California Los Angeles (UCLA) with both Joan and Lynn. Not only is the Black Lady highly educated, she also has a work ethic that is second to none.

Black Ladies are known as relentless hard workers (Shaw 1996). They maintain careers that are elite in nature and often hold roles in which they are in charge of others. They know exactly how they have achieved success in their career because they have had to work twice as hard as everyone else. Childs was a successful real estate agent in LA whose clientele included celebrities. During Season 2 on the "Childs in Charge" episode, she opened her own independent firm through convincing one of the most successful Black developers in LA to give her seed money after putting together an in-depth pitch. Yet still, she was not truly fulfilled. Throughout the show she sought to date, or dated, men that she classified as being rich. It is evident that she was looking to move up on the financial totem pole by way of marriage; however, her pursuit would not be easy because of how the Black Lady is perceived.

Collins (2004) offers the notion that Black Ladies have benefited from policies such as affirmative action, which have effectively placed them at the top of the career hierarchy in American culture. As a threat, Black Ladies hold jobs that should go to white men (Collins 2004). Due to the racial and gendered means of discrimination in America, Black women, in essence, sit atop a career pyramid in which they are followed by white men, white women, and then Black men. In understanding this, Edwards (2011) posits this hierarchy automatically places Childs at odds with Black men as she takes away their agency across political, economic, and social landscapes because of her chosen career and the financial and social benefits that come with it. Arguably, it would make sense that although Toni dated many Black men, she ultimately married a white man out of compatibility.

In terms of visually conforming, Childs perfected the look of the Black Lady, embracing European standards of beauty. Her character always wore her hair straight, either permed or via a wig. Reid-Brinkley (2012) suggests this is because Black Ladies must appear as respectable, "engaging in a persistent, performative replication of propriety" (42). She must be "free of dreadlocks, braids, and other indicators of nappy hair, gracious and accommodating, loyal to the institution that employs her" (41). They also must speak the part, speaking standard English over African American vernacular or Ebonics (41). Childs exhibited her lack of an affinity toward anything that was outside of standard English. This can be most closely seen by the way she felt about Maya's son's, Jabari, name. In her opinion his name was ghetto, and she underscored this sentiment by purposely calling him by the wrong name over the course of the show. On different occasions she referred to him as "Jingle Jangle, JaCarter, and Jam On It." The names that she ascribed to him were meant to mock him and demonstrate her disdain.

Reid-Brinkley also notes this idea of violating the ascribed tenets of the Black Lady, which Toni Childs violated. "Black women's performances of appropriate femininity are always already suspect within white supremacist discourse" (42). Therefore, "successful black women are masculine and aggressive, making them unattractive to men" (43). Childs, however, embraces her femininity and excessively comments on her good looks. Also, the Black Lady can be a sexual being, yet that sexuality must be contained within the confines of traditional heterosexual marriage. Childs had a very active dating and sex life. As well, she was assertive and aggressive, which would make her undesirable as a mate. This proved untrue as it was indeed her behavior that attracted her future husband.

EMASCULATION AND SAPPHIRE

The controlling image of Sapphire was named for the fictional television show character Sapphire Stevens from the *Amos 'n' Andy* show. She was most well-known for berating Black men, specifically in her case, her husband. Sapphire's character paved the way for the derogatory and stereotypical connotation of Black women as being angry (Owens Patton and Snyder-Yuly 2016). Over the years Sapphire-esque characters have appeared in media as darker hued (Kanyeredzi 2018). This move was likely intentionally done to reinforce their Blackness and legitimize racist Blackface comedy, which many considered *Amos 'n' Andy*. Toni Childs had much in common with Sapphire. Toni was a dark-skinned woman and berated men, particularly her husband Todd. Todd Garrett was a white, Jewish, plastic surgeon. Toni met him during Season 3's episode "Secrets & Eyes" where she had a bad Botox job and she went to him to get it fixed. They began dating which led to a marriage proposal over the course of a few short months and then a quick wedding. During their interactions Toni berated Todd about his height and his income. For their wedding, Toni had extravagant ideas including asking Todd to rent out an expensive villa for them to stay in just before the wedding. She planned their honeymoon to be on a private island in the Indian Ocean. When he rebuffed her request for yet another expense, a helicopter for them to fly on after the wedding, they got into a heated argument:

Todd: "What am I to you? Your bank? A new accessory? Your new handbag?"
Toni: "Listen! If I were marrying for money, I wouldn't be marrying you . . . I've got money! I can pay for it myself! I don't need you!" (Akil 2003).

Although Todd was rich, he was not rich enough by her standards. She had no problem expressing that she had money too back in his face and that she did not need him. Later in Season 6, when Toni went into labor with her and Todd's daughter, they were not at a good place in their relationship. They were separated and were going back and forth on whether or not to divorce. Todd was living in New York while she was still in LA. After she went into labor early, he arrived to greet their daughter Morgan and to discuss her request for a divorce, Toni says, "What am I doing? We can't get a divorce. Maybe I was just scared. Or maybe it's that postpartum thing like you said. Or maybe I'm angry that you weren't here for the birth. Or maybe it's some weird delayed reaction to the fact that you're short, I don't know" (Prince-Blythewood 2005). It is surprising that Toni would choose to have such a conversation at what is supposed to be a happy time, the birth of a child, the first for both her and him. She further demonstrates her traits as a Sapphire by using the discussion of such a serious topic, the prospect of getting a divorce, to poke fun at his height. As always Todd does not laugh but does go on to tell her that she was right and that they should divorce.

THE GOLD DIGGER: OBSESSION WITH MONEY

The Gold Digger goes after rich men so that she can use his money to buy things for herself (Stephens and Few 2007; Weitzer and Kubrin 2009). She enjoys the finer things in life although quite often she does not have the means to purchase them on her own. But for the Gold Digger, it's not just all about the money. It's also about power. The Gold Digger seeks out rich men because being with them helps to raise her profile (Jones 1994). She gets to be in social circles with the elites, something that she has probably only ever dreamed. The Gold Digger is willing to do whatever she needs to in order to get what she wants. She will sleep with a man if she thinks he fits the description for what she is seeking (Jones 1994). As one can see her interests are very superficial. She's only interested in you if you can make her dreams come true.

Although Toni Childs was a successful business woman in her own right, she was always chasing after rich men over the duration of the show. Prior to meeting Todd, she was interested in a man named Anthony. Anthony was a wealthy developer who she tried to goad in vain to ask her on a date. Anthony could see right through Toni and called her out on her reasons for trying to go on a date with him. He said to her, "Toni, you're superficial . . . where's the substance?"(Garner 2002). He then asked her to think about what her legacy will be in the future. After pondering this she decided to open her own agency and asked him to invest in her procuring an office space. In their conversation he tells her exactly what he thinks about her:

Anthony: "I invest in people who make me money, not take my money . . . The only thing I've ever seen you apply yourself to is the pursuit of rich men."
Toni: "So you think I'm just a gold digger?"
Anthony: "Your words, but yes."
Toni: "And what does a gold digger do Anthony?"
Anthony: "Separate good men from their money."
Toni: "Ok, ok that's your perspective. But isn't it also possible that she does her very best to make men feel complete and add exponentially to their happiness quotient? . . .The point is whether its separating people from their money or making people feel complete, both are essential components for selling high end real estate, and I figured out a new way to do it. Anthony do yourself a favor, you're gonna hate yourself if you miss out." (Garner 2002)

Anthony lets Toni know right up front that he is nobody's fool. He has seen exactly what Toni has been up to and sees that she preys upon rich men, solely for their wealth. He also makes a value judgment about "gold digging" women. They are solely looking to take from men, separating him from that which makes him good and gives him his status, his money. But Toni quips back with a new spin on the role of the Gold Digger. She rejects the public perception that Gold Diggers are not good people as they are only in relationships for the benefits that they will reap. Toni asks Anthony if he has ever thought about the benefits that the man in the relationship will receive as well.

In Toni's mind, a man is not "complete" without the companionship of a woman. Although the Gold Digger is in the relationship for her own personal gains, she brings a sense of completeness and happiness to the man that she is with. Indeed, the relationship between the Gold Digger and the benefactor is one that is all about perspective. She then applies this reframing of the situation to real estate to show him how she has the rhetorical chops to sell houses to anyone in any situation. She then closes with a plea for him to invest in her business, which is also a double entendre about him asking her out on a date. It's interesting that even though Toni makes very good money on her own, she was looking for more money from someone else. Indeed, a man's money was her primary motivation for wanting to date them. Toni made it very clear over the course of the show that her love life was motivated primarily by the amount of money that a man had. She was not interested in the idea of actually falling in love nor was she overly concerned with his looks; she only wanted to know that his bank account was full of zeros.

An example was in an episode when she was in the early dating stage with Todd. She invited him over to Joan's house to eat, drink, and chat with her girlfriends, Joan's current boyfriend, and Joan's coworker, William. The topic of conversation for the evening was how men judge women and vice versa. In the midst of the conversation Todd turned to the women and said,

Todd: "You judge us by superficial standards. He's too short. He's too bald . . . Talk about degrading and offensive. All you women want are men with big penises and deep pockets."
Toni: "We can be flexible. I mean in my case, the deeper the pockets, the smaller the penis can be . . . See we want to feel secure and protected. . . ." (Garner 2002)

In his comments Todd depicts all women as only being interested in men who can give them pleasurable sexual experiences and those who are also rich. In her comments Toni affirmed this but pushed back on his sweeping claim. She let him know that the quality of sexual experiences is not all that important to her in a relationship so long as the man makes great money. Perhaps this was also a personal message for Todd that no matter how well-endowed he was or was not, it did not matter to her because he had money. In this conversation Toni also shared why she has embraced a Gold Digger's mentality. Money brought Toni a sense of safety and security that nothing else in the world seemed to give her. If she had money, then she had the ability to take care of herself. The more money she has, the better the quality of life she can provide herself. Money gave Toni a false sense of security. Yet, money could not save Toni from the real-world problems that she would go on to encounter including being accused of being a bad wife and mother, in essence becoming the antitheses of a widely known controlling image.

THE ANTITHESES OF THE SUPERSTRONG BLACK WOMAN/SUPERWOMAN

Toni Childs was a self-professed bad wife and bad mother, yet there were no specific controlling images that represented either of these concepts in the ways that she did. It could be assumed that Sapphire was a bad wife because she was always berating her husband, but this was not the focus of her image. Sapphire was the original angry Black woman. As it pertains to motherhood there was the image of the Bad Black Mother, which would later evolve into the Welfare Mother (Collins 2004). This woman was "abusive and neglectful" toward her children. She was poor, unemployed or underemployed, or working class. Toni was not an abusive mother or poor, but she was neglectful due to her work. Toni was the opposite of two controlling images the Superstrong Black Woman and the Superwoman.

The Superstrong Black Woman is a figure who is the epitome of motherhood. She sacrifices everything for the benefit of her family, but specifically for her children (Collins 2004). Her life is all about rearing her child. Her sole focus is on making sure that her child is taken care. She dotes on her child, loving them fiercely, and being there for them in a number of supportive ways. For middle-class women this image often seems to go hand-in-hand with that of the Superwoman. This is a woman who in addition to being a great wife is also a great mother. When thinking of the most well-known Black media image of this figure, Clair Huxtable of *The Cosby Show* fame immediately comes to mind. Clair had it all in terms of career and home life. She made her profession as a lawyer and had a wonderful relationship with both her husband and her children (Press 1991), all while managing to look beautiful for her husband (Collins 2009). She navigated her career, marriage, and motherhood flawlessly, managing everything with ease, and doing everything well (Chambers 1997). Toni was the exact opposite of Clair Huxtable.

Toni was not a great wife to Todd. Over the course of their short-lived marriage they had many problems. They argued over things such as differences in their respective faiths as she was Christian, and he was Jewish. After they were married Todd shared that he was in $750,000 of debt and she wanted to immediately divorce him upon learning this. Toni also developed feelings for an ex-boyfriend which led to conflict, among other things. Deep inside Toni knew that she was not good to Todd. And this was reflected in a conversation that she had after signing her divorce papers: "It just all went wrong, and it was all my fault . . . I can be a real self-centered, spoiled bitch sometimes" (Garretson 2005). In this moment Toni recognized that she played a major role in the way things went between her and Todd. Her focus was hardly ever on what was best for the two of them; it was mainly about what was best for her. For example, even after finding out that Todd was in debt, she decided to buy a Birkin handbag which is known for being very expensive. When her dysfunctional mother prompted her to pick between either staying married to Todd or trying to mend a relationship with her, Toni initially chose trying to appease her mother. Over the duration of the show in many ways she still had the mentality of a single person, only thinking about what was best for her versus what was best for the both of them. In another episode when talking to Todd as his now ex-wife she said to him, "All my life I've made knee jerk decisions. I mean come on Todd our marriage was knee jerk" (Truesdell 2006). She initially said yes to marrying Todd just because of his status, but she never stopped to think about what it would be like to be a wife, and to be willing to put someone else's needs before her own. Her selfish attitude also served as a part of the reason why she was perceived as a bad mother. Toni never truly seemed to be interested in motherhood. Much of the discourse around her relationship with her child was about how she had to be "stuck" with her all the time, unable to do the things that she wanted to do such as hanging out with her friends, working, and dating. She further demonstrated her lack of interest in mothering in the actions that she took after just having her daughter Morgan.

In Season 6, episode 3, after being up all night with Morgan who had been crying, Toni places her in the crib, still crying, and goes out in the hallway to read a book. Todd was in town for the weekend to visit the baby. He encounters Toni sitting in the hallway on the way to her apartment. Todd asks why Toni is sitting in the hallway and she tells him that it is his turn to watch the baby and that she was going out. She hops on the elevator and closes it before he can ask another word. When he tries to open Toni's apartment door to get to Morgan who is still crying, he realizes that Toni has locked it. Later when she returns, he confronts her and lets her know that he was only able to get in because of the maintenance man. This incident demonstrated how Toni cared more about herself and meeting her own self-fulfilling needs. She was more interested in getting away from Morgan's crying than trying to diagnose what was wrong with Morgan, no matter how long this might have taken. It demonstrated her carelessness.

When confronted, Toni scoffed off locking Morgan inside the apartment as no big deal. Instead of taking ownership for her mistakes she opted to hire a nanny for Morgan, even though both she and Todd agreed that they would wait until they both had more time to bond with the baby before doing this. Later in the episode she discussed her mothering woes with Maya over lunch saying:

Toni: "I don't have any business being somebody's mother . . . I just feel like such a failure, everything I touch goes bad. Look at my marriage, look at me . . . I don't even want to be around her because I don't want to mess her up. That's why I'm here with you instead of at her first doctor's appointment . . . All I know how to do for Morgan is shop." (Belli 2006)

As previously demonstrated, Toni makes the decision to prioritize her well-being over the well-being of her child. She decided to go shopping and have lunch with Maya instead of being present for her daughter's first doctor's appointment. She had her newly hired nanny take her to the doctor instead. She recognizes that motherhood was not for her. Todd takes her to court for custody of Morgan in which his lawyer described Toni as "self-centered, irresponsible, and a danger to the child" (Allen 2005).

DISCUSSION

The findings from this chapter reveal that the Toni Childs character was a combination of three controlling images: The Black Lady, Sapphire, and Gold Digger. She was the opposite of the Superstrong Black Woman/Superwoman as she was consistently depicted as a bad wife and careless mother. While the Toni character was not as likeable as some of the other characters on *Girlfriends*, it was encouraging that Brock Akil embraced the idea that Black women are more than one dimensional. They have personalities that are nuanced, complicated, and multifaceted, which she embodied through the themes that permeated through Toni. On the other hand, it is a bit disappointing that Brock Akil had the power to write Toni's character as a professional Black woman in a non-stereotypical light but did not. Brock Akil failed to fully move beyond controlling images, even though she does in some ways put a new spin on them.

One interesting perspective is that in her characterization of Toni as a Black Lady, Toni did marry a white male doctor which could represent that he was the most suitable partner for her from an economic standpoint. It is also important to note the power dynamic between white men and Black women. As a Sapphire, Toni berated her husband who happened to be white. This is a slant on the power dynamics in which Toni finds her agency, yet it is not helpful in maintaining a healthy relationship, interracial or otherwise.

Another updated image is Brock Akil's presentation of Toni as a Gold Digger. While she was gainfully employed and firmly in the middle class, she had dreams of becoming rich through marrying up. Through Toni, Brock Akil bucked the idea of the independent woman who is making it happen for herself. On the contrary, Brock Akil communicated the idea that dependency on a man might not be a bad thing if it ultimately gets a woman the wealth and status that she is seeking. However, this style of thinking is in opposition of Black feminist thought (BFT) and liberation movements as it rests on hegemonic patriarchy.

Brock Akil also presents a new controlling image that challenges the Superwoman stereotype, as Toni is considered a bad mother and wife, even though she has financial means, a husband, and a support system with her friends. The notion of "having it all," meaning everything from a career to a family to friendships is not always easy to negotiate in all aspects of life. The pressure of balancing everything causes a person to withdraw from the most unpleasant parts of their lives, while devoting their time to the aspects that they enjoy. Toni seemed to revel in this behavior, in which she was frequently characterized as selfish. And in doing so, she did irreparable damage to vital relationships in her life.

After analyzing the Toni Childs character on *Girlfriends*, this research argues that Brock Akil developed a lead character that displayed multiple controlling images. Future researcher should analyze how other female lead characters from in her subsequent shows may also represent hybrid controlling images. Perhaps Melanie Barnett of *The Game* embodies characteristics of the Black Lady and the Gold Digger or Mary Jane Paul of *Being Mary Jane* represents the Black Lady and the Jezebel. It may even be worthy to do a further analysis on the other characters of *Girlfriends*, as they too may represent hybrid of controlling images as well. What is abundantly clear is that Brock Akil's characters represent the full spectrum of the Black experience, be it good or bad.

REFERENCES

Akil, Salim, dir. "*Girlfriends*" Season 3, episode 24, "The Wedding." Aired May 19th, 2003 on UPN.

Allen, Debbie, dir. "*Girlfriends*" Season 6, episode 7, "Trial and Errors." Aired November 7th, 2005 on UPN.

Amazon. "Girlfriends: The Complete Series." Accessed January 29, 2019. https://www.amazon.com/Girlfriends-Complete-Reggie-Hayes/dp/B076DQZ41G.

Belli, Mary Lou, dir. "*Girlfriends*" Season 6, episode 3, "Game Over." Aired February 28th, 2006 on UPN.

Belli, Mary Lou, dir. "*Girlfriends*" Season 3, episode 22, "Blood is Thicker Than Liquor." Aired May 5th, 2003 on UPN.

Belli, Mary Lou, dir. "*Girlfriends*" Season 3, episode 3, "Secrets & Eyes." Aired October 7th, 2002 on UPN.

Biography.com. "Clarence Thomas." Accessed January 29, 2019. https://www.biography.com/people/clarence-thomas-9505658.

Bobo, Jacqueline. 1995. *Black Women as Cultural Readers*. New York: Columbia University.

Boylorn, Robin M. and Mark C. Hopson. 2014. "Learning to Conquer Metaphysical Dilemmas: Womanist and Masculinist Perspectives on Tyler Perry's For Colored Girls." In *Black Women and Popular Culture: The Conversation Continues*, edited by Adria Y. Goldman, Vanatta S. Ford, Alexa A. Harris, and Natasha R. Howard, 89–108. Lanham: Lexington Books.

Braun, Virginia and Victoria Clarke. 2006. "Using Thematic Analysis in Psychology." *Qualitative Research in Psychology* 3, no. 2: 77–101.

Burke, Kenneth. 1969. *A Rhetoric of Motives*. Berkeley: University of California Press.

Campbell, Shannon B., Steven S. Giannino, Chrystal R. China, and Christopher S. Harris. 2008. "*I Love New York*: Does New York Love Me?" *Journal of International Women's Studies* 10, no. 2: 20–28.

Chambers, Veronica. 1997. *Having it All? Black Women and Success*. New York: Broadway Books.

Christiansen, Roger, dir. "*Girlfriends*" Season 6, episode 3, "And Nanny Makes 3." Aired October 3rd, 2005 on UPN.

Collins, Gail. *When Everything Changed: The Amazing Journey of American Women from 1960 to the Present*. New York: Hachette Book Group, 2009.

Collins, Patricia Hill. 2004. *Black Sexual Politics: African Americans, Gender, and the New Racism*. New York: Routledge.

———. 2000. *Black Feminist Thought: Knowledge, Consciousness, and the Politics of Empowerment, Second Edition*. New York: Routledge.

———. 1998. *Fighting Words: Black Women and the Search for Justice*. Minneapolis: University of Minnesota Press.

Donahoo, Saran. 2017. "An Examination of Black Women as Students in College Films: Where My Girls At?" In *Critical Perspectives on Black Women and College Success*, edited by Lori D. Patton and Natasha N. Croom, 59–74. New York: Routledge.

Edwards, Erica R. March 2011. "The Black President Hokum." *American Quarterly* 63, no. 1: 33–59.

Epps, Sheldon, dir. "*Girlfriends*" Season 4, episode 16, "On The Couch." Aired March 1st, 2004 on UPN.

Epps, Sheldon, dir. "*Girlfriends*" Season 4, episode 2, "Don't You Want Me Baby." Aired November 24th, 2003 on UPN.

Epps, Sheldon, dir. "*Girlfriends*" Season 4, episode 3, "Snoop, There It Is." Aired September 29th, 2003 on UPN.

Garner Jr., Leonard, dir. "*Girlfriends*" Season 4, episode 2, "If It's Broke, Fix It." Aired September 22nd, 2003 on UPN.

Garner Jr., Leonard, dir. "*Girlfriends*" Season 2, episode 17, "Childs in Charge." Aired March 18, 2002 on UPN.

Garner Jr., Leonard, dir. "*Girlfriends*" Season 3, episode 10, "A Little Romance." Aired November 25th, 2002 on UPN.

Garretson, Katy, dir. "*Girlfriends*" Season 5, episode 13, "All in a Panic." Aired February 7th, 2005 on UPN.

IMDB. "Mara Brock Akil." Accessed January 29th, 2019. https://www.imdb.com/name/nm0015327/.

Jewell, K. Sue. 1993. *From Mammy to Miss America and Beyond: Cultural Images and the Shaping of US Social Policy.* London: Routledge.
Jones, Lisa. 1994. *Bulletproof Diva: Tales of Race, Sex, and Hair.* New York: Doubleday.
Kanyeredzi, Ava. 2018. *Race, Culture, and Gender: Black Female Experiences of Violence and Abuse.* London: Palgrave MacMillan.
Lubiano, Wahneema. 1992. "Black Ladies, Welfare Queens, and State Minstrels: Ideological War by Narrative Means." In *Race-ing Justice, Engendering Power*, edited by Toni Morrison, 323–363. New York: Pantheon.
Owen, W. F. 1984. "Thematic Metaphors in Relational Communication. A Conceptual Framework." *Western Journal of Communication* 49 Winter: 1–13.
Pannell, Ni'Kesia. "Where Are They Now: The Cast of 'Girlfriends'." Accessed January 29, 2019. https://www.essence.com/entertainment/where-are-they-now-cast-girlfriends/.
Patton, Tracey Owens and Snyder-Yuly. 2016. "The 'Tyra Tyrade': Reinforcing the Sapphire Through Online Parody." In *Black Women's Portrayal on Reality Television: The New Sapphire*, edited by Donnetrice Allison, 127–148. Lanham: Lexington Books.
Press, Andrea L. 1991. *Women Watching Television: Gender, Class, and Generation in the American Television Experience.* Philadelphia: University of Pennsylvania Press.
Prince-Blythewood, Gina, dir. "*Girlfriends*" Season 6, episode 2, "Odds & Ends." Aired September 26th, 2005 on UPN.
Reid-Brinkley, Shanara Rose. 2012. "Mammies and Matriarchs: Feminine Style and Signifyin(g) in Carol Moseley Braun's 2003–2004 Campaign for the Presidency." In *Standing in the Intersection: Feminist Voices, Feminist Practices in Communication Studies*, edited by Karma R. Chavez and Cindy L. Griffin, 35–58. Albany: State University of New York Press.
Sharetv.com. "Joan Clayton." https://sharetv.com/shows/girlfriends/cast/joan_clayton.
Sharetv.com. "Lynn Searcy." https://sharetv.com/shows/girlfriends/cast/lynn_searcy.
Sharetv.com. "Maya Wilkes." https://sharetv.com/shows/girlfriends/cast/maya_wilkes.
Sharetv.com. "Toni Childs." https://sharetv.com/shows/girlfriends/cast/toni_childs.
Shaw, Stefanie J. 1996. *What a Woman Ought to Be and to Do: Black Professional Women Workers During the Jim Crow Era.* Chicago: The University of Chicago Press.
Stephens, Dionne, P. and April L. Few. December 2007. "Hip Hop Honey or Video Ho: African American Preadolescents Understandings' of Female Sexual Scripts in Hip Hop Culture." *Sexuality and Culture* 11, no. 4: 48–69.
Thompson, Lisa B. 2009. *Beyond the Black Lady: Sexuality and the New African American Middle Class.* Urbana: University of Illinois Press.
Truesdell, Keith, dir. "*Girlfriends*" Season 6, episode 12, "The Music In Me." Aired January 16th, 2006 on UPN.
Variety Staff. "'Girlfriends': Mara Brock Akil takes the High Road." *Variety.* https://variety.com/2008/tv/news/girlfriends-mar-21202/.
Weitzer, Ronald and Charis E. Kubrin. October 2009. "Misogyny in Rap Music: A Content Analysis of Prevalence and Meaning." *Men and Masculinities* 12, no. 1: 3–29.

Chapter 3

Real, Respectable, or Both

Respectability on Being Mary Jane *through the Words of Mara Brock Akil*

Natasha R. Howard

> "42% of Black women have never been married. This is one Black woman's story . . . not meant to represent all Black women." (Pilot, *Being Mary Jane*)

This quote opened the 2013 pilot episode of Black Entertainment Television's (BET) *Being Mary Jane*. Described in its tagline as "beautifully flawed," *Being Mary Jane* focused on the ups and downs of its main character Mary Jane Paul's—whose given name is Pauletta Patterson—encounters in her personal and professional life. Mary Jane represents an often explored demographic in the media: the successful, single Black woman. Despite this disclaimer of not representing all Black women, the goal of creator Mara Brock Akil seems to be to present a character in which Black women can relate. This is evidenced by the #IAmMaryJane hashtag created during the first season that encouraged viewers to tweet and explain why they identified with the lead character. Arguably as well, with the comparatively small number of lead roles for Black women in Hollywood, each one automatically becomes looked at as a representation of Black womanhood by default. Although the show covers a variety of topics, the balance between the personal and professional life of Mary Jane is at the crux of the show, with side storylines including members of her family. Additionally, because Mary Jane appears to have achieved financial and career success, her personal life and desire to find love and start a family becomes her biggest area of concern. This depiction of the successful and single Black woman and the themes and messages regarding respectability and sexuality on *Being Mary Jane* are worth examining.

Historically women have dealt with troubled representations of their sexuality and quest for relationships. In fact, researchers found that media representations, especially in the 1990s and 2000s, portrayed women as being more concerned about romance than their own career (Douglas 2010; Holtzman 2000). This desire for romance is so intense that, according to some media messages, it often leads to troubled relationships among women who aren't opposed to be fighting over a man (Douglas 1994). As a result, women often receive mixed messages from the media regarding sexuality, relationships, and what is socially acceptable. Black women, in particular, have had to contend with historical stereotypes that have painted them either as the asexual "Mammy" or a hypersexual, promiscuous "Jezebel." The battle between fighting these images has been further complicated by respectability politics that have facilitated a binary of "good girls" versus "bad girls" in terms of the expectations regarding Black women and their openness and expressions of sexuality. Brock Akil acknowledged this challenge in describing the complexities of Mary Jane's character:

> Oftentimes the African American audience will ask for a positive image because so much of the stereotype has been what gets in the landscape of our images. They want to counteract that with a positive image, but I personally believe strongly that the positive image is just as damaging as the negative image. Humanity does not exist in those polar extremes. One day you can be both good and bad. Your intentions can be good, your actions can be bad. Oftentimes you'll see Mary Jane doing a good deed but frustrated and agitated in the doing. (Brock Akil as quoted in Gaffney 2015)

In many ways, the images seen in popular culture today both play with and defy the constraints of respectability, particularly in their "[deconstruction of] conventional borders of female sexuality" (Lee 2010, xii). Brock Akil's work both on *Being Mary Jane* and *Girlfriends,* in which she also created, serve as examples as the characters had respectable sensibilities and explored their sexual desires. As Jordan (1991) stated "the politics of sexuality are the most ancient and probably the most profound arena for human conflict" (12). Corresponding with respectability politics, "the politics of sexuality subsumes all of the different ways in which some of us seek to dictate to others of us what we should do, what we should desire, what we should dream about, and how we should behave ourselves, generally, on the planet" (Jordan 1991, 12). Thus, the treatment of Black women's sexuality and approach to relationships in media and the messages that audiences receive—these images continue to be an area that need to be interrogated.

With the growing prevalence of social media, reality television, and audiences that self-produce their own media, there is a fresh opportunity for newer images of women in media as it relates to relationships and their sexuality, particularly with Black women such as Brock Akil, at the helm of a show. Brock Akil has an established history with creating, producing and writing for primetime television programs with Black women as lead characters such as *Girlfriends*, *The Game*, and *Being Mary Jane*, and more recently *Black Lightning* and *Love Is*. However, research has shown us that newer images may not always translate to better quality images (Cramer and Creedon 2007; Croteau and Hoynes 2003; Douglas 1994, 2010; Holtzman 2000; Meyers 1999). In fact, it has been debated if complicated Black female lead characters such as Mary Jane are a sign of progress or regression. While Mary Jane appears to be a successful and thriving Black woman, her interactions with men romantically have been criticized as stereotypical. Authors Jeffries and Jeffries (2015) note that while *Being Mary Jane* may be a show in which the main character is not objectified and subject to the white male gaze, "Mary Jane's character portrayal still illustrates a relationship dependent, promiscuous, and sexualized image" (130). This chapter examines that debate using a thematic analysis employed with a hip hop feminist lens to explore episodes of *Being Mary Jane* to identify themes pertaining to Black women, respectability, and sexuality.

BACKGROUND

Respectability Politics

The term "respectability politics" stems from the efforts of the Black women's club movements and church organization of the early nineteenth century to challenge stereotypes of Blacks as hypersexual, immoral, and lazy (Higginbotham 1993). Aimed at challenging and dispelling negative stereotypes of Black people, the tenets of respectability politics functioned under the premise that Blacks were always under scrutiny of the white gaze. Therefore, the Black Baptist women condemned behaviors deemed to be immoral and reflective of negative stereotypes. The overall belief was that each person represented the race, and so the individual actions and behavior of one, reflected upon all. In order to disprove and fight stereotypes, these women fought to prove and demonstrate "ladylike" behavior and morality, qualities that were only afforded to white women. As such, they emphasized that Black women had good manners and morals, were clean, did not indulge in drinking, were sexually pure, thrift, modest in dress, and also fought for racial equality.

In pushing a specific set of characteristics and behaviors on Blacks, respectability politics in many ways blames Blacks for socioeconomic status and unfair treatment by putting the sole burden on them. Black women, in particular, are burdened with this responsibility in that they have to exemplify respectability and be responsible for when others do not exemplify it due to their roles as caretakers and the models of it (Higginbotham 1993, 202). This amplifies the good woman versus bad woman dichotomy. Instead of rejecting this ideal, many Black women have struggled to be reclassified as good women rather than expose the bankruptcy of the entire system (White 2001, 35).

Class became a factor in respectability politics when Black Baptist women identified more with the working poor, championing strong work ethic, and opposed lower-class idleness (Higginbotham 1993, 187). This would not change until years later when more Blacks gained affluence and created middle-class status via occupations as doctors and lawyers. Moral standards were traded with material items of status in terms of representing indicators of class (Frazier 1969). In his study of consumption and stigma management in the contemporary Black middle class, Crockett (2017) found that having the material trappings of what looks like success continues to be one of the significant attributes of respectability. Still in keeping with the tradition of monitoring what is considered appropriate behavior of the Black community, respectability is still expressed and upheld among the upper and middle classes of the Black community. "Now that Black elites are part of the mainstream elite in media, entertainment, politics, and the academy, respectability talk operates within the official sphere, shaping the opinions, debates, and policy perspectives on what should—and should not be done on the behalf of the Black poor" (Harris 2014, 33). Indeed as Crockett noted, "Normative respectability retains a prominent place in the cultural repertoires of the [B]lack middle class, despite substantial doubts about its ability to make their lives more tolerable" (576).

Mary Jane's choices reflect her adherence to respectability expectations as a successful Black woman journalist and for her family. Changing her professional name to Mary Jane Paul from Pauletta Patterson is an example. Frazier (1969) argues that the "Black Bourgeoisie" or "respectable Negroes" attempted to conform to the behavior and values of the white community in the most minute details. Similarly, Smith-Shomade (2002) points out that contemporary members of this group often include Black business owners, educated white-collar owners, professional athletes, academics, and entertainers including politicians and media workers—such as Mary Jane.

Black Women on Television and Sexuality

In this country, race and sexuality are inextricably linked (White 2001). White argues that in terms of sexuality, often times we have allowed our history under racism to dictate what we tell about ourselves (24). Television reflects this when it comes to portrayals of Black womanhood historically, as

Black women have been portrayed stereotypcially in such roles as the asexual Mammy or the hypersexual Jezebel. However, in response and defiance of these two archetypes, additional archetypes have emerged including "The Black Lady" and the "Educated Black Bitch." "The Black Lady" stereotype has been embodied by characters such as Claire Huxtable from the Cosby Show. She is middle, upper-middle, or upper class, smart, beautiful, and classy. Countering the Jezebel archetype, she was generally in a relationship—always heterosexual—and allowed to be a sexual being unlike the asexual Mammy (Collins 2005, 139). Even if she was single she was not portrayed as promiscuous. This archetype mirrored the idea of respectability in that these characters appeared to be morally upright through their suppression of the sexual performance of Black women, thereby mirroring the characteristics ascribed to respectable Black women (Thompson 2009).

The other archetype that has recently emerged is the "Educated Black Bitch" or "Bad Bitches." These Black women are portrayed as being beautiful, sexual, having money, power [to a degree], and good jobs. They appear to be successful in every way except their love lives (Collins 2005, 145). Unlike "The Black Lady," the "Educated Black Bitch" is shown working to balance her personal and professional life—struggles the Black Lady isn't often seen having—often to her detriment. Collins (2002) expounds, "These representations are used to explain why so many African American women fail to find committed male partners—they allegedly work too hard, do not know how to support Black men, and/or have character traits that make them unappealing to middle-class Black men" (146). Still, they also appear to represent aspects of respectability outside of their love lives due to their upper or middle-class lifestyles and accompanying outward displays of upper-class sensibilities.

Yet even with, and in fact because, of these changing archetypes, the need for examination of how Black women are represented and portrayed in the media continues. "The ideological power inherent in Black screen representations creates possibilities as well, since Black audiences' engagement with Black characters on-screen is at once a matter of fantasy projection as well as the reification of a collective sense of self" (Cartier 2014, 152). Therefore, these images can be powerful in that they allow Black people to see themselves on-screen, either challenging, uplifting, or providing them the opportunity to reimagine what is possible and reflect on their own realities. This is particularly important for young women and men who are inundated constantly with messages from the media they consume. "Because of its authority to shape perceptions of the world, global mass media circulates images of Black femininity and Black masculinity and, in doing so, ideologies of race, gender, sexuality, and class" (Collins 2002, 121). Additionally, popular culture can function as a location for feminist politics by affording women access to subversive sexual scripts and new discourses of sexuality (Lee 2010, 8).

Hip Hop Feminism

Drawing from Black feminist studies, hip hop feminism is a cultural, intellectual, and political movement grounded in the situated knowledge of women of color from the post–civil rights or hip hop generation who recognize culture as a pivotal site for political intervention to challenge, resist, and mobilize collectives to dismantle systems of exploitation (Durham 2007, 305). Not drawing strictly from or being about just hip hop music, hip hop feminism instead refers to the generations that grew up with and/or in hip hop culture and have been influenced by it. This study thus employs this theory partly because the main characters, and Brock Akil herself, represent the hip hop generation, and the show in many ways is influenced by the shifting themes and ideals presented in hip hop culture. Additionally, hip hop feminism invites new questions about representation offering alternative models for critical engagement that lean past challenging stereotypical archetypes of Black women, which some researchers argue Black feminism has sometimes gotten hung up on (Durham, Cooper, and Morris 2013; Lee 2010). In particular, some works critique Black feminist scholarship for having yet to "generate a discursive attack against middle-class systems of sexual regulation that monitor black female sexuality" (Lee 2010, xi). That isn't to say that Black feminism has not discussed Black female sexuality, but, as Morgan (2015) argued, "From academia to the blogosphere, we've become feminist fluent in theorizing the many ways in which our sexuality has been compromised. We've been considerably less successful, however, moving past that damage to claim pleasure and a healthy erotic as fundamental rights" (36). Hip hop feminism, instead, faces these questions head on. Like Black feminism, hip hop feminism still places value in examining and holding value for the experiences and realities of Black women. Yet still, one of the struggles for hip hop feminism has been to amplify an "unapologetic pro-sex stance" amidst the lingering of respectability politics in many Black feminist discussions. As Durham, Cooper, and Morris (2013) note:

> There are often serious reprisals for people of color, and women of color in particular, when we freely express sexual agency and desire. Engagement with respectability politics, then, continues to be vitally important to hip hop feminism. In tackling these challenges hip hop feminism pushes the conversations about black sexual politics, respectability and "compulsory heterosexuality within . . . the culture at large" (730).

METHODOLOGY

For the purpose of this study, a deductive thematic analysis was conducted in order to examine the themes related to respectability politics and sexuality presented in *Being Mary Jane*. Thematic analyses can be helpful in examining images and storylines in the media because they can be used to examine social constructions of meaning of said images and storylines (Braun, Clarke, and Terry 2015, 96). Using the descriptions ascribed to the idea of respectability politics, the episodes were observed for the presence and representations (both in adherence to and against) of the following themes: cleanliness of person and property, temperance (or lack thereof), sexual purity, and racial uplift. In terms of cleanliness, images where Mary Jane or one of the supporting characters is seen doing any kind of domestic work such as cooking, cleaning, and so on were noted. For temperance, the use of alcohol and the settings and connotations of it were also noted and described. Particularly, situations where the use of alcohol factored into specific conversations and/or decisions of the characters were observed. Sexual purity (or lack thereof) was recorded as any conversations about sex as well as any sexual encounters. Finally, racial uplift was defined and examined as all situations where characters discussed, spoke out against, or were depicted as participating in situations related to issues and concerns plaguing the Black community.

In order to examine Brock Akil's most direct connection to the images and dialogue pertaining to the themes being examined, this study examined nine episodes from Seasons 1 to 3 of *Being Mary Jane* that Brock Akil specifically wrote or cowrote (see table 3.1).

Table 3.1 Being Mary Jane Episodes Written/Cowritten By Mara Brock Akil

Season, Episode Number	Episode Name
Season 1, Episode 1	Pilot
Season 1, Episode 3	"Girls Night In"
Season 1, Episode 9	"Uber Love"
Season 2, Episode 1	"People"
Season 2, Episode 3	"Jane Knows Best"
Season 2, Episode 7	"Let's Go Crazy"
Season 2, Episode 12	"Signing Off"
Season 3, Episode 1	"Facing Fears"
Season 3, Episode 10	"Some Things are Black and White"

Credit: N. Howard.

Table 3.2 Cast of Characters in Featured Episodes

Characters	Brief Description
Mary Jane Paul (also known as Pauletta Patterson)	Main character of the show. News correspondent with SNC Network (Seasons 1–3). Daughter of Paul Patterson Sr. and Helen Patterson.
Paul Patterson, Sr.	Mary Jane, Patrick, and PJ's father. Helen's husband. Retired.
Helen Patterson	Mother of Mary Jane, Patrick, and PJ. Wife of Paul Patterson Sr. Recently diagnosed with lupus. Retired principal.
Patrick Patterson	Oldest son of Paul Sr. and Helen. Father to Niecy. He formerly worked in the nightclub industry. Currently seeking stable work and living with Paul Sr. and Helen in the beginning of the show. Recovering addict.
Paul Patterson, Jr. (PJ)	Youngest son of Paul Sr. and Helen (they refer to him as their "surprise baby"). In college for multiple degrees. Also sells marijuana on the side and wants to get in the marijuana dispensary business when he graduates (which he does in Season 2).
Niecy Patterson	Daughter of Patrick. Has two children by two different men (is pregnant with her daughter in the Pilot episode). Unemployed but seeking to begin nursing school.
Kara Lynch	Producer of Mary Jane's show at SNC during Seasons 1–3.
David Paulk	Ex-boyfriend of Mary Jane.
Andre Daniels	Beau of Mary Jane who she discovers is married in the Pilot episode.
Dr. Lisa Hudson	Long-time friend of Mary Jane.
Sheldon DeWitt	Older beau of Mary Jane in Season 3.
CeCe	Bookstore owner who is involved in the car accident with Mary Jane at the end of Season 2, beginning of Season 3. Later begins extorting Mary Jane through Season 3.

Credit: N. Howard.

FINDINGS

Cleanliness

The pilot episode of *Being Mary Jane* begins with Mary Jane baking a cake at 2 am in the morning for her mother's birthday the next day. Later in the episode after Andre has thrown up, she cleans up after him, puts a cold compress on his neck and later cleans his clothes off of the floor. While cleaning up after oneself and cooking are normal parts of life, the way the camera lingers on Mary Jane cleaning or baking puts these traits as a focal point. Although being able to cook does not necessarily correlate with cleanliness, both correlate with the idea of traditional domesticity. The show seems to make a point of repeatedly showing her baking and decorating cakes with detail. In fact the end of the pilot shows her baking another cake, this time for Niecy's baby shower.

Cleaning again becomes a focal point of activities for Mary Jane in the "Let's Go Crazy" episode. As the episode opens, David, who Mary Jane had unprotected sex with the night before in the effort to get pregnant, wakes up to find Mary Jane vacuuming in the morning. She says that she couldn't sleep so she thought she would get up and clean. Even after her conversation with David, she is shown continuing to clean out rooms in her house, reflecting on events in her life up to that point and appearing to be symbolically purging her house the same way she has decided to purge David out of her life if their effort at getting her pregnant have not been successful. Indeed whenever Mary Jane is cleaning she seems to be deep in thought and reflecting about her life and/or relationships as well.

Temperance

This is one of the areas pertaining to respectability that completely is not adhered to on *Being Mary Jane*. In the pilot episode the man she is seeing, Andre, who is drunk and drove over to her house, visits Mary Jane at 2 am. After having sex with him, the next morning she is seen praying God to give her a sign if he is the one and he in turn wakes up and throws up on her. The next Brock Akil-written episode we see Andre is in the "Girls Night In" episode. In this episode Andre references this same event, saying that he had to get drunk to go over to Mary Jane's because he had realized he loved her and needed the alcohol to tell her that and to propose.

In general alcohol use, even in social settings, is often shown as being the impetus for confessions—some of which lead to arguments. The entire "Uber Love" episode is an example of that. The episode begins with David coming over to Mary Jane's house to ask her to take a pregnancy test in front of him after finding out that she had frozen sperm from him after their last liaison. She in turn offers him a glass of wine in an effort to dissuade him, which leads to them having a conversation about their failed relationship. Later in the episode Mary Jane's friend Lisa comes over, and over another bottle she finds out that Lisa is the one that told David about having the sperm. The two of them then get an Uber and head to David's house where Mary Jane meets David's current girlfriend. Lisa later sends Mary Jane to her friend Kara's, where they continue drinking, and Mary Jane confesses to Kara that Andre was married—which Kara takes personally as her own marriage ended due to her ex-husband having an affair. Kara's suggestion, as they continue drinking, is that Mary Jane should go over to Andre's house and apologize to his wife—which they do. After this night of drinking Mary Jane eventually returns home via the Uber.

In Season 2, alcohol again inspires confessions, and also Mary Jane's reliance on alcohol as dependency. The "People" episode shows Mary Jane getting drunk at a dinner party she is hosting at her house and in turn insulting her little brother and her friends. Later in the episode she wakes up finding she has wet her bed, which is suggested to be possibly linked to either Mary Jane's drinking or her stress—as her friend Valerie suggests later in the episode. Two episodes later during the "Mary Jane Knows Best" episode, Niecy, who Mary Jane has allowed to move into her house temporarily, is searching for lotion in Mary Jane's bathroom and instead finds bottles of alcohol under her sink. Niecy later views Mary Jane's security camera and pays witness to how much Mary Jane is drinking. Mary Jane again struggles between drinking in the "Let's Go Crazy" episode when in a cleaning fit she pours out all the liquor in her house, but later on after getting a string of negative pregnancy tests, pours a glass from a new bottle she recently purchased, sniffs, and then thinking of all her recent incidents with liquor, leaves it. In the last episode written by Brock Akil, "Signing Off," Mary Jane is showing signs of her alcohol issues. In this episode, while at a new love interest Sheldon's house, she again wets the bed—again crediting it to stress. The irony of how this episode ends and Season 3 begins is that Mary Jane, who has been working on avoiding alcohol, gets in a car accident; despite having a blood alcohol level that is below the national level and not being drunk, her network goes into defense mode to avoid it being assumed that she was under the influence. She ends up spending most of Season 3 being blackmailed by the woman that was in the accident with her over this very assumption.

Sexual Purity

If there is one thing completely not present in *Being Mary Jane*, it is sexual purity. From the beginning of the pilot where Mary Jane cleans herself up in preparation of the sex she has with Andre in the hallway of her house minutes later, to the end of the episode when she masturbates in her office before heading to an impromptu invitation to dinner from David, sex a is major part of this show. In fact at the end of the pilot episode, Mary Jane gives in and has sex with David—later extracting the semen from his condom with a turkey baster which she then puts in a jar that is placed in her freezer. Indeed while Mary Jane is searching for love and desires to start a family, sexual purity is not her route.

One of the themes that is a major part of Season 1 due to Mary Jane's back and forth relationship with Andre, who is still married, is infidelity. In fact while sex is shown and discussed frequently, the idea of being a mistress is still a taboo. In the episode "Girls Night In," Mary Jane and her friends have enjoyed a strip tease from a stripper that was hired—again, not in line with sexual purity—they share secrets in a circle in the kitchen. One reveals that she is involved with a married man and the reaction she receives is disparagement. Meanwhile Mary Jane keeps Andre's marital status to herself. Similarly Kara, Mary Jane's producer, revealed that she had had sex with one of her interns. Even that is viewed lightly, primarily because the idea of infidelity is not a part of it. Being a "mistress" is still displayed as being frowned upon, even as Mary Jane participates as one. This guilt is part of what leads her to apologize to Andre's wife in the "Uber Love" episode. Later in the "Mary Jane Knows Best" episode when arguing with David who has come on to her, she laments about "how hard she has worked to not be this side chick," reflective of both her involvement with Andre and with David's attempts to seduce her despite being in a relationship and expecting a child with his current girlfriend. Another aspect of this is shown in the "Facing Fears" episode when Lisa tries to explain to Helen, Mary Jane's mother, about her relationship with David. Lisa remains silent when Helen asks her directly if she had sex with David. Helen then lectures Lisa on her wrong as she is considered family. Again the link of betrayal via sex is condemned.

Season 2 is filled with Mary Jane vacillating with her feelings for David. Brock Akil depicts her almost having sex with David in the "People" episode, to actually waking up from the night before having sex with him in the "Let's Go Crazy" episode. Mary Jane also has a friend she has nicknamed "Cutty Buddy" in her cell phone that she meets for sex. By Season 3, when she is exploring an interracial relationship, the "Some Things are Black and White" episodes start with Mary Jane waking up in bed with her Caucasian love interest. In many ways, the different types of relationships she has with these three men serve as context for comparison of how Mary Jane approaches handling her sexual desires. For example, she has a long history with David, and she has vacillated in desire to have a child with him. Sex with him complicates her feelings, so she is more cautious. With Cutty Buddy, however, the situation is completely reversed. Their interactions are all based on Mary Jane fulfilling her sexual urges outside of the confines of a relationship. Cutty Buddy at one point even lets Mary Jane know that he would be open to them developing something more, which she basically brushes off. There is not a back-and-forth and resistance as with David. In fact Mary Jane is seen as being the initiator at times with meeting up with Cutty Buddy. Her Caucasian love interest in Season 3 serves as a middle ground of sorts in that Mary Jane's interest in him originally was just physical but morphed into him being an actual potential relationship interest. Still, with the newness of their relationship, she is sexually free with him without the complications that can arise later in a relationship.

Even aside from the depictions of sex, conversations about outcomes from sex are a current theme in the show as well. The episodes of Season 1 feature Mary Jane pondering using David's sperm to inseminate her. In fact, toward the end of the "Uber Love" episode, Mary Jane calls Lisa to come over and help her with the insemination which she backs out of at the last minute. Additionally during the "People" episode, Mary Jane agrees to go through with doing the process of freezing her eggs on air for her show—showing her receiving shots and in further episodes undergoing the effects of the hormones and the shots for the process. An additional component to the effects of sex is shown in the "People" episode where further conversations between Mary Jane and David reveal that back when they were together she had gotten pregnant by him and had an abortion. This is later revealed in the "Let's Go Crazy" episode as being part of why she is obsessed and angry regarding David because someone else is having a baby with him—the man she loves—and not with her.

Community Uplift

As a journalist with a desire to bring attention to issues that matter to her and are related to the Black community, community uplift is mainly represented while Mary Jane is at work. During Season 1 Mary Jane strives to get a story on air about the "Ugly Black Woman" article posed by an issue of *Psychology Today*. Despite lack of interest from her management, Mary Jane is portrayed trying to pitch the idea while explaining why it is so important to her. This desitre to do shows about issues relevant to the black community is seen again in during the "Let's Go Crazy," when Mary Jane, who is tired of being a team player and ready to tell the stories she is interested in, tells Kara that she wants to all Black topics about Black women and the Black community. Similarly in the "Some Things Are Black and White" episode, Mary Jane's interns suggest to her to do shows related to issues like police brutality. As this episode ends, this particular issue comes close to home as Mary Jane sees a live video of the police tasiher niece Niecy. Outside of the news, during this same episode Mary Jane is seen giving a speech in a bookstore championing the need for books, education, and knowing one's history.

Another way the idea of community uplift is displayed is via conversations that Mary Jane has with her family and friends. Among her friends, Mary Jane discusses issues plaguing the Black community at her dinner party in the "People" episode. Toward the end of the "Some Things are Black and White," her blackmailer, CeCe, has a monologue about how her bookstore is important for the youth because of the knowledge that books have which the younger generation need. Mary Jane's conversations with members of her family, especially Niecy, represent the concept of upliftment as well. In the pilot episode, Mary Jane laments the fact that Niecy does not seem to have any real career aspirations and laments that her niece is a teenage parent. This is seen again during the "Mary Jane Knows Best" episode when Mary Jane is trying to encourage Niecy to take her health seriously and embrace a healthier lifestyle. In this conversation, Mary Jane refers to the issues of poor diets leading to a high occurrence of heart disease and diabetes in the Black community as a way to make Niecy embrace the changes she is suggesting. Finally the values of education as a way of uplift are encouraged throughout the "Signing Off" episode. With her brother Paul Jr. finally graduating from college, he thanks his parents for their support and encouraging him to finish his education, which he notes is "the key to true freedom." As Higginbotham (1993) pointed out, the idea of uplift at times relates to trying to encourage others in the community to behave better or achieve more as a way to better their overall lives.

DISCUSSION

Mary Jane is seemingly the perfect woman—she is smart, beautiful, and financially secure. She also can cook and is displayed as enjoying taking care of the men around her. The depiction almost begs the too commonly heard of question of "if she's so perfect, why is she single?" The fact that Mary Jane is so desperate to be married with children only plays more into this idea, bringing to life the idea that she, like many other Black women who are in a similar situation, "are deficient if their lives do not fit neatly into these prescribed roles," of wife and mother. (Harris-Perry 2011, 291) Mary Jane bemoans this herself during the pilot episode when she says, "I did everything right. What do I have to show for being a good girl?"

While the idea of respectability heralds holding oneself up as a model citizen of the community that embodies the image of upper-class sensibilities, with Mary Jane, Brock Akil paints a picture of someone who grew up following the rules of respectability according to what was expected of her, yet she still does not have everything she desires. For respectable people, vices are not heavily indulged in, yet on *Being Mary Jane*, alcohol is seen as almost a catalyst for truths to come out. Later on in Season 2 alcohol is seen as a symbol of Mary Jane's unraveling. In many ways she personifies the "Educated Black Bitch" Collins (2005) described. Despite not having reached her ultimate career goal, she is still very successful and working in a highly sought-after industry. She is even shown achieving greater success at the end of the "Signing Off" episode. In her personal life, however, things are more complicated.

Mary Jane both represents a sex-positive woman, and a woman whose personal desires motivate her to use her sexuality in questionable ways. Brock Akil depicts Mary Jane's sexual choices as a mix of both being in love—particularly in her interactions with Andre and David—and being in lust with other male interests. She seeks love and a family, and as the traditional way has not come about, in terms of her sexuality she has abandoned the prescribed puritanical ideal. She embraces her sexuality and makes no apology for it, except for the infidelity with Andre. Walking away from the mistress role, Mary Jane agonizes about being put in that position which reflects her displeasure with the nature of that role. In many ways this presentation is a more modern reflection of how many women embrace their sexuality. Instead of being a pawn or subject to the whims of the men in her life, Mary Jane dates, has sex with, pursues, and breaks up with the men in her life as she so chooses. Yet at the same time, the way that she goes about trying to get pregnant and find love at times put her in the position of appearing desperate for the role of motherhood, and maybe even wife. She goes back and forth with whether she wants David, their history, and whether there could be a future with him. Her feelings about the subject seem to depend upon the episode. The interrogation by all of her friends about David's life in the "People" episode after finding out that he is going to be a father makes her appear almost pushed to insanity. This is further fueled by her growing alcohol dependency in that season. In this way, despite displaying healthy sexuality, her actions related to her motivations in some of her relationships hinder this. While the complexities of Mary Jane's love life are designed to keep the storyline of the show going—as it is a television drama—in many ways it still represents past images of women being consumed primarily with romance and love (Douglas 2010; Holtzman 2000).

Aside from sexuality, when it comes to respectability, the inner workings of how important image is to those that uphold respectability politics is one that Brock Akil enforces in Mary Jane's world. Physical image and reputation are everything, much like they are for all celebrities. One scene toward the end of the "Let's Go Crazy" episode illustrates this clearly. Mary Jane, who has just taken out her weave, is panicked when finds out that her appointment for her hairstylist the next morning has to be canceled. Although she is able to get Niecy to come over and do her hair for her, she confesses to Niecy that part of her urgency with trying to get Niecy to come was because she was afraid of facing the world without her weave because she feared people at work looking at her like she was just average and not special. Her hair, just a part of her appearance—which is put at odds in the "Facing Fears" episode as Mary Jane recovers from reconstructive surgery on the scars from her accident—is a big part of her image as Mary Jane Paul.

Yet even aside from outside appearance and reputation, the materialism both for Mary Jane and those within her personal circle, people that are not in the public eye the way she is, are displayed almost as a way of firmly identifying them as members of the upper middle and upper class. Mary Jane attends exclusive "invite only" charity events such as the one during the "Mary Jane Knows Best" episode where she meets Sheldon. Those with whom she surrounds herself have the trappings of financial abundance, such as Sheldon who collects slave love letters from auctions and David whose success with his company has Paul Jr., Mary Jane's younger brother, seeking his help for investment in his proposed entrepreneurial venture. Aside from just the houses and clothes, this world maintains the image of success. Yet with all this success, as Black people, that feeling of uplift inherent in respectability is still there.

Aside from the discussions held about issues occurring in the Black community, a lot of attention is paid to how Mary Jane and her parents support Mary Jane's brothers and her niece Niecy. In this sense, the realities of how affluence may be attained by singular members of a family who in turn have to care for other members of the family are portrayed. As a result, conversations reflecting racial uplift are often with Mary Jane and her parents with Patrick or Niecy. The "Mary Jane Knows Best" demonstrates this in one scene where Patrick and Paul Sr. are on the golf course and Paul Sr. offers to help connect Patrick with some people for a job opportunity and later introduces him to an acquaintance that he thinks could help Patrick. Paul Sr. later complains to Helen that Patrick had too much pride and wouldn't accept help. Mary Jane's efforts to help Niecy, asking her about the cost for the nursing program Niecy wants to attend and even discussing career plans with Niecy also reflect this. Harris-Perry (2011) notes that many Blacks in the middle class often have family members who do not have the same material items or assets as them. In turn they may often find themselves in the position of having to take care of, whether it is physically, emotionally, and definitely financially, those family members. *Being Mary Jane* reflects this reality of how upliftment can therefore be on a more personal level.

CONCLUSION

Harris-Perry (2011) notes that "if a claim to full citizenship rests on the assertion of a narrowly defined, sexually repressive respectability, then [B]lack women must adhere to a rigidly controlled public performance of themselves. Such rigidity can leave little room for complicated realities" (62). *Being Mary Jane* attempts to present these complicated realities, displaying the tensions of balancing respectability, and adhering to this idea of positive representations of Black womanhood, while at the same time challenging the good versus bad woman dichotomy in the displays of sexuality. Mary Jane seems to mix the idea of both being "The Black Lady" and also being the "Educated Black Bitch" in the sense that while she lives up to the image of what the Black Lady is, a key storyline in the show is that of maintaining and balancing her career and her love life—much like the quintessential "Educated Black Bitch." Often the idea of these two archetypes is that they are opposites in that the "Black Lady" has it all, whereas the "Educated Black

Bitch" has flaws that keep her from having it all—specifically not being able to obtain a relationship. Much like hip hop feminism asserts, this dichotomy fact simplifies this notion about Black women's lives. Like many women, Mary Jane represents aspects of both.

The way that Mary Jane is depicted as living up to the idea of being a respectable Black woman—particularly in terms of being about cleanliness or domesticity—highlights the "Black Lady." In particular, one area that seems to be subtly emphasized with Mary Jane is her pride in her home, her body, and her talent for domesticity. For example, Mary Jane not only cooks but she is also apparently known for her ability to bake and displays professional-cake design and baking tools. She is seen having a housekeeping service and yet also makes a point of cleaning her house on her own anyway—particularly when she is stressed. The way these scenes are interwoven into storylines, for example showing her baking in the middle of the night alone in her kitchen and then turning on the television just in time to see a commercial featuring a family—which in turn makes her cry—serve as a point of contrast. Mary Jane is clearly made out to be a woman who not only can cook and clean—areas that often are not ascribed to successful career women—but also desiring of having her own family. The "Black Lady" not only has a family and/or a successful love life, but also has the skills to take care of home and those in it. Mary Jane has the skills to take care of her home, but just lacks having anyone in it.

In terms of balancing this split between being the "Black Lady" and the "Educated Black Bitch," it can be argued that Mary Jane's embrace of her sexuality is a component of being the latter. And yet, while the "Black Lady" may not always be seen as sexual, she likely does have sex with her husband. The difference here is that on *Being Mary Jane* an emphasis is placed on displaying how Mary Jane is in touch with her sexuality. Just as the "Educated Black Bitch" is considered beautiful, and sexual, but struggling to find a relationship they seek, Mary Jane is locked in the same battle. Sex is not something that Mary Jane shies away from. As a product of the postfeminist movement and hip hop generation, Mary Jane represents many women who have chosen to not run from embracing their sexuality or looking at sex as something that is a taboo and to be confined. Yet at the same time, coming from an upbringing where she was raised to aspire to be a wife and mother, steeped in these middle-class values of respectability, the balance of fulfilling these sexual needs as a single woman is one she still struggles with. Mary Jane acknowledges her sexual desires, but also knows that they could put her in a position to cloud her judgment, particularly in the relationship arena. The scene where she masturbates before going to out to meet with David in the pilot episode represents that. Mary Jane knows she is attracted to David and, that with the history they have, he is an area of weakness for her. In the end when she calls to cancel on him, she even acknowledges that his late invite to dinner was likely his way of trying to eventually have sex with her. She could have bypassed masturbation and just carried out her desires with him. But instead she takes care of her urges beforehand using masturbation as a tool to prevent her desire from making what could possibly be a bad choice. She takes marriage seriously and despite her drama in her relationships, a major part of that seems to be her desire to not make a mistake and be with the wrong person.

Another representation of this idea of balancing the need for sexual fulfillment with that of also seeking the way she approaches her relationships is the difference with how Mary Jane treats sex with David and Cutty Buddy in Season 2. In many ways the way that Mary Jane explores her sexual empowerment is with her Cutty Buddy. As a sexual partner, Mary Jane only contacts him when she desires sex and their contact and interactions appear to be on her terms. In one scene he mentions to her that he does have more to offer than just sex, if she ever wants that. While she kisses him before leaving, she is not seen in these episodes taking him up on that offer and contacting him for anything other the sex in the future. This is in contrast to men like Sheldon, who she waits to become intimate with as she is getting to know him. So when Mary Jane has sex in these episodes that Brock Akil has written, the men she is with fill one need or the other. Cutty Buddy represents the one uncomplicated relationship in her life because he fulfills one need only. Mary Jane, through this relationship with Cutty Buddy, shows that despite looking for love and desiring a relationship, it is possible for a woman to have a purely sexual relationship with a man without those desires for more. And yet, just by being able to balance both desires, with Mary Jane, Brock Akil has created a character that is not just either/or in terms of being able to be a lady or a bitch. While she has sexual desires, she also wants love. As such she pursues both, sometimes with the same person and sometimes with different people, much like many men and women do in real life.

For Mary Jane, having it all means having the family and the career. When looking at her life, Mary Jane considers how she played all the rules of respectability to have the career and financial trappings she was raised to seek. She went to college, waited to start a family until she was married, and worked hard to get the career she desired. But amidst her wait, like a lot of women, she found that life doesn't necessarily work out as you have planned just because you follow the rules. For example it was revealed on the show that Mary Jane previously had an abortion when she was younger and dating David. The explanation was that the time was not right and they both felt they were not ready to be parents. At the same time, for someone like Mary Jane, that lived up to the ideals of respectability, having a baby earlier than planned without all the success she dreamed would not have fit in the life plan she had. The irony of course is how despite following these rules and getting to where she wanted in her career, she was at a point in present day, where she was going through desperate moves to have a baby with David. Like many women, Mary Jane represents the reality of Black women that work to live up to these ideals of what the respectable Black woman should be, only to find themselves unhappy in many parts of their life and switching up to embracing whatever will make them unhappy—even if it is outside the confines of the traditional respectability they were raised to pursue. As Morgan (1999) points out, "Even our existences can't be defined in the past's simple terms: house nigga vs. field nigga, ghetto vs. bourgie, BAP vs. boho because our lives are usually some complicated combination of all of the above" (62).

Future studies examining respectability on *Being Mary Jane* may further observe the show's supporting characters such as Mary Jane's family members. Additionally, while this study focused on those written by Brock Akil, an examination of the trajectory of the show in terms of these themes, particularly in the last season of the show when Brock Akil Productions was no longer affiliated, would be interesting. In the end, the world of Mary Jane sought to provide a look into the complex realities of a specific demographic of Black people in this world.

REFERENCES

Braun, Virginia, Clarke, Victoria, and Terry, Gareth. "Thematic Analysis." In *Qualitative Research in Clinical and Health Psychology.* Edited by Poul Rohleder & Antonia C. Lyons, 96. New York: Palgrave Macmillan, 2015.

Cartier, Nina. "Black Women On-Screen As Future Texts: A New Look at Black Pop Culture Representations." *Cinema Journal* 53, no. 4 (2014): 150–57.

Collins, Patricia Hill. *Black Sexual Politics: African Americans, Gender, and the New Racism.* New York: Routledge, 2005.

Creedon, Pamela J. and Cramer, Judith. "Introduction: We've Come a Long Way, Maybe." In *Women in Mass Communication*, 3rd edition. Edited by Pamela J. Creedon & Judith Cramer, 3–8. Thousand Oaks, CA: Sage Publications, 2007.

Crockett, David. "Paths to Respectability: Consumption and Stigma Management in the Contemporary Black Middle Class." *Journal of Consumer Research* 44 (2017): 554–81.

Croteau, David and Hoynes, William. *Media/Society: Industries, Images, and Audiences*, 3rd edition. Thousand Oaks, CA: Pine Forge Press, 2003.

Douglas, Susan J. *Where the Girls Are: Growing Up Female With the Mass Media.* New York: Times Books, 1994.

———. *The Rise of Enlightened Sexism: How Pop Culture Took Us From Girl Power to Girls Gone Wild.* New York: St. Martin's Press, 2010.

Durham, Aisha. "Using Living Hip hop Feminism: Redefining An Answer (To) Rap." In *Check It While I Wreck It: Black Womanhood, Hip-hop Culture, and the Public Sphere.* Edited by Gwendolyn Pough, et al., 304–12. Boston, MA: Northeastern University Press, 2007.

Durham, Aisha, Cooper, Brittney C., and Morris, Susana M. "The Stage Hip-hop Feminism Built: A New Directions Essay." *Signs: Journal of Women in Culture and Society* 38, no. 3 (2013): 721–37.

Frazier, E. Franklin. *Black Bourgeoisie.* London: Collier, 1969.

Gaffney, Adrienne. "*Being Mary Jane* Creator Mara Brock Akil on Her Flawed Heroine, the Rise of Diverse TV, and Why She Hates Color-Blind Casting." Last modified February 3, 2015. https://www.vulture.com/2015/02/being-mary-jane-mara-brock-akil.html.

Harris, Fredrick C. "The Rise of Respectability Politics." *Dissent* (2014): 33–37. https://www.dissentmagazine.org/article/the-rise-of-respectability-politics.

Harris-Perry, Melissa. *Sister Citizen: Shame, Stereotypes, and Black Women in America.* New Haven: Yale University Press, 2011.

Higginbotham, Evelyn Brooks. *Righteous Discontent: The Women's Movement in the Black Baptist Church, 1880-1920.* Cambridge, MA: Harvard University Press, 1993.

Holtzman, Linda. *Media Messages: What Film, Television, and Popular Music Teach Us About Race, Class, Gender, and Sexual Orientation.* Armonk, NY: Routledge, 2000.

Jeffries, Devair and Jeffries, Rhonda. "Mentoring and Mothering Black Femininity in the Academy: An Exploration of Body, Voice, and Image Through Black Female Characters." *The Western Journal of Black Studies* 39, no. 2 (2015): 125–33.

Jordan, June. "A New Politics of Sexuality." *Progressive* 55, no. 7 (1991): 12.

Lee, Shayne. *Erotic Revolutionaries: Black Women, Sexuality, and Popular Culture.* Lanham, MD: Hamilton Books, 2010.

Meyers, Marian. "Fracturing Women." In *Mediated Women: Representations in Popular Culture.* Edited by Marian Meyers, 3–24. Cresskill, NJ: Hampton Press, 1999.

Morgan, Joan. *When Chickenheads Come Home to Roost: A Hip-hop Feminist Breaks it Down.* New York: Touchstone, 1999.

———. "Why We Get Off: Moving Towards a Black Feminist Politics of Pleasure." *The Black Scholar* 45, no. 4 (2015): 36–46.

"Pilot." *Being Mary Jane.* Directed by Salim Akil. Written by Mary Brock Akil. July 2, 2013. Los Angeles, CA: BET Networks.

Pough, Gwendolyn D. *Check It While I Wreck It: Black Womanhood, Hip-hop Culture, and the Public Sphere.* Boston, MA: Northeastern University Press, 2004.

Smith-Shomade, Beretta E. *Shaded lives: African American Women and Television.* New Brunswick, NJ: Rutgers University Press, 2002.

Thompson, Lisa B. *Beyond the Black Lady: Sexuality and the New African American Middle Class.* Urbana and Chicago: University of Illinois Press, 2009.

White, E. Frances. *Dark Continent of Our Bodies: Black Feminism and the Politics of Responsibility.* Philadelphia: Temple University Press, 2001.

Chapter 4

"Girl, You Know I Got You"

The Ideology of Sisterhood on Being Mary Jane

Shauntae Brown White

I[1] must admit when *Being Mary Jane* was first broadcasted in 2013, I was turned off by what I thought was the premise—an African American, single woman involved in an affair with a married man. After much buzz in social media, I was enticed to check it out. I was pleasantly surprised the show was more than what I thought. While Mary Jane was in an adulterous relationship with a married man of whom she did not initially know was married, it was clear that the main character nor the show's writers were not condoning the behavior. Other than knowing it was an original show produced on Black Entertainment Television (BET), I knew nothing about the producers or writers. However, I was more than confident. African American women had significant roles at the writers' table. *Being Mary Jane* captured the nuances of Black women's experiences—the loving and supportive, but meddlesome and emotionally manipulative mother; though Mary Jane was enormously successful, she still had ties to her family, extended family, and the Black community. Mary Jane was at the top of her game professionally, and yet racism and sexism were always prominently discussed in her life. The one thing that stood out to me the most was the intimate, complex, yet beautiful relationships she had with other women. They were supportive. They were encouraging. They had conflict. But, at the end of the day, they loved each other.

From scripted shows, such as *Julia* or *Scandal*, that don't show Black women connected to any community of Black women to reality shows, such as *The Real Housewives of Atlanta*, that often show women rife with petty jealousy, conflict, and aggressive tactics for conflict resolution, the portrayal of positive friendships among African Americans is welcome, refreshing, and should be studied. This chapter explores the representation of sisterhood on

Being Mary Jane. It will provide a brief historical context of African American women's portrayals on television, a theoretical framework using black feminist thought (BFT), and use ideological criticism to analyze scenes from *Being Mary Jane* related to her relationship with her niece, her coworker/friend, and childhood friend.

HISTORICAL OVERVIEW OF BLACK WOMEN ON TELEVISION

Over twenty-five years ago in the concluding remarks of the seminal work *Split Image: African Americans in the Mass Media*, Dates and Barlow (1993) discussed the dual strategy black image makers used to control the black image: (1) Be a media professional insider of corporate media working to broaden and upgrade the image of African Americans; and/or (2) Be cultural entrepreneurs and activists who develop alternative media products, outlets and services that target the interests and needs of African American audiences and consumers. They ended the chapter and the book with a call to make a concerted and systematic effort within the media mainstream, academia, and industry to ensure the future of Black images would be different from the past. Needless to say, over twenty-five years ago there was a dearth of dramatic television lead characters which featured smart, complex, and multidimensional Black people that also addressed issues that were both significant and germane to the Black community. One could only hope this call would be answered.

Media scholars and Black popular culture critics have long called for media images of African American women to be more authentic and fully represent their humanity (Bogle 2001; Cheers 2018; Dates and Barlow 1993; Gammage 2016; Gray 2004). From Ethel Waters, the first African American woman to appear on television in 1939 on the *Ethel Waters Show* to today, the portrayals of Black women have been problematic at best. Over its nearly 100-year history, the television representations of African American women have shown women who have been virtually nonexistent, consumed in roles that serve as controlling images justifying white supremacy and patriarchy, featured women with no connection to the Black community nor their experiences with racism, or are consistently featured as bad girls who are aggressive, negative, loud, bitchy, and sexually promiscuous (Allison 2016; Cheers 2018; Gammage 2016).

These characters often lack context and relational connections with other African Americans. Conversely, portrayals of Black women's friendships on television are not nonexistent.

In her analysis of African American women on primetime television, Merritt (1994) documented several friendships of Black women in television history. Characters such as Julia (*Julia*, 1965–1966), the first television series to feature a lead African American woman and Nell (*Gimmie a Break*, 1984–1989) nearly twenty years later, portrayed women who were disconnected from the Black community and addressed no issues of race or racism. This is important in that the absence and/or presence of those portrayals contribute to how an idea, person of group is perceived (Gray 2004; Merritt 1994). While Julia had no Black female friends, and Nell had one, Addie, who Merritt argues was most times antagonistic and not always supportive of Nell. However, television viewers were also exposed to Florida Evans and her neighbor and friend Willona Woods on *Good Times* (1979–1983), Louise Jefferson, Helen Willis and employee Florence on *The Jeffersons* (1978–1985), and the friendship circle of four diverse women—Mary, Sandra, Pearl and Rose—on *227* (1986–1990). These relationships, Merritt argues were warm, supportive, genuine and positive. In addition to friendships with peers, Claire Huxtable on *The Cosby Show* (1983–1993) was shown to have healthy intergenerational relationships with her mother and mother-in-law.

In a more recent study on *Black Women's Portrayals on Reality Television: The New Sapphire*, Allison (2016) argues that while the 1990s scripted show *Living Single* provided a refreshing portrayal of Black women's friendships that were a portrayal of loyalty and solidarity, the reality shows that came after leave much to be desire. From the 1990s *The Real World*, to show such as *The Bad Girls Club* (2006), *The Real Housewives of Atlanta* (2008), *Basketball Wives* (2010), *Love and Hip Hop* (2011), Black women are often shown as difficult and regularly exhibit bad behavior—that is, bitchy, aggressive, loud, unsupportive, hypercritical, and confrontational (Allison 2016; Cooper 2016; Gammage 2016). The relationships with each other are riddled with conflict, and unhealthy conflict resolution strategies from screaming matches to physical fights. Not all reality television shows depict African American women exhibiting physical aggression, but the passive-aggressive representations are just as problematic. In her analysis of friendships on the reality show *The Preachers of L.A.* Cooper (2016) argues,

> Overall, these women offered a negative portrayal of black womanhood by suggesting that within black female friendships there is a lack of trust surrounding how much information can be shared, because there is always a perceived possibility that what is shared will be talked about in separate conversations— behind your back. This can also cause difficulty in women's desire to share; and because this is a religious context, judgment may be even harsher. (pg. 11)

These and other portrayals of Black women and friendships among them distort the image of Black women, minimizes their humanity, and sends the message that Black women are incapable of healthy relationships with other women (Gammage 2016).

Answering the Call: Mara Brock Akil

As both a corporate media professional insider and a cultural entrepreneur and activist Mara Brock Akil answered the call that Dates and Barlow issued over twenty-five years ago to create diverse, multidimensional characters that affirmed the humanity of African Americans, and women specifically. Throughout each of her long-running shows, *Girlfriends* (2000–2008), *The Game* (2006–2015), *Being Mary Jane* (2013–2017), and most recently *Love Is* ____ (2018), Brock Akil tells the stories of everyday characters through the lens of Black women (Asare 2013). She has articulated in many interviews, her goal for *Being Mary Jane* was to bring humanity to the character (Witherspoon 2015; Terrero 2015) and create real, authentic, and relatable experiences about Black women (Stack 2015). Brock Akil has created characters and are multidimensional and flawed. In fact, the promotional ad for *Being Mary Jane* was the tagline "beautifully flawed." In a 2015 interview, she said "Trying to shape my characters' humanity is so much part of my work. One of the things I think has been missing from the landscape of talking about black characters is talking about our humanity, and the fact that we come from somewhere" (Terrero 2015). Though she has a commitment to telling real, authentic stories about African American people, Brock Akil also argues her stories are universal:

> Any form of media is an opportunity to be a mirror and reflection of what we are experience more in the details of our life. . . . What makes it fun and unique in a lot of ways is how that journey is changing just by the mere fact of the current time. I love writing about black women, but if you go beyond that, we're human beings—and because we're human beings, it's universal for everybody. (Brock Akil as cited in Asare 2013)

Brock Akil's work gives voice to the everyday, average Black woman's experience. This is a tenant of Black feminist thought.

BLACK FEMINIST THOUGHT: A THEORETICAL FRAMEWORK

Black feminist thought is critical social theory that gives voice and visibility to Black women and their experiences (Collins 2000). The theory is concerned with the multiple jeopardies and interlocking identities Black women face and their response to them. Thus, there is no one experience or response to oppression. Instead, Black women share a collective standpoint that acknowledges there is not one experience that is more accurate, or a response to oppression that is more correct, than another woman's experiences, "Black women's standpoint eschews essentialism in favor of democracy" (268). One of the safe spaces for Black women to construct individual and collective voices is the location in Black women's relationships with others including family, friends, and community. Safe spaces represent places where Black women could freely examine issues important to them—usually free of men or non-Black people. It is a place to develop empowerment, generate understanding or their realities and develop strategies for dealing with those interlocking oppressions.

There are multiple themes about Black women's relationships with each other that Collins documents in literature. Fundamental to all healthy relationships with other women is affirmation and support: (1) Black women affirm each other humanity—each other's specialness and right to exist. (2) Black women listen to each other in order to support, and/or aid in each other's growth, well-being, and renewal. Though the first two themes are common and essential to sisterhood, because we are complex human beings, we can also experience difficulties in our relationships with other women. (3) Those difficulties in affirming each other can happen for a variety of different reasons. (4) Control and repress (i.e., an overbearing mother). Women can experience all these themes in one relationship.

Collins argues that people become more human and empowered primarily in the contexts of a community, and "the power of the word generally, and dialogue specifically, allows this to happen" (261). It is the dialogue we have with others where we can access our knowledge claims and assign meaning to our lived experiences. Researcher Marsha Houston (2004) utilizes Black feminist thought to explore Black women's talk with each other. The facets of everyday talk include care talk, personal accountability, and triumph stories. Collins argues that the ethic of caring or "talking with the heart" consists of three parts: an emphasis on individual uniqueness affirming everyone's value, appropriateness of emotions—which indicates a speaker's belief in the validity of a knowledge claim—and the idea that emotions and intellect are not separate developing the capacity for empathy. She argues that the ethic of personal accountability is equally important, where people hold each other responsible for their own knowledge claims:

> Assessment of an individual's knowledge claims simultaneously evaluate an individual's character, values and ethics. Thus, it is appropriate to probe into a person's personal viewpoints to assess personal accountability. "Knowledge claims made by individuals respected for their moral and ethical connections to their ideas will carry more weight than those offered by less respective figures. (Collins 2000, 265)

Houston's (2004) study on how African American women conceive their talk included a theme of celebration, which included wisdom, fortitude, and caring. Black women's talk characterized as wise referred to her knowledge about a topic. That knowledge could be considered caring which includes demonstrating concern, compassion, being sensitive, warm, and humanistic. When the dimensions of fortitude and wisdom are combined, Houston argues it indicates Black women value, "speaking out and speaking strongly, but not without a basis in knowledge and experience" (162).

With Collins' assessment that women's relationships with each other is a safe space for them to develop both individual and collective voice, and Houston's application of the ethics of caring and personal accountability in everyday talk, I argue *Being Mary Jane* exhibits an ideology of sisterhood embedded in the main character's relationship with other women, and the show creates a space for her to be supported, grow and renew, yet be held accountable for her personal actions.

METHODOLOGY

This chapter utilizes ideological criticism to analyze what messages are embedded in *Being Mary Jane* about Black women's relationships. In an ideological analysis, the critic is "looking beyond the surface of an artifact to discover the beliefs, values, and assumptions its suggestions" (Foss 2009, 209). According to Foss, the first step is to select the artifact. This chapter presents and analyzes six scenes from *Being Mary Jane* from Seasons 1 to 3 which highlight the relationships Mary Jane has with her niece, Niecy, her colleague and friend Kara, and her childhood friend Lisa. All three women play a significant role in Mary Jane's life. All three scenes depict tension and conflict at a particular time in their relations. One could also argue that these tensions were significant moments in the relationship between women. The second step is analysis of the artifact, identifying the assumptions that construct a particular ideology. For this study, the analysis evaluated the assumptions made about the construct of sisterhood. Once the assumptions were identified, the ideology is formulated. Thus, this study asks the following research question: What is the ideology of sisterhood embedded in the text of *Being Mary Jane*?

ANALYSIS

Family and Community as a Safe Space

Before examining Mary Jane's relationships with other women, it is important to understand her connection to her family and the community. Depicting represents the fullness of their [...]tion to the African American [...] awareness of issues that [...]. The [...] *Mary Jane* consistently re[...] see Mary Jane in her pro[...] the things that all professiona[...]nce, professional developments, and office [...] racism and sexism. It is also in this context we could see Ma[ry Ja]ne's connection and commitment to the African American community and issue germane to them with the stories she pitched and fought to get on the air.

In addition to seeing her in a career context, we see that Mary Jane was very much a part of the lives of her immediate family which included her parents, two adult brothers, and her nieces, the daughters of her older brother. It is in the scenes with her family that the audience gained more insight into the character's humanity. Mary Jane is the name she used professionally as well as with newer or adult friendships and romantic relationships. Pauletta is the character's birth name where the audience only sees her family calling her that.

There is no universal image of the African American family; however, the writers of *Being Mary Jane* captured some of the nuances that are familiar to many in family dynamics. Mary Jane grew up in a stable, two-parent family where her retired father, Paul, was one of the first African American pilots for an airline. Mary Jane's mother Helen is active in her community and the social organizations of Atlanta's Black elite. It is clear to the audience that her parents are supportive of their children, had expectations of all of them to be productive citizens of the world. They are profoundly disappointed and hurt by their oldest son Patrick's years of drug use. Although they had higher expectations for Patrick, they celebrate his small victories of continued sobriety and maintaining employment. Mary Jane's single status worries her mother. Helen is supportive of her daughter, proud of her (she likes to brag to her friends about her daughter being on the air), has a mother's critical eye when she calls Mary Jane to give her a critique of her outfit or makeup when she was last on the air, is overly dependent on Mary Jane—the responsible one of her children, meddlesome in her daughter's love life, and emotionally manipulative at times. Helen's characteristics show the audience a multidimensional mother who generally is loving and supportive of her children while simultaneously being overly dramatic, emotionally manipulative, and critical.

In addition to Mary Jane's immediate family, she is still connected to her extended family. When Patrick, her older brother, discovers Mary Jane is in an adulterous relationship, he confronts her and attempts to get her to see the behavior she has exhibited about her affair (the lying, denial, inability to let go) are very similar to his addictive behavior about drugs. When Mary Jane calls him to help support her in resisting Andre, her lover, Patrick takes Mary Jane to the place where he goes when he is trying to resist the temptations of drugs: Aunt Toni's house—their father's sister. Aunt Toni's house is certainly more modest than Mary Jane's and even Mary Jane's parent's home. Paul and Helen appear to live in a solidly middle-class neighborhood. Aunt Toni appears to live in the "hood" which Mary Jane implies when she asks Patrick, "Aren't you going to lock your car doors?" Yet, the home had all the markers familiar to many African American family gathering houses: lots of intergenerational family and extended family; enough food for everyone even those who dropped by unexpectedly; and Aunt Toni making them feel included in the family dinner rituals by putting Patrick and Mary Jane to work as soon as they walked in to stir the cabbage and set the table while she multitasked on something else. Though this scene is not essential to the storyline, it, and others like it, provides the audience with a view of Mary Jane's familial experiences that give us insight into who she is and helps to create characters that are familiar, authentic, and relatable.

In the Company of Women: Safe Space in a Sister Circle

Familial connections are but one safe space for Black women to be supported. Equally important is being in the company of women. In Season 1, episode 3, "Girls Night In," Mary Jane is in her kitchen, a familiar gathering place for Black women, with four of her friends. They all have professional jobs—a doctor, two in the news industry, and a publicist. In this safe space, "my sister's kitchen," the women discussed topics that are both varied and commonplace among women: work, men, and relationships. The women also shared secrets—secrets they each seem a bit embarrassed to admit. One friend who was recently engaged admitted she purchased her engagement ring because her fiancé purchased one that was too small. Mary Jane admitted that she had "stolen" her ex-boyfriend's sperm and frozen it to use for later. Lisa admits that she did not vote for Obama. It is in this same scene that the audience also realizes that neither Mary Jane nor her friends condone marital adultery. Even though this is a safe place where the women are each sharing secrets, Mary Jane does not disclose that she is having an affair with a married man. Further, the body language of two of her friends when one friend, Nichelle, admits to an affair demonstrates this is not regarded favorably by the women. Kara directly asks, "Oh, so you are a homewrecker? You actually celebrate the destruction of families?" [32:30]. After Kara questions her some more, Nichelle asks, "Oh come on. So, I am the only one who has had an affair with a married man?" To which the other women answer, "Yes."

Mary Jane remains silent, and when Nichelle asks her for her answer, she replies "Don't look at me!" The women challenge Nichelle, and Nichelle apologizes to Kara whose own marriage ended for multiple reasons including her husband's unfaithfulness. This scene with the collective women shows women who were vulnerable to one another, held each other accountable, and did not pass some much judgment as to shame another woman. In essence, each woman's experiences and personhood were affirmed. These friendship characteristics represent the type of relationship Mary Jane had with various women individually.

Mary Jane and Niecy: My Sister's Keeper

Mary Jane has a close and supportive relationship with her niece Niecy. In many aspects, the relationship is unequal. Mary Jane is a successful professional woman who lives in a comfortable lifestyle. She can afford nice things including her own luxury home and car to being able to splurge on designer purses and shoes. Clearly, Niecy looks up to Mary Jane. Niecy on the other hand is nineteen and has two children by two different men, unmarried, overweight, and lives with her grandparents because she cannot support herself and her children on her own. She has few skills that will lead her to upward mobility. Despite the differences, the two women love each other. Mary Jane is an active and involved great aunt with Niecy's children, and is always encouraging Niecy to do and be better. Sometimes those encouragements come off as harsh, judgmental admonishments, but the ultimate desire Mary Jane has is for Niecy to be her best self.

In Season 2, Niecy and her grandmother have an argument and she and her two children move in with Mary Jane. Niecy cramps Mary Jane's style. Frustrated with several things, but in particular the junk food wrappers found under the bed, Mary Jane decided to confront Niecy, not about being a slob, but instead about being overweight. Though the conversation was hurtful to Niecy, Mary Jane was thoughtful about it as the audience observes her in the mirror practicing what she is going to say, and then the next scene cuts to the confrontation already taking place:

"By whose standards?"
"America! There is the First Lady's "Let's Move Campaign"
  there is the American Diabetes Association."
"I am healthy, I am just thick."
"This is me trying to be motivational."
"Well, I don't feel motivated. I feel ridiculed and forced to be a size 2."
"This conversation is about your health. About diabetes, cholesterol.
  No. No. Don't get me started on the 'I'm thick' conversation."
"Well go ahead and get started, please!"

"Why does every overweight black woman in the hood think she is thick?
We don't eat well. We don't exercise and then we justify our diabetes,
high cholesterol by saying, 'I was born this way. God made me 60 pounds
overweight.' Because you know what, it's all fun and games until you lose a
foot at 40. Ain't nobody going to call you thick when you have three toes."
"Auntie you have been brain washed."
"No, no Babydoll, you were the one who was crying
because you didn't feel beautiful."
"I am not saying I can't stand to lose some weight. I can. But
I am not going to let you or anyone else convince me that
skinny is it when models are passing out on runways."
"And you cannot walk down up a flight of stairs without
breathing heavy." [S2:3, 1:18–3:05]

Confronting any person, especially a woman, about his or her weight is a difficult conversation as evidenced by Mary Jane practicing what she was going to say. Mary Jane attempts to demonstrate both care and concern while holding Niecy personally accountable for her weight. In her persuasive attempts she moves the focus of the conversation from more than her opinion, Mary Jane invokes the credibility of The First Lady Michelle Obama's "Let's Move campaign and the American Diabetes Association." Mary Jane doesn't just confront Niecy about her weight, she also helps and supports her. The remainder of the episode is scenes showing Niecy and her exercising and cooking together. This segment shows healthy relationships with other women require forthrightness in conversation and balanced with support. It would not be enough for Mary Jane to bring the conversation up about Niecy's weight without helping her to develop new strategies for health and wellness.

Throughout the next two episodes Niecy continues to live with Mary Jane and Mary Jane, in the position of authority based on her status of being her aunt, being older and being established and successful in her career, continues to give Niecy advice and support to be better. She also critiques of some of the choices she makes. A turning point in their relationship came in Season 2, episode 4 "Sleepless in Atlanta," when Mary Jane found Niecy having sex with her older child's father in Mary Jane's bed. After Niecy apologizes Mary Jane asks her, "Are you tired of being sorry and making promises you can't keep." From that question, a hostile exchange erupts:

"Auntie, I made a mistake."
"I know, you are always making a mistake. My question is are you
tired of it? Cause here I am thinking, "Wow, Niecy is really getting
her life together." And then you go a pull a stunt like that . . .
. . . Baby, you are never going to attract more than how you feel about yourself . . .

... I love you. Baby, I do. But your life cannot revolve around
  a dude. There is more to life the men and kids."
"Like what, freezing your eggs and drinking tequila?"
"Excuse me, little girl?"
"Oh, no, you made it very clear that I'm a big girl. And since we are talking truth,
  let's talk about the empty tequila bottles that I found under your bathroom sink."
"Wait, wait. You have been snooping around my house?"
"I was looking for lotion."
"Ain't this about a blimp. You use Treyvion to get Cameron
  to come over here and then I call you on it, and now you
  are trying to come at me sideways over a drink?"
"So, you can critique me on everything—everything! But, I can't say
  anything about the fact that you drink all the time and by yourself?"
"I don't have to answer to you, Niecy. I am a grown-ass woman."
"Yeah, and you're twice my age, and you have to sneak around your
  own house hiding alcohol. Is that what grown women do?"
"No, grown women have jobs. Contrary to the belief of the blogs
  and reality shows, being a baby mama is not a career!"
"I'm taking care of my kids."
"No! I am taking care of your kids. You have no job, no skills, and
  two mouths to feed. You show up at my doorstep, and you are
  surprised that I'm drinking? Oh baby, you are lucky that is all I'm
  doing living with your ungrateful ass." [S2:4, 14:50–16:59]

This exchange, too, uses direct, forthright communication, but different from the exchange about Niecy's weight. Though Mary Jane expresses care and concern with using the endearing term "baby" when she addresses Niecy and making the statements such as "you are never going to attract more than how you feel about yourself," the spirit behind the statements were not as warm or supportive as the first conversation. She also was quick to remind Niecy of the power dynamics in the relationship when she addressed her as "little girl," a reminder that she was the aunt, the adult, and the one who had her life together more than a nineteen-year-old teen mother who cannot take care of herself or children. In turn, Niecy invokes the use of the ethic of personal accountability—the idea that your words need to match your own life and personal ethic. For Niecy, Mary Jane cannot critique her when her own life is not without reproach. Instead of direct communication to build each other up, the goal for both the women is to bring the other woman down a notch— for Mary Jane it was about being challenged by a child about her drinking, and for Niecy it was about being criticized by someone who was not perfect herself. Though Niecy and her grandmother are not on speaking terms—the reason she was living with Mary Jane—she calls her grandfather to come pick her and her children up from Mary Jane's. Paul tries to get the women to reconcile before leaving with Niecy and her children to no avail.

Mary Jane and Niecy maintain their standoff with each other for three episodes until "Let's Go Crazy," Season 2, episode 7, when Mary Jane's regular beautician cancels her appointment after she has removed her weave in preparation for a new one. Mary Jane begs Niecy—who doesn't have a cosmetology license but is skilled at doing hair—to come rescue her. It is a switch in power dynamics in their relationships where Mary Jane usually holds the resource that Niecy needs be it money, advice, or encouragement to now Niecy has something Mary Jane needs. The women reconnect in the safe space of the familiar Black girl/woman ritual of getting her hair done. As a safe space, it provides the opportunity for women to talk about a myriad of topics for what could take multiple hours. It is here the audience witnesses the women reconnecting while Mary Jane is sitting on the floor between Niecy's legs while Niecy sewing in Mary Jane's weave. The scene is significant in its portrayals of Black women's relationships with each other in that it shows that even though there is conflict, there is still trust, love, and intimacy between them. There is an ethic of caring where both women demonstrate an emotionality that is vulnerable. Niecy admitted her feelings were and still are hurt, especially when the comments were from her aunt to whom she looks up and wants her approval. Mary Jane admits that her hair "emergency" was motivated by her own insecurities and terrified of going to work without her weave and not feeling beautiful. Though this statement is not unpacked in the dialogue, it is an issue that the majority of Black women influenced by the standards of Eurocentric beauty would understand. Mary Jane admits she is human, and the pedestal Niecy had her on was too high. Moreover, there is the ethic of personal accountability. Mary Jane apologizes for hurting Niecy's feelings. Niecy doesn't back away from her aunt's drinking pointing out while she has been doing her hair Mary Jane was on her third glass of wine. The scene ends with Niecy saying, "But, seriously Auntie. I worry about you" [35:31–38:11]. The relationship between Mary Jane and Niecy shows that though women can show care, concern, and support, they can simultaneous be destructive with their words because they are flawed and human. However, genuine sisterhood that more often than not exhibit care and concern leaves room for human flaws and even more room for vulnerability and forgiveness.

Mary Jane & Kara: Personal Accountability

Kara is Mary Jane's producer for her news show. It is clear they have a partnership with each other. Kara is Latina, who shares her own gendered and raced experiences in her professional and personal life. Kara is comfortable in Mary Jane's world evidenced by the social contexts she is in with Mary Jane outside of work. In the scene mentioned earlier in the kitchen she is the only Latina of the group of women. She is also comfortable discussing her own experiences—different from the others—primarily in her attraction for white men, yet she shares several commonalities with the African American women dealing with both racism, sexism, and work–life balance.

Kara is a divorced mother of two boys. The audience is privy to her struggle of trying to balance home life and her ambition at work. In her eyes, she has failed as a wife stating she deserved to be cheated on by her husband because she checked out of the marriage. She also feels she comes up short in mothering, for instance purchasing store bought baked goods for her son and feeling like the other mothers judge on her because of it. In an act of support, when she shows up at Mary Jane's door after midnight to ask her to make some brownies because she burned hers earlier in the evening, Mary Jane does it without questions asked. Acts and conversations such as these give the audience the impression that Mary Jane and Kara have had a long and supportive history together.

Mary Jane has concealed her affair in the entirety of Season 1 and finally confesses it to Kara in the season finale. Kara, whose marriage ended because of her ex-husband's infidelity, has strong and harsh judgment for Mary Jane.

"I think you should have to sit with what you have done."
"I pray like 50 times a day they get back together."
"Um. Um hum."
"I am hoping that my affair just brings them back together in a real way."
"You know what? I am going to stop drinking right now because
 all I can see in you is John's wench, and I all can think
 of doing to haul off and punch you in the face."
"But you always said, 'John deserved to cheat.'"
"Yeah, I can say that because that's how I cope, but your ratchet
 ass went back to him after you found out he was married."
"Please don't judge me."
"It's too late for that. And you went back and told the wife? Really?"
"See I was doing that in solidarity. I probably didn't think it through."
"Oh! And then you slipped on his penga. Um hum.
You need to apologize to here. That is what I wanted. Weird. I know.
 But I just wanted that bitch to say, 'sorry' to me. To acknowledge
 me. To see me. And to accept my existence and that she participated
 in hurting me, even if I deserved to be cheated on."
"I would apologize. I just don't know where they live." [S1: 9 25:35–27:13]

Kara is angry and disappointed with Mary Jane, and she does not hold back in showing it. Mary Jane, like her husband's mistress, violated the first principle of sisterhood, which is to affirm one's humanity, her specialness, and right to exist. No matter how badly a marriage is going, Kara's words express that no woman has a right to violate another woman in the way Mary Jane has done. Kara's speech is forthright in chiding Mary Jane to take personal responsibility for her anti-sisterhood actions. Later in the episode, Kara and Mary Jane go to Avery, Andre's wife, so that Mary Jane can apologize. While there Kara clearly expresses her disgust to Avery about Mary Jane's behavior, "Look Avery, I think my friend is despicable. I mean I can barely look at her right now. She saw me. Held me . . . as I cried . . . snot coming down myself before I entered my office. Because my heart was so broken. And the thought that she participated in doing this to another woman sickens me. Sickens me. It does" [31:00–31:38].

The safe spaces of sisterhood does not excuse each other when there is a violation done to other women. Kara called Mary Jane on her contribution to the destruction of another woman's marriage and didn't let up. Kara expressed her disapproval of Nichelle's affair in episode 3, "Girls Night Out," but she expresses her disgust with Mary Jane for whom she had greater expectations not just because of the close relationship they share but because Mary Jane watched her walk through the breakdown of her marriage. Thus, her judgment and words were much harsher for Mary Jane. However, one of the themes of sisterhood is encouraging each other to be and do better. Mary Jane is taken aback that Kara said that she was "sickened by her" in front of Avery, and that motivates her to also apologize to Kara. Kara accepts her apology on behalf of all women done wrong. She and Mary Jane embrace; they both say, "I love you," and Kara assures Mary Jane everything is going to be alright. Kara is angry and disappointed with Mary Jane. Yet, she still encourages her to take responsibility for her actions. Because Mary Jane like all people is flawed, and her actions cause conflict with her relationships with her friends. Equally important to holding Mary Jane accountability is also extending her grace. As an act of affirming her humanity, Kara communicated both love and forgiveness.

Mary Jane and Lisa: Transitions

Mary Jane and Lisa have been friends since childhood, and their relationship is the most complex among her sister circle. Lisa is close to Mary Jane's family. In fact, Mary Jane's mother refers to her as a daughter. In one scene the audience sees Lisa visiting Mary Jane's mother and comfortably sitting in Helen's bed with her talking and watching television, an act that connotes intimacy between the women. The first scene in "Storm Advisory," Season 1, episode 2, is Mary Jane breaking into Lisa's house to rescue her from an attempted suicide with a drug overdose. Mary Jane stayed at Lisa's house for several days to take care of her. Lisa, a medical doctor, is professionally accomplished and committed to the community through various acts of volunteer service, but she is emotionally troubled and suffers from depression.

The audience witness cracks between Lisa and Mary Jane in Season 2. "No Eggspectations" is a turning point in their relationship. Mary Jane perceives Lisa as being non-supportive and judgmental in her quest for fertility suggesting that perhaps she is not ready or fit to become a mother. Mary Jane suggests they get to the bottom of the riff between them which began five years ago where she started a relationship with David, Mary Jane's long-term ex-boyfriend who was Lisa's friend first.

"I know where this is really coming from. We've been having
   the same argument in some way, shape or form for the last five
   years. Why are you only mad at me and not David?"
"Because you were my friend, and you're supposed to be loyal to me."
"There we go. There we go. Now we're getting somewhere. Now we are finally
   getting somewhere, you finally admitted it. I can't believe I'm about to
   have this stupid-ass high school discussion, but here we go. Since you love
   revisionist history, let me give you a little reminder. You kept calling David
   your friend, so he asked me out. I did not accept until you said, 'Okay.' So,
   don't come in my house and try to lecture me about accepting my decisions.
Wait a second, Lisa. Lisa, wake up. He didn't want you."
"Well, now you know how that feels." [S2:5, 10:42–14:40]

For Lisa, Mary Jane violated a sister-friend ethic—even though she said David was her friend, she expected Mary Jane to know she had feelings for him. For Mary Jane, this was an unfair expectation to have when Lisa was not honest about her feelings and Mary Jane did ask for her permission before she got involved. After this exchange Mary Jane does not speak to Lisa for the remainder of the season. An even more significant turn of events for the two women is when David accidentally butt-dialed Mary Jane and she overheard a conversation between him and Lisa where Lisa was expressing her feelings for him—something David seemed unaware even though Lisa had lent him start-up money for his business and performed oral sex on him—at a time he and Mary Jane had broken up. While listening to the conversation, Mary Jane has a life-threatening car accident which is the season finale.

Season 3 opens with the aftermath of Mary Jane's car accident, Lisa attempting to apologize and Mary Jane icing her out. In Season 3, episode 3, Lisa commits suicide. Even though Lisa violated the bond between she and Mary Jane and Mary Jane had not spoken to Lisa in over a year, Mary Jane was fiercely protective of her in the planning of her funeral and determining how her legacy would be shaped. She was angry with her mother, Helen, who called Lisa's parents to tell her she died—Lisa had not spoken to them in fifteen years. Mary Jane made it very clear that Lisa's stepfather was not welcomed at the funeral and instructed him not to come. When he did, she said this in her eulogy:

> I realized that I am a liar. I am a big liar and a good liar. We all are. We are all just pretending that we are ok when we are really not. It is not enough for just us to lie. We really expect for everyone else to lie, too. It's like we are all afraid that the whole world is going to come falling down if we are honest with one another all the time. I absolutely now believe that the lies we tell each other that's what killed my friend Lisa. My sister. So, I know a lot of you here know that Lisa was originally from Ohio and moved to Atlanta when she was 8 and that she was a straight A student and graduated from Meharry Medical School. Lisa was also molested by her stepfather from the time she was nine until the time she was 16 and she carried that pain with her everyday for the duration of her life. Her whole life she was in pain. She also suffered from depression. She suffered from un-requited love, and she suffered from the silent treatment way too many times. I must have asked her 1000 times, 'how are you?' But, I don't know if I actually wanted to hear her truth. I don't think any of us did. Lisa touched so many lives. She literally brought life into the world and I think the best way to celebrate her life is to stop being liars. To actually embrace the truth. Just make sure that you tell everyone that you love that you will love them no matter how ugly their truth is. You will still love them. [S3:3, 35:06–40:03]

The deterioration of Mary Jane and Lisa's friendship represent the reality that people and relationships change. Sometimes events happen and words are said that change the course of a friendship permanently. That is part of the human experience. Even though Lisa had betrayed Mary Jane and Mary Jane had ignored Lisa's multiple calls and attempts to apologize for over a year, she still felt responsible for her death. She knew Lisa would not have wanted her parents, especially her stepfather to attend her funeral. In another scene several friends are gathered with Mary Jane, and Mary Jane suggests they can honor her legacy by living life. As Collins highlights, sometimes women are unable to affirm other women for a variety of reasons. Despite their broken sister bond, Mary Jane understood that Lisa was a broken, wounded soul and needed more than she could give her. In the end, Mary Jane told Lisa's truth. Some could perceive it as a violation of Lisa's privacy, but in some ways sharing Lisa's truth as a chastisement to all of those in her life who did not want to hear it while she was alive. She included herself in the list of rejections Lisa experienced when she stated Lisa suffered from the silent treatment. Here is an example of a sisterhood gone wrong, But, ultimately, Mary Jane was protective of her friend in the death that same way she had been at one time in life. She was protective of how her life would be celebrated. She was protective of not leaving the shame and burden of suicide solely with Lisa, but instead her stepfather should most certainly share that burden and the others who did not protect her in life.

CONCLUSION

Being Mary Jane shows women's relationships that are realistically complex. It is both in community with family, extended family, the African American community at large, and her sister circle, that help the audience assign meaning to Mary Jane's lived experiences. The ideology embedded in each of these and other relationships on *Being Mary Jane* is sister/friends are supportive, protective, honest, vulnerable, and encourage personal accountability. Sister/friends are also flawed human beings who come up short and will require forgiveness. Women can be their sister's keeper love and support their women friends. Simultaneously they also can be disappointed by their choices and hurt by each other. In both storylines with Niecy and Kara, the audience sees the women encouraging personal accountability for their choices and behaviors. Sometimes the other woman feels judged, but there is never a question of the love and support they have for each other. *Being Mary Jane* supports Houston's (2004) claim that Black women's talk has forthrightness to it, and that forthrightness is not only a demonstration of care but also a demonstration of personal accountability. Audiences frequently see portrayals of the Black woman who "tells it like it is." However, that is only one aspect of Black women's forthright talk. *Being Mary Jane* shows that Black women's talk is concerned, compassionate, warm, intelligent, and assertive. The characters demonstrate this in a way that is familiar and resonates with the audience.

The ideology embedded in this series is consistent with the goals Brock Akil has for characters on her other shows—*Girlfriends*, *The Game*, and *Love Is___*. These works provide a mirror for Black women to see authentic and relatable representations of themselves. Instead of the steady diet of dysfunctional women relationships on reality television or scripted characters that have no connection to community or other Black women, viewers see friendships that are supportive and encouraging while holding sister/friends accountable. Black women are not monolithic. They are not representations of perfection. Instead, Black women are complex. They are multidimensional. They are flawed. They are human.

NOTE

1. Black feminist epistemology utilizes lived experience as a criterion of meaning. The lived experiences of either the scholar and/or other African American women are invoked in selecting topics of investigation. Thus, the author's use of the pronoun "I" is appropriate (Collins 2000, 257–58).

REFERENCES

Akil, Salim, dir. *Being Mary Jane*. Season 1, episode 3, "Girls Night In." January 14, 2014 on BET.

———, dir. *Being Mary Jane*. Season 1, episode 9, "Uber Love." February 25, 2014 on BET.

———, dir. *Being Mary Jane*. Season 3, episode 3, "Sparrow." October 27, 2015 on BET.

Allison, D. C. (2016). Introduction. In D. C. Allison, *Black Women's Portrayals on Reality Television: The New Sapphire* (pp. ix–xxvii). Lanham, MD: Lexington Books.

Asare, A. (2013, November 25). *Entertainment Weekly*. Retrieved January 18, 2019, from https://ew.com/article/2013/11/25/mara-brock-akil-being-mary-jane-interview/.

Bogle, D. (2001). *Primetime Blues: African Americans on Network Television*. New York: Farrar, Strauss, Giroux.

Cheers, I. (2018). *The Evolution of Black Women in Television: Mammies, Matriarchs & Mistresses*. New York: Routledge.

Cooper, E. W. (2016). High Tea, Church Hats, Pastors' Wives and Friendships. In D. C. Allison, *Black Women's Portrayal on Reality Television: The New Sapphire* (pp. 3–16). Lanham, MD: Lexington Books.

Dates, Jannette L., and William Barlow. (1993). Conclusions: Split Images and Double Binds. In J. L. Dates, *Split Image: African Americans in the Mass Media*, 2nd Edition (pp. 495–528). Washington, DC: Howard University Press.

Foss, Sonja K. (2009). *Rhetorical Criticism: Exploration and Practice*, 4th Edition. Long Grove, IL: Waveland Press, Inc.

Gammage, M. M. (2016). *Representations of Black Women in the Media: The Damnation of Black Womanhood*. New York: Routledge.

Gray, H. (2004). *Watching Race: Television and the Struggle for Blackness*. Minneapolis: University of Minnesota.

Harris, Alexa A. and Adria Y. Goldman. (2014). Black Women in Popular Culture: An Introduction to the Reader's Journey. In V. S. Adria Y. Goldman, *Black Women in Popular Culture: The Conversation Continues* (pp. 1–12). Laham: Lexington Books.

Hill-Collins, P. (2002). *Black Feminist Thought: Knowledge, Consciousness, and the Politics of Empowerment*, 2nd Edition. New York: Routledge.

Houston, M. (2004). Multiple Perspectives: African American Women Conceive Their Talk. In Ronald L. Jackson, *African American Communication & Identities* (pp. 157–64). Thousand Oaks: Sage Publications.

King, Regina, dir. *Being Mary Jane*. Season 2, episode 3, "Mary Jane Knows Best." February 17, 2015 on BET.

———, dir. *Being Mary Jane*. Season 2, episode 4, "Sleepless in Atlanta." February 24, 2015 on BET.

———, dir. *Being Mary Jane*. Season 2, episode 7, "Let's Go Crazy." March 17, 2015 on BET.

Merritt, B. D. (1994). Illusive Reflections: African American Women on Primetime Television. In M. H. Alberto Gonzalez, *Our Voices: Essays in Culture, Ethnicity, and Communication* (pp. 48–53). Los Angeles: Roxbury Publishing Company.

Stack, T. (2015, February 10). *Entertainment Weekly*. Retrieved January 21, 2019, from https://ew.com/article/2015/02/10/being-and-making-mary-jane-gabrielle-union-creator-mara-brock-akil/.

Terrero, N. (2015, December 8). *Entertainment*. Retrieved January 22, 2019, from https://ew.com/article/2015/12/08/being-mary-jane-post-mortem-showrunner-mara-brock-akil/.

Witherspoon, C. (2015, February 4). *The Grio*. Retrieved January 12, 2019, from https://thegrio.com/2015/02/24/mara-brock-akil-being-mary-jane-sexual/.

Writght, J. (2014). Scandalous: Olivia Pope and Black Women in Primetime History. In V. S. Adria Y. Goldman, *Black Women in Popular Culture: The Conversation Continues* (pp. 15–32). Lanham: Lexington Books.

Chapter 5

What *Love Is* ___ and Is Not
A Critical Discourse Analysis
Roslyn M. Satchel

Mara Brock Akil has been breaking racist and sexist barriers with unprecedented success via several hit television shows that go back to the 1990s. It is no wonder that she could assemble an incredibly talented cast of veterans and newcomers who leap off of the screen and into our hearts. *Love Is* ___ stars Michele Weaver, Will Catlett, Wendy Davis, Clarke Peters, Idara Victor, Tyrone Brown, Kadeem Hardison, and Yootha Wong-Loi-Sing. *Love Is* ___ also features Emmy-winner Loretta Devine, NAACP Image Award-winner Tim Reid, NAACP Image Award-nominee Vanessa Bell Calloway, and Tammy Townsend—each with a recurring role. Brock Akil and her husband Salim's love story is legendary in an industry (and our modern reality) where divorces are commonplace, and according to the Akils *Love Is* ___ tells a story inspired by their own. *Love Is* ___ surely takes me back to the best years of my life—as well as many of my worst decisions.

Love Is ___ captures a time of empowerment, fun, innocence, and simplicity for African American culture and especially my generation—the Hip Hop generation. While I won't claim innocence or simplicity, we were powerful and focused on the good times. We were surrounded by ideals of justice, mainly due to efforts of abolitionists, suffragists, and civil rights pioneers. "No" was not an answer we abided, for we were determined to take advantage of the opportunities that our ancestors and elders fought for and propelled us toward.

Our righteous indignation about our collective inheritance of racism, sexism, classism, ableism, heterosexism, xenophobia, and other white supremacist ideologies inspired us to rise up. We read, recited, and recorded our literature, art, sermons, and scientific discoveries poetically, prolifically, and prophetically. Whether in our music or relationships, we not only partied up—and down—with Prince and MJ but also with KRS-One and Public

Enemy, and even more so with Queen Latifah, MC Lyte, Monie Love, YoYo, and yes, the Sistah Souljah. As proud Black women, we loved up our men and children, we cleaned up our communities, and we dressed up in our African kente cloth and medallions with our fists in the air, exclaiming, "Fight the Power!" Unfortunately, though, we often didn't fight for ourselves against the patriarchal forces repressing us in our churches, mosques, temples, schools, communities, and government.

Untainted by social media's instant gratification, we waited in lines stretched around corners and down streets to get into this week's party of the century so we could party like it was 1999. Dances like the kid-n-play, the running man, the prep, the reebok, the alf, and eventually the butterfly jumped off on dance floors while the cool people chilled in heels, leather, and miniskirts in the VIP sections. Bass reverberated through our hearts and veins as the lighting, clothes, music, sights, and sounds of the 1990s made us believe, "Baby, I'm a Star!" all the while waiting for equality and an end to violence against women.

Love Is ___ helps those of us born between 1965 and 1975 remember a time that we didn't know passed. Many of my peers and I are around that midlife crisis point that lends to reflection on what we did and what we should have done. So, when the score to *Love Is* ___ booms with music from our favorite artists or when we watch a scene where Ruby's sitting on the couch watching TV shows like *Living Single*, our minds go back to that simpler time and our eyes light up, our ears tune in, and our interest is piqued. *Love Is* ___ also speaks to a younger generation of hopeful romantics who hear 1990s R&B songs and remember parents who divorced or were ruined by the war on drugs, some of whom post online that they find hope in this show. Surely, Mara Brock Akil knows how to accentuate the purity of those moments by foreshadowing pivotal shifts in plotline, setting, and mood with the techniques that draw in target audiences deeper and deeper into the Akils world.

Like Nuri, reality often hit us like deer caught in headlights as we blindly struggled to find our way through our first adult jobs, marriages, and other forces into adulting. Most of us made the mistake of over-romanticizing our futures. Many of us had no idea how hard life could be, how painful the consequences of our mistakes would be, or even how the best made plans can fail. Similarly, Season 1 of the autobiopic, *Love Is* ___, presents the idealized life of Nuri, a woman of African descent living and working in Los Angeles, through three unique stages of her life: (1) her free-spirited early to mid-twenties as a single woman, (2) her complicated late twenties at the beginning of her intimate relationship with Yasir, and (3) her reflective fifties in the latter years of their relationship. By no surprise, Nuri over-romanticizes everything.

Primarily set in 1996 and 1997, the first season of *Love Is* ___ opens with Nuri (Wendy Davis) reflecting upon her man's positive impact on her life at the celebration of their twentieth anniversary. Her man, Yasir (Clarke Peters), eventually joins her on the couch with a disgruntled tone, challenging her and the director about the scope of the program—as well as antagonizing Nuri about her clothing until she relents and changes her attire. This scene is emblematic of the type of controlling behavior, from the male lead, that caused many women to bristle at the portrayal of Nuri and Yasir's relationship in *Love Is* ___. Audiences posted comments and questions in social media discussion groups across various platforms, arguing about whether Yasir was controlling, manipulative, or abusive? Was he "a user" or "a con man" playing on women's insecurities? Was he "lazy" or "a gold digger" riding on her coattails?

PLOTLINE

Nuri and Yasir chase their dreams and learn to follow their hearts—often impulsively and irresponsibly. Told from the perspective of the couple's present-day selves, the romantic dramedy also revisits the social issues and vibrant African American culture of the 1990s. The "wiser" couple reflects on how circumstances shaped the couple they have become nearly twenty years later—a formidable intimate and professional partnership navigating a complex set of social codes while also balancing successful careers and a beautiful family. Drawing inspiration from creators Mara Brock Akil and Salim Akil's own relationship journey, "the series explores the highs, the lows, and the magic of falling (and staying) in love" (Pena 2018).

The cast includes several series regulars including Michele Weaver as the younger "Nuri," who is a bubbly personality with big dreams, struggling to make a name for herself as a sitcom staff writer. At the same time she is juggling an assortment of romances that only leave her partly fulfilled. Will Catlett takes on the role of "Yasir," an aspiring writer/director who is down to his last two unemployment checks and lives (unhappily) with his on-and-off again ex-girlfriend "Ruby," played by Yootha Wong-Loi-Sing. Tyrone Marshall Brown portrays "Sean," Yasir's opinionated friend who possesses great taste and is full of ideas but lacks follow through. Additionally, Idara Victor stars as "Angela," a member of the same writing staff with Nuri. Angela doesn't always agree with everything Nuri says, primarily since she is a disgruntled drama writer stuck in a comedy she doesn't believe in. TV veteran Kadeem Hardison is "Norman," the executive producer of the hit sitcom "Marvin," presented as the tough boss of Nuri and Angela who is hard to impress and even harder to amuse. As mentioned above, Clarke Peters portrays the present day "Wiser Yasir," while Wendy Davis is the "Wiser Nuri," portrayed to be a more relaxed, happy, and comfortable version of herself both in life and in her marriage.

On November 20, 2018, a lawsuit was filed against Salim Akil for domestic violence, breach of contract, and copyright infringement. In her petition, Amber Dixon Brenner claims that Salim Akil repeatedly brutalized her physically, emotionally, and sexually throughout their ten-year romantic relationship that ended in the summer of 2017 (Brenner v. Akil 2018). These allegations sent shockwaves through Black Hollywood and its loyal #BlackLove fanbase. Salim Akil is one of the executive producers on *Love Is ___*, and according to the show's website, the TV memoir was inspired by the real-life love story of married producers Mara Brock Akil and Salim Akil (Pena 2018). However, Brenner alleged that Salim stole the idea from a script she wrote based on her abusive relationship with him. Brenner contends that she pitched the story to Salim and shared the script with him in 2016 as a potential collaboration with her. Unaware of the dispute, The Oprah Winfrey Network (OWN) launched the show on June 19, 2018. On July 31, 2018, OWN renewed *Love Is ___* for a second season, but OWN subsequently cancelled the series on December 19, 2018, amid the allegations of domestic violence against Akil (Wills 2018), stating simply, "OWN has decided not to move forward with the second season of *Love Is ___*." Ultimately, the most important question is whether this depiction of what "love" is actually presents the dangerous message that infidelity and other forms of abuse are acceptable.

THEORY AND METHOD

Critical discourse studies set the groundwork for developing media literacy (Satchel 2016). Therefore, expounding on the latent meaning from television shows as texts is the primary concern of this study. Qualitative analyses are the best method for examining untapped significance in small samples, such as this analysis of the ten episodes of *Love Is ___* as media texts. Such an analysis is a suitable method for analyzing the episodes in this study because it is a particularly effective investigative strategy in analyzing meaning making through "a careful, detailed, systematic examination and interpretation of a particular body of material in an effort to identify patterns, themes, biases, and meanings" (Berg 2007, 303–4).

This type of qualitative critical discourse analysis aids in interpreting how media content creators treat images, montages, dialogue, and related social and political issues in the context of American media (Denzin and Lincoln 2011, 7). I use this approach in examining intersectional race, gender, and class representations and their equivalents when present (e.g., religion, sexual orientation, age, ability, ethnicity, nationality, language, etc.).

This essay, therefore, acknowledges entertainment media as essential components of the emerging media environment instead of the archetypal hegemonic role of news media as the only shapers and suppliers of public opinion. Movies, television, music, novels, and newspapers are media texts that also influence popular culture commodities—objects of commercial desire—for which large, ever-conglomerating corporations calculate efforts to appeal to the largest part of the target audience (Kolker 2006, 173). Coherence, system, and order in entertainment produce and reflect a meaning-making process that affirms or denies beliefs born of class, gender, race, education, acculturation, and ideology (172–73). Culture, therefore, in this research, can be understood as the text of our lives, the ultimately coherent pattern of beliefs, acts, responses, and artifacts that we produce and comprehend every day. As such, media content creation is a cultural practice that generates, reinforces, reproduces, challenges, and transforms understandings of subcultures and individuals in the society (Kolker 2006, 174). As platforms converge, filmmakers and showrunners are increasingly taking advantage of the blurring of lines between television and film content in these regards.

What makes this critical discourse study unique is the linking of media framing and media representations to social functions such as reinforcing social hierarchies, perpetuating/rejecting ideologies, or promoting/threatening democracy. In turn, the following analysis critically examines frames and representations in *Love Is ___* as mechanisms for cueing beliefs and representational schemas in audiences. In so doing, this research also acknowledges the intertwining of race, gender, religion, ability, and other forms of social classification as determinants of power and privilege.

Triangulating Co-cultural Standpoints

Throughout this essay, I triangulate theoretic approaches so that theories produced by Black scholars to explain African American culture, epistemologies, and media representations might be juxtaposed with theories that were produced by counterparts to accent European American culture, epistemologies, and media representations. This functions as an equal valuing of co-cultural standpoints (Jackson 2002). I recognize that no method is perfect or without limitations, and likewise neither is this integrated approach.

In reading media, beginning with what Roland Barthes (1977) identifies as "the rhetoric of the image" is beneficial (161). In an image, Barthes argues, a discontinuous set of elements signifies an ideology and integrates with an iconic discourse that denotes and naturalizes its symbols to produce rhetorics. In other words, a picture's meaning does not lie exclusively in the image, but in the conjunction of image and text or context. Frequently, it is the caption that identifies one out of the many possible meanings from the image, and anchors it with words (Hall 2013). In effect, two discourses—the discourse of photography and the discourse of written language—are required to produce and fix the meaning of an image (Hall 1972; Hall 2013). Respectively, these function as signifier and signified. Together, they produce a sign.

In essence, any physical sign can constitute visual rhetoric. Using images instead of using words to convince people is a staple of visual rhetoric (Handa 2004). Semiotics is the study of signs and the socially produced meanings from the structural relations in sign systems. As tools of visual rhetoricians, signs and their science are integral to rhetorical analysis. Semiotics, like texts, is based on our prior knowledge of an object or idea, combined with its presentation context and resulting meaning or sets of meanings (Handa 2004). Daily, and in almost every moment of our lives, semiotics enables us to recognize cues and incorporate them into our lives. To understand how visual images function similarly to verbal images, we must start with socially constructed knowledge and shared meanings as the building blocks for our interpretive lenses. After all, visual images too have been learned and established over time (Handa 2004).

Semiotics helps us see the otherwise invisible process that occurs when a rhetor's (producer's) visual image produces a linguistic understanding in auditors (audiences). For instance, a contortion of facial features leads audiences to think and feel fearful. Following this reasoning, "rhetoric inheres in the words that a visual image activates," so that the rhetoric of a television show, for example, becomes the verbal understanding that accompanies its viewing (Covino and Jolliffe 1995, 6). Whether verbal, aural, or visual, talented writers, directors, and producers use all available methods to send messages to audiences.

Studying visual rhetoric in media is indeed "the study of symbolic inducement" (Blakesley 2004, 113). This is to say that we must examine the connection created between the content and the audience. Visual rhetoricians contend that audience identification occurs not only in relation to media content broadly, but also in shot composition, scene construction, and visual representations. Skilled directors can literally lure audiences into an imagined world by using visual elements such as "camera movement, placement in the frame, color, spatial relationships among characters and between the viewer and the visual material, special visual effects, visual editing, and so on" (Blakesley 2004, 115). When breaking down the rhetoric of a scene, it is important to consider all of these elements make up the composition of the shots because viewers used this composition to make connections between themselves and the character(s).

In this way, semiotics contributes greatly to media literacy by teaching us to read, analyze, and decode media texts (Kellner and Share 2005). Barthes (1998) explained that semiotics aims to challenge the naturalness of a message, the "what goes-with-out-saying" (11). Likewise, in critical media literacy, practitioners analyze media culture as products of social construction and ideological struggle. They teach that audiences must be critical of media representations and discourses, while also stressing the importance of learning to use the media as modes of self-expression and social activism. In fact, the principle of nontransparency is the foundation of media education (Masterman 1994). "Media do not present reality like transparent windows or simple reflections of the world because media messages are created, shaped, and positioned through a construction process" (Kellner and Share 2005, 374). As discussed above, this construction and its implicit framing bias involve many decisions about what to include or exclude and how to represent reality.

Building on Barthes's semiotic conceptions, Hall (1980b) argued that reading media requires distinguishing between the encoding of media texts by producers and the decoding by consumers. In relation to the production and reception of media content, Hall (1997) explains that frameworks of knowledge, relations of production, and technical infrastructures encode meaning structures into media content as "meaningful discourse" that can be visual and aural (94). Audiences then decode the meaning structures with differing degrees of symmetry into personal frameworks of knowledge that may be reproduced, negotiated, or rejected as limits and parameters. While this book is not about reception or effects, I adopt Hall's (1997) definition of production as the encoding of meaning as discourse. Consequently, I analyze media representations and their relationships to one another for whether they constitute socially shared models or constructs that encode "meaningful discourse" into media as a type of hegemonic code. If so, then the presence and relations of laudatory and derogatory stereotypes in media content with the greatest influence warrant ideological scrutiny.

As a caveat, I acknowledge viewers' capacity to produce their own readings and meanings to decode texts in aberrant, resistant, or transformative ways as well as the "preferred" ideological ways (Kellner and Share 2005, 375). Although I agree with Ien Ang (2002) that "a certain text can come to mean different things depending on the interdiscursive context in which viewers interpret it" (180), I also concur with bell hooks (1996) that "there are certain 'received' messages that are rarely mediated by the will of the audience" (Kellner and Share 2005, 3). Audiences are neither powerless nor omnipotent when it comes to reading media and this study demonstrates a process by which viewers may negotiate meaning. My goal is to empower viewers through critical thinking inquiry to negotiate different readings and challenge the power of media to create preferred readings.

Discourse analysis, according to Berg (2009), offers researchers a method for examining not only what is said or which words are used, but also the social construction and apprehension of meanings created through discourse. Examining a discourse looks for patterns of the language used in the communications exchange as well as the social and cultural contexts in which these communications occur (Berg 2009). The relationship between the exchange and its social context "requires an appreciation of culturally specific ways of speaking and writing and ways of organizing thoughts"—including "how, where, and when the discourse arises in a given social and cultural situation" (353). Further, Berg (2009) argues as follows:

> ... this sort of content analysis should include examining what a given communication exchange may be intended to do or mean in a given social cultural setting. In effect, the ways in which one [speaks] in a given communication exchange are also important in terms of constructing certain views of the social world. Counting terms, words, themes, and so on allow the researcher to ascertain some of the variations and nuances of these ways parties in a communication exchange create their social worlds. (353)

Given common perspectives and aims, conceptual and theoretical frameworks such as critical discourse analysis, qualitative content analysis, and frame analysis are closely related. Each provides a complementary set of tools for scrutinizing latent meaning in media texts. Whereas content analyses measure instances, qualitative content analyses also examine the contexts of those instances. Additionally, frame analyses investigate the overarching themes that instances and contexts create, adding the supplemental layer of critical discourse analysis. This then interrogating the deployment of specific discourse structures in reproducing social dominance, irrespective of medium, genre, or context. Using these techniques together provides a comprehensive approach to deriving manifest and underlying meaning from media content.

Critical discourse analysis occurs as a type of analytical method that investigates how social power abuse, dominance, and inequality are created, reproduced, and resisted through text and dialogue within social and political contexts (van Dijk 2001). Yet, there is no unitary theoretical framework because critical discourse analysis is not a direction, school, or specialization, but rather it offers a "mode" or "perspective" of theorizing, analyzing, and applying knowledge that varies based on the type of data collected (van Dijk 2001). Illustratively, this critical analytical approach involves scrutiny of concepts and language such as power, dominance, hegemony, race, interests, institutions, and social structure (van Dijk 2001), which are also central to the phenomenon presently under study.

Critical discourse studies explicitly link patterns of framing in media texts to predictable priming and agenda-setting effects, as consistent with Entman (2007). Entman (2004), in fact, exposes linkages between the elite discourse, government discourse, news discourse, and public discourse using a type of critical discourse analysis for examining news media frames. Similarly, Stuart Hall (1993, 1997, 2013) unambiguously endorses discourse analysis in describing and evaluating racial representation in media texts. Hall (1997) expounds upon Michel Foucault's (1977) original conceptualization of discourse as a system of representation that produces knowledge through language, images, and other symbols.

ANALYSIS

Ideological analysis requires complex interrogation of not only the media text but also "the intricate cognitive representations and strategies used in the production and comprehension of the text" (van Dijk 1998, 118–19). van Dijk (1998) refers to socially shared event, mental, and context models as social cognitions that are the interface between a media text and its context:

> If social cognitions about different social groups and social events are similar, we say that they are being monitored by the same fundamental interpretation framework, that is, by the same ideology. Such an ideology features the basic norms, values, and other principles which are geared towards the realization of the interests and goals of the group, as well as towards the reproduction and legitimation of its power. (118)

Through a detailed account of social cognitions such as laudatory and derogatory representations, critical discourse analysis enabled this researcher to relate discourse and speakers with social structure and culture because "social cognitions also allow us to relate the micro-structures of discursive action and communication with the societal macrostructures of groups . . . and institutions" (119). For example, use of the term or image of "Mammy" in a film enables the researcher to analyze the units of analysis with the myths, ideologies, legends, history, culture, and social structures in which "Mammy" originated (Satchel 2016).

Drawing connections between the media text and the societal discourse is the goal. Critical discourse analysis of social representations (such as media stereotypes) is an established technique for media research on socio-cognitive models that characterize groups. This study, in turn, uses critical discourse analysis (CDA) to describe and evaluate media frames with the tools provided within CDA's analytic approach. Images, themes, words, actions, and scenes are not only identified but also discussed in relation to each other and the historical contexts, ideologies, myths, and legends that make them discursive.

What makes this approach unique is that it addresses critiques of prior content analyses by following a model for critical discourse analysis espoused by Tyree (2007) and Fairclough (1989, 1995). This model consists of three interrelated processes of analysis that are tied to three interrelated dimensions of discourse. Janks (1997) summarizes the three dimensions as follows: (1) the object of analysis (including verbal, visual, or verbal and visual texts); (2) the processes that produce the object and through which human subjects received it (writing/speaking/filming and reading/listening/viewing); and (3) the sociohistorical conditions that govern these processes. These three dimensions require the following type of analysis: text analysis (description), processing analysis (interpretation), and social analysis (explanation) (Fairclough 1989, 1995). Further, Janks (2001) explains how beneficial critical discourse analysis can be to the analysis of texts within a historical context:

> What is useful about this approach is that it enables you to focus on the signifiers that make up the text, the specific linguistic selections, their juxtapositioning, their sequencing, their layout and so on. However, it also requires you to recognize that the historical determination of these selections and to understand that these choices are tied to the conditions of possibility of that utterance.

This is another way of saying that texts are instantiations of socially regulated discourses and that the processes of production and reception are socially constrained. Fairclough's approach to CDA is so useful because it provides multiple points of analytic entry. It does not matter which kind of analysis one begins with, as long as in the end they are all included and are shown to be mutually explanatory. It is in the interconnections that the analyst finds the interesting patterns and disjunctions that need to be described, interpreted, and explained.

To simplify and make relevant Foucault's (1977) concept for its application in this study, a media text cannot be analyzed without examining the entire discursive formation to which that text and its related practices belong (Hall 1997). In other words, investigating only a television show or a showrunner is insufficient in discourse analysis because either are merely a subject of the discourse. For Foucault (1982), no individual (showrunner) or thing (TV show) produces knowledge or meaning. Rather, a proper assessment must include analysis of the historical context, regulations of conduct, practices, language, and systems of knowledge and power that produce each show's content.

As Hall (1997) explains, the discourse produces and subjectifies each subject. Cultural and historic contexts create discourse by attaching sets of meaning to certain symbols (Potter 1996). Foucault and discourse are difficult to summarize, but it is sufficient for our purposes to focus on the relationship between knowledge and power, and how power operates within an institutional apparatus and its technologies. This study, therefore, recognizes media as a technology involved in strategic transmissions of meaning through the content analyzed herein. The analysis of each, therefore, takes into consideration not only the content but also the medium, content creators, studio systems, socio-historical context, and socially shared cognitive models. As a result, I analyze the collected materials in a manner that was mindful of both the historical and social forces that helped create them.

Racial Representations

The lineage of racist discourse, troubling stereotypes, and the specific representations is well established in multiple literatures. Distinctively, however, *Love Is* ___ clearly arises from those ashes with creativity and beauty about Black love in a way that likely will inspire storytellers to step away from the antiquated imagery of white supremacy's past. For example, Brock Akil challenges stereotypes such as the mammy, coon, buck, or jungle bunny that were used by white filmmakers and politicians of prior generations in justifying colonialism, enslavement, and segregation through nineteenth-century eugenics and literature. Instead, Black women are brilliant, complicated, sophisticated, and involved in their own children's lives. Black men, likewise, are hardworking, resilient, complex, and take care of their families to the extent of their abilities. Akil's character-development decisions completely reverse naturalizations in racist discourse that reduce Black and Brown people as a race, or species, to permanent childlike, culture-less, lazy, unstable tricksters in need of whites' civilizing through slavery and subjugation.

Admittedly, I am always thrilled to see Black actors in complicated and developed character roles in film and television. I celebrate each time a Black content creator or showrunner succeeds in Hollywood. I rush to the page to write about Black content creators who are changing the ideological slant of the industry with counter-hegemonic narratives that show us in our beautiful complexities.

One such complex issue that raises ideological concerns is colorism. Colorism occurs when preferential treatment goes to people with lighter complexions over those with darker complexions (Satchel 2016). The phenomenon is usually present in members of marginalized ethnic groups who internalize white supremacist aesthetics. In *Love Is* ___, Yasir arguably practices colorism in choosing Nuri, a light-skinned woman, over his prior girlfriends who had darker complexions.

Of course, proving the intentions and motivations of any real person is difficult—so, I will not attempt to psychoanalyze a fictitious character. Still, however, the dialogue between Yasir and his friend in episode 1 repeatedly refers to Nuri as "light skinned with long, curly hair." In intra-communal conversations, particularly while admiring another as the male characters were doing, this would communicate a preference for that look as an ideal beauty. Such colorism has plagued Black communities since the days of colonialism and slavery when enslavers gave light-skinned enslaved Africans better conditions of confinement and those who were dark skinned were treated worse. In fact, eugenics followers often argued that the darker Black people were an indicator of them being more evil, mean, or dirty.

Such fallacious absurdities are deeply rooted in Western thought. One of its earliest recorded manifestations attributes to Aristotle the Pythagorean Table of Opposites (Satchel 2016). The table was used to teach logic by associating certain character traits with whiteness and others with blackness. The positive traits belonged to all that was white and the converse was true for blackness. Then, the European colonizers used that so-called logic in teaching religion to the conquered peoples—teaching them that colonizers were white and therefore good, and that all others fell to the logical extreme and polar opposite. Mara Brock Akil clearly rejects white supremacist logic in the beautiful, light, and airy ways she films and presents Blackness. In this and other regards, *Love Is ___* is a counter-hegemonic narrative that challenges dominant culture ideologies. Here, Black love is not oxymoronic; instead it is fun, kind, warm, and longsuffering—irrespective of the gender of its source.

Racial representations impact people's perceptions of others and themselves. Brock Akil makes every hue and shade of brown skin in the Black community look rich, supple, and sweet. Grable (2005) argues that this is important because people in audiences learn about themselves and society's expectations of them when they see racial group members with whom they identify in the media. Her "Looking Glass Theory of Media Influences" adapts symbolic interactionism to help explain how a person's self-image can develop by viewing media content (Grable 2005). For example, African American women see other Black women portrayed in entertainment media and ask, "How are the portrayed people treated by others in the content? Are they treated as inferior? Are they rejected? Under what circumstances are they accepted?" Media portrayals send not-so-subtle messages to viewers about themselves and how other people regard them. Movies, television, or other media, therefore, offer a kind of "social mirror" through which similarly situated people gather clear indications about their status in society (Grable 2005). Perhaps, this is why the show did relatively well for a new primetime cable television show. Brock Akil established the following among Black viewers, especially women, because the imagery about Black people and Black communities were positive, fresh, and new.

Another counter-hegemonic move Brock Akil makes is in the context of religion. Nuri and Yasir are (or were) Muslim. This show may be primetime television's first romantic drama or comedy with lead characters who practice Islam. Moreover, Nuri definitely is the first Muslim woman in a lead role on primetime television show. Even the reality genre has not created a character who was a product of domestic American Islam. Nuri grew up in the Nation of Islam, then explored religions with her mom; and Yasir grew up as a Christian, then converted to Islam as a young adult. His conversion to Islam represents a common journey for Black people who develop a critical consciousness and embrace an African-centered identity and cultural orientation. His decision to change his name to Yasir and fast during Ramadan is refreshing to many viewers who leave white Judeo-Christian traditions. Similarly, the National of Islam, from which Nuri comes, is a faith community where these types of conversions often occur. This is a story that has not previously been told—one that the Akils know intimately.

Finally, and perhaps most controversially, additional intersectional questions arise as we consider #BlackRage or #BlackMaleRage in the context of intimate partner violence as represented in *Love Is* ____. More of the combustible side of Yasir erupts in episodes 9 and 10. Here, as Nuri's career crescendos, Yasir is angry and sulking because Nuri is prioritizing work over him by not calling once she got to work as he requested. She apologizes and explains, ad nauseam. This pattern develops into a rhythm drumming upon our hearts with increasing fear of an explosion—an inevitable violent eruption. "You're working" becomes the way he mocks her, leaving her feeling guilty for staying focused and working hard to achieve her dreams.

Nuri is constantly apologizing for making big strides at work that distract her from tending to his needs or that make her so tired that she doesn't see things that he does—but he also doesn't tell her he did them. Rather than just say, "Baby, I left your dinner on the counter," Yasir sets the trap and then stands back to watch Nuri get caught in the trap. Why the test to see if she sees it and says thanks? It's that kind of cunning and sulky behavior that makes me question Yasir's motivations and volatility. He's looking for something to fight about or feel victimized by, which is when his rage is most expressed. In his subsequent rant with his friend at the coffeehouse, the two dejectedly "guy-talk" against the independent and successful Black women these days who "wear the pants" in their relationships who don't see the sweet things they do. Then, Yasir shares vulnerability saying, "I wanna celebrate my girl, not ride her success." As they commiserate about the downside of being in relationships with successful women, the two men get to a point where it becomes unclear which of them is the butt of a joke about the trifling men who impregnate women so they can stay home all day while the woman works.

After reluctantly agreeing to go to Nuri's big night only after opting to use it as an opportunity to pitch his best script to Nuri's agent, Yasir lashes out at Nuri in public at her job on the biggest night of her career because his name was not on the list. Sure, no one enjoys being interrogated, harassed, or talked down to, especially not when you're already nervous for other reasons. When stopped at the gate by the officer, Yasir likely felt like most Black men—fearful, defensive, and on guard. The longstanding tensions between law enforcement and Black and Brown communities have a painful history that goes back to the Fugitive Slave Law and the ways in which the state has sanctioned ongoing violence against Black and Brown bodies. This torturous history of barbarism, enslavement, kidnapping, brutality, mutilations, violence, child abuse, and murders with impunity is often unknown to non-Black people despite that the historical records exist. As a communal ethic, many marginalized people try to avoid interactions with law enforcement due to that history. Yasir's tension and anxiety is evident in his suspicious eyes, his nervous gestures, and his cadence of speech.

Just then arrives a production assistant with whom Yasir knows Nuri had a prior sexual relationship. After several minutes of questions, horn blowing, and an officer's condescending attitude, the production assistant gets the officer to let in Yasir. By the time he arrives at the studio stage door where Nuri's show is taping, the private duty security guard is direct and unrelenting about not letting Yasir in—even getting in his face and insulting him by calling him, "Son." In the African American community, only an elder of high esteem or a parent may call a Black man "Son" or "Boy." After a long history of racist taunts and systemic negations, that is a non-negotiable aspersion cast—particularly between Black men. Viewers can read this added cutting insult and fiery anger boiling within Yasir in the non-verbal eye contact communicating a "recognition of meaning" between Yasir and the security guard. While this is not something that everyone can or will read, many of us can translate the intracommunal messages linked to our cultural heritage and identify with the combustible rage in Yasir that builds to eruption.

Finally, someone calls Nuri about the ongoing dispute, and, upon overhearing it, her boss warns her about bringing drama to the lot. Clearly, this altercation upsets him and reflects unfavorably on Nuri. She leaves the control booth at a moment when she was being recognized on stage as the writer of what could have been the show's final episode. What greets her is chastisement from Yasir in public at her job about his unfounded assumptions that she forgot to put him on the list and brought him to the studio lot to parade him around her exes. He accuses her of breaking promises and starts to storm off while she cries and pleads with him. Coming to her senses, she returns to the stage door only to realize that now she cannot get inside either and misses her moment. On the biggest night of her career, the talk among her colleagues was about her boyfriend showing up broke with a script in his hand looking for a job—so much so that her mentor checks her about being used by men and performing better at work.

Nuri confronts Yasir in the kitchen at home, "You embarrassed me in front of my boss and my coworkers." He responds, challenging her because she "put [him] in that position." Nuri checks Yasir, saying, "Maybe we should take a break. I don't think love is supposed to be this hard. I know you will fulfil your dreams, but maybe it's too hard for you to watch me live out mine." Yasir relents and apologizes the next morning, but in so doing, triggers a brief psychotic episode in Nuri related to being molested by her stepfather when she was a child. Yasir says they have that in common. They cry together. This moment of woundedness and tears shared between men and women of African descent is far too rarely represented in media content.

These tender moments of humanness remind us to handle each other with care, for we never know that with which others are struggling. Even if Yasir (Salim) is abusive, he is not disposable. Wonderful programs like Men Stopping Violence in Atlanta have a long and rich history of rehabilitating male violent abusers. But that is not my concern here. I focus on the victims and survivors, as many of the most vulnerable among vulnerable populations. What is encouraging is seeing the caring conversation between Nuri and Yasir about the child abuse she experienced. When threatened with harm to loved ones, victims—especially child victims—turn inward because, in Nuri's words, "There's nowhere to go but to God." Nuri's shift to spiritual talk signifies the way in which many victims of violence go inward to find safety after surviving abuse. In Nuri's words, "Now our relationship is so sweet, so safe."

Episode 10 ends oddly with Nuri's ex, Derrick, proposing to her. She neither accepts or denies and keeps the ring. Then, Nuri asks Yasir to marry her while sitting in the jeep in the driveway in front of her house when she's on her way to take Yasir to Ruby's house. Yasir says yes. And then there's the violence . . . again . . . when Yasir fights Ruby's new love interest. Finally, we see Wiser Yasir's anger emerge as he learns for the first time of Derrick's proposal and the ring that Wiser Nuri still has.

Gender Representations

Research evaluating the ideological relationships between the stereotypes of dominant and non-dominant social groups occurs primarily in the context of gender relations (Satchel 2016). Race and gender norms function similarly. Like race, gender is a social construct, and one of the major ways that human beings organize their lives. Each ascribes a place to individuals with certain immutable characteristics within the ruling hierarchy (Jost and Hamilton 2005, 219). None of these marginalizations, however, are experienced in isolation. Instead, their manifestations are intersectional; meaning, multiple interlocking systems impact each life so we must consider the particularities and commonalities that present themselves when multidimensional oppressions impact an individual's efforts to secure human dignity and rights.

As with race, gendered norms and expectations, as a social institution, create "distinguishable social statuses for the assignment of rights and responsibilities" (Lorber 1994, 280). These ranked statuses structure inequality and stratify families, organizations, and processes such that "what men do is usually valued more highly than what women do because men do it" (Lorber 1994, 281). The "devalued genders have less power, prestige, and economic rewards than the valued genders" (Lorber 1994, 281). This gender inequality—"the devaluation of 'women' and the social domination of 'men'"—has social functions and a social history "produced and maintained by identifiable social processes and built into the general social structure and individual identities deliberately and purposefully" (Lorber 1994, 282).

Majority rule, even if merely perceived, functions to justify a societal ranking that places white males at the top—as those in power at the time of the country's framing—and all others beneath (Satchel 2016). Gender and race play significant roles in ordering the remainder of society's hierarchical structure. A purely patriarchal structure would accord the next level of privilege to males of other races in some systemically racialized manner. On the other hand, a solely white supremacist structure would accord the next level of privilege to white women and then rank subjugated races according to male-female complementarity. Arguably, race and gender privilege may differ according to context because the U.S. system functions as a mix of these two models.

As a cisgender woman of African descent who is identified as a Christian, heterosexual, and working class in a heterosexist, patriarchal, capitalist society, I have a responsibility to use my societal privilege and resources to empower marginalized groups when possible. In this context, the area of urgency is with misogyny and the abuse of women. So, without conflating sexuality and gender, this section highlights progress and concerns arising from gender representations in *Love Is* ___.

Seeing Black women in simplistic and unrealistic media roles is so commonplace that any complex characters—even if not true to my own experience—are an absolute delight. In fact, my heart skipped a few beats in elation when I first watched *Love Is* ___. Nuri's character was far more complex and realistic of women in my generation than the dominant media representations. Women like Nuri (and the rest of us) tried to have it all, do it all, and be it all. We sought (and seek) equality and success in career, in family, and in love. As many *Love Is* ___ fans on Twitter often live-tweeted during the season, "I've been every female character in this show at different times in my life." More often than not, though, I identified with Nuri because Nuri represents the romantic in us all.

Nuri is a talented writer working on the studio-based creative team of a fictitious Black sitcom. Not surprisingly, the writers of *Love Is* ___ develop Nuri's character so well that we learn extraneous details about her coworkers, friends, family, and neighbors that matter to no one. Initially, it seems

Nuri has a full life, but then a shift to focus on her relationship with Yasir occurs in the latter half of the season. After the shift, the story begins to read like a tragedy where we see Nuri spiraling downward toward the destructive end that comes from searching for the solutions to personal issues outside of ourselves.

Well, candidly, the rush to close the deal immediately after the first date was the first red flag about Yasir's character for me. Yasir's manipulation at the table to get Nuri to say she loved him was coercive and I wished it was as off-putting to Nuri as it was for me. I felt like screaming "No! Don't do it!!! Don't fall for that old trick!" Nuri often seems so desperate to be loved and in love. She is struggling to create it with a man who seems to be a manipulative narcissist. I worried that she gave in so quickly to his advances. Perhaps I worried most because I've been her and made similar naive decisions that I lived to regret.

The concern is that the show romanticizes this type of behavior in ways that send dangerous messages. I wanted Nuri—or anyone on the show—to question his conduct, challenge him on his intentions, and warn her about the possible effects of her decisions. Where was the wise woman figure in her life? Why isn't someone there for young women to caution them against the dire consequences of their poor judgment calls? I guess I just wished Brock Akil was using this outlet as a guide, to lovingly help women make better choices in protecting themselves. Perhaps, however, she is too close to tell that story.

The allegations against Salim Akil concern me. As a womanist, women's stories are important, and I always try to believe women's stories about their own experiences. In fact, I give all victims the benefit of the doubt. They are innocent until proven guilty, as is the accused. There is never cause to put victims on trial. In the final analysis, however, the wealth and status of men like Salim Akil today are determinants of power and privilege. So, when it comes to violence against women, as a survivor and as an advocate working with victims/survivors, I applaud OWN for stepping away from *Love Is* ___ until a thorough investigation can be completed.

SES/Class Representations

How media represents the working class has been a controversial issue from early images of the late 1940s to those on display in recent situation comedies, dramas, and "reality" programs. This issue clearly resonates with Mara Brock Akil, who deliberately challenges assumptions, stereotypes, and ideologies about socioeconomic status (SES). Nuri's character is gainfully employed in a middle-class occupation as a Hollywood writer on a hit show. In her, we see what it was like to be among the first few Black people, especially Black women, in executive level jobs in Hollywood in the 1990s. She wears designer clothes, shops on Melrose Boulevard, drives a fancy jeep, and owns her own home in an elite Los Angeles neighborhood.

On the other hand, Yasir is unemployed, houseless, carless, and unable to pay his pager bill. Subsequently, however, what emerges in the storyline is that Yasir could have paid his bills but chose to put his last money into piano classes to enrich his son Deonte's life. Such a distinction is important to value the sacrifices that working-class people are making every day to care for their children. This representation of masculinity, and Black manhood in particular, is countering the negative stereotypes and ideologies about houseless people, Black fatherhood, and masculinity in general. The irony is in Yasir not having a house but having so much love to give Nuri, and Nuri having a huge house that is empty until Yasir moves in.

In *Love Is* ____, Mara Brock Akil is presenting through Nuri and Yasir a realistic economic dynamic with which many working-class couples in America struggle. Single and childless, Nuri may be of a higher socioeconomic status than she would be if her salary was being stretched to provide for dependents—especially another adult. Often, women are having to choose between their own upward mobility and having a marriage or family with a partner who is unemployed or underemployed. In episode 8, for example, Yasir's ex-wife alludes to his running through the money of the women he dates. Still, Nuri chose Yasir and was financially secure enough to provide for him as needed. Fortunately, he contributed to her life in ways that were meaningful enough to satisfy her needs. Some women do not mind earning more and being the family's primary breadwinner; some even consider such actions as chipping away at patriarchy. One may ask, "Why does the man have to be bigger, stronger, wealthier, or working outside of the home if we have gender parity?" Whether a man can withstand the social criticism associated with such choices for extended periods of time, however, is ultimately the test to which many victims of abusive marriages can attest.

Even Yasir's mother, Rose (Loretta Devine), expressed concerns about Nuri's involvement with her son in episode 8. When the two women have a moment alone to talk, Rose refers to her as a type she's seen before—one of those "privileged cute girls from across the Bay curious about the hood boy you just met." In saying this, Rose as the sage is telling Nuri colloquially, "I see you." She goes on to say, "He doesn't have the privilege to be distracted or heartbroken. . . . Some of us are really counting on [him]." Without saying it Rose makes clear that Yasir has responsibilities back home in Oakland—responsibilities to his son, her, and his ex-wife, Destiny. They apparently are in need of a return on their investments in him—a sense that his ex-girlfriend, Ruby, shared. In a way, Rose steps into the wise woman position in cautioning Nuri to think clearly about that into which she is walking. Nuri seeks to assure her of her commitment to Yasir, saying, "I was born in Compton, so this is not new to me. . . . I'm not thrill seeking with your son . . . I love him." The two women share a uniquely intracommunal moment of recognition and acceptance through the "proper" pronunciation of an explicit term with intracommunal significance for working and low SES communities.

As the scene progresses, we learn that Rose's diabetes and other health challenges are worsening. She becomes faint while trying to de-escalate a dispute between Yasir and Destiny that erupts in front of Nuri, Rose, Bill, and little Deonte. Destiny's tears clearly reflect residual feelings for Yasir, and she was not aware that Yasir was dating a new woman and was upset that Yasir had their son around someone who was a stranger to her. Yasir becomes verbally combative with Destiny and storms toward her until Rose stops him by reminding him that that's not the way she raised him. This is the moment that Nuri identifies as the first time she saw that side of Yasir in the show's dialogue. Viewers now are wondering how many more times Brock Akil or other women saw that side of Salim Akil.

As only a mother can, Rose steps up to check Yasir thusly, "I'm gonna translate for ya. She's mad because every six months you wanna roll up in here and tell people what to do, but this is a 24/7 job. Do you understand me?" Devine set the screen afire with her amazing performance. She checked Destiny also, but pulled no punches in correcting Yasir about Destiny being a good mother whose sacrifices and works hard to enable him to go off to pursue his dreams in Hollywood. It was the speech that every mother wishes someone would make on her behalf. Tears flowed on screen and in most homes that tuned in. Powerful. Deep. Beautiful.

CONCLUSION

What makes this critical discourse study unique is the linking of media framing and media representations to social functions such as reinforcing social hierarchies, perpetuating/rejecting ideologies, or promoting/threatening democracy. In turn, the following analysis critically examines frames and representations in *Love Is* ___ as mechanisms for cueing beliefs and representational schemas in audiences. In so doing, this research also acknowledges the intertwining of race, gender, religion, ability, and other forms of social classification as determinants of power and privilege.

Here, love occurs at the intersection of power and privilege. Yasir's male supremacy and Nuri's economic privilege. *Love Is* ___ captures the beauty and romance of infatuation. What worries me is that the show does not represent the consequences that come from the decisions made by the characters. The episodes display more about what love is not than what love is. Candidly, if this is love, then maybe love is not for me. In the words of a dear friend, "The only value of this relationship I see . . . is using it to dialogue with my daughters [about how] not to let a man with no job, car, address, pot or window to move into your house and drive your car while you get up and go to work every day."

Media literacy is important for consumers who are facing domestic abuse and intimate partner violence. Media literacy empowers readers with (1) awareness, (2) analysis, (3) activism, (4) advocacy, and (5) access (Earp 2015). "Awareness" about the pervasiveness of the media in their lives helps audiences identify the ubiquitous messages inundating their lives. "Analysis" empowers viewers to discuss the forms and contents of the media's various messages as well as the intent of most media to persuade an audience. "Activism" helps audiences develop their own opinions about the negative and positive effects of the media and decide to do something about it—this can be in the form of praise for healthy media, protest of unhealthy media, or development of campaigns to educate others with regard to the media, to change media messages, and so on. "Advocacy" educates others on how to work with media and use their own media to develop and publicize messages that are healthy, constructive, and all too often ignored by our society. "Access" to the media—radio, newspaper, internet, television, and so on—provides opportunities for viewers to spread their own message (Earp 2015). This in turn leads to further awareness of the media and how it works, which leads to a deeper analysis and so on. As a result, in the context of domestic abuse, victims and survivors can deconstruct what they see on shows like *Love Is* ____ and experience empowerment through tools that can enable them to question and challenge content that may send mixed messages that may be dangerous for them.

Ultimately, I am grateful for the beautiful counter-hegemonic narratives that *Love Is* ____ represents. Perhaps, as Black people unlearn slavery and all people unlearn white supremacy, there also will be an unlearning of the ways in which people internalize harmful messages that may lead them to harm each other. In the words of an ancient sacred text,

> If I speak in the tongues of mortals and of angels, but do not have love, I am a noisy gong or a clanging cymbal. And if I have prophetic powers, and understand all mysteries and all knowledge, and if I have all faith, so as to remove mountains, but do not have love, I am nothing. If I give away all my possessions, and if I hand over my body so that I may boast, but do not have love, I gain nothing.
>
> Love is patient; love is kind; love is not envious or boastful or arrogant or rude. It does not insist on its own way; it is not irritable or resentful; it does not rejoice

in wrongdoing, but rejoices in the truth. It bears all things, believes all things, hopes all things, endures all things.

Love never ends. . . . Now I know only in part; then I will know fully, even as I have been fully known. And now faith, hope, and love abide, these three; and the greatest of these is love. (1 Cor. 13: 1-13, NRSV)

REFERENCES

Barthes, Roland. (1977). *Rhetoric of the Image*. New York: Hill and Wang.
Barthes, Roland. (1998). *Image, Music, Text*. New York: Hill and Wang.
Barthes, Roland. (1998). *Mythologies*. New York: Hill and Wang.
Berg, Bruce L. (2007). *Qualitative Research Methods for the Social Sciences* (6th ed.). Boston, MA: Pearson and Allyn and Bacon.
Berg, Bruce L. (2009). *Qualitative Research Methods* (7th ed.). Boston: Allyn & Bacon.
Blakesley, David. (2004). "Defining Film Rhetoric: The Case of Hitchcock's Vertigo." In *Defining Visual Rhetorics*, eds. Charles A. Hill and Marguerite Helmers. Mahwah, NJ: Lawrence Erlbaum Associates, 112–17.
Brenner v. Akil. (2018). 18STCV05673 (Superior Court of Los Angeles for the County of Los Angeles, November 20).
Covino, William A., & Jolliffe, David. (1995). *What Is Rhetoric? Rhetoric: Concepts, Definitions, Boundaries*, 3–26. Boston: Allyn & Bacon.
Denzin, Norman K., & Lincoln, Yvonne S. (2011). "Introduction: The Discipline and Practice of Qualitative Research." In *The SAGE Handbook of Qualitative Research*, eds. N. K. Denzin and Y. S. Lincoln (4th ed.). Thousand Oaks, CA: Sage Publications, 1–42.
Earp, Jeremy. "Rich Media, Poor Democracy." *Media Literacy Circle of Empowerment. Amherst: Media Education Foundation* (2015): 19. Accessed January 30, 2019. http://www.mediaed.org/discussion-guides/Rich-Media-Poor-Democracy-Discussion-Guide.pdf.
Entman, Robert M. (2004). *Projections of Power*. Chicago: University of Chicago Press.
Entman, Robert M. (2007). "Framing Bias: Media in The Distribution of Power." *Journal of Communication* 57(1): 163–73.
Foucault, Michel. (July 1982). "The Subject and Power." *Critical Inquiry* 8(4): 777–95.
Grable, Betty. (2005). *African American Women's Reception, Influence and Utility of Television Content: An Exploratory Content Analysis* (Unpublished Doctoral book). The Manship School of Mass Communication, Louisiana State University, Baton Rouge, LA.
Janks, Hilary. (1997). "Critical Discourse Analysis as a Research Tool." *Discourse: Studies in the Cultural Politics of Education* 18(3): 329–42.

Hall, Stuart. (1972). "The Social Eye of Picture Post. Birmingham Centre for Contemporary Cultural Studies." *Working Papers in Cultural Studies* (3): 71–120.

Hall, Stuart. (1980b). "Encoding/Decoding." In *Culture, Media, Language*, ed. S. Hall (pp. 128–38). London, UK: Hutchinson.

Hall, Stuart. (1997). *Representation: Cultural Representations and Signifying Practices*. London, UK: Sage Publications.

Hall, Stuart. (2013). "The spectacle of the 'Other.'" In *Representation*, eds. S. Hall, J. Evans, and S. Nixon (2nd ed.), 213–71. London: SAGE.

Handa, Carolyn. (2004). *Visual Rhetoric in a Digital World: A Critical Sourcebook*. New York: Bedford/St. Martin's.

Jackson II, Ronald L. (2002). "Exploring African American Identity Negotiation in The Academy: Toward A Transformative Vision of African American Communication Scholarship." *Howard Journal of Communication* 13(1): 43–57.

Kolker, Robert. (2006). *Film, Form, & Culture*. Boston: McGraw Hill.

Kellner, Douglas, & Share, Jeff. (2005). "Toward Critical Media Literacy: Core Concepts, Debates, Organizations, and Policy." *Discourse: Studies in the Cultural Politics of Education* 26(3): 369–86.

Masterman, Len. (1994). *Teaching the Media*. London: Routledge.

"Nielsen Ratings Chart Love Is: Season One Ratings." *TV Series Finale Cancelled & Renewed TV Shows*, December 20. Accessed January 30, 2019. https://tvseriesfinale.com/tv-show/love-is-season-one-ratings.

Pena, Jessica. (2018). *Love Is: Season Two Renewal Announced by OWN*. Press Release, OWN.

Potter, James W. (1996). "An Analysis of Thinking and Research About Qualitative Methods." *Howard Journal of Communications* 17: 183–203.

Tyree, Tia C. M. (2007). *The Pursuit of Movie Money: A Textual Analysis of Rap Artists As Actors In Hollywood Films*. Doctoral book Howard University, Washington DC.

van Dijk, Teun A. (1998). *Ideology: A Multidisciplinary Approach*. London: SAGE Publications.

van Dijk, Teun A. (2001). "Critical Discourse Analysis." In *The Handbook of Discourse Analysis*, edited by Deborah Schiffrin, Deborah Tannen, and Heidi E. Hamilton. Hoboken, NJ: Blackwell Publishers, LTD.

van Dijk, Teun A. (2001). *Text and Context: Explorations in the Semantics and Pragmatics of Discourse*. London: Longman.

Wills, Courtney. "'Black Lightning' Showrunner, Salim Akil Sued for Domestic Violence and Breach of Contract." *theGrio*, November 2018. Accessed January 29, 2019. https://tinyurl.com/yaq5t74g.

Part II
AUDIENCE RECEPTION/SOCIAL MEDIA INTERACTION

Chapter 6

Relating to *The Game*

Meaning Making Among Fans

Lisa M. Paulin

While the ways people watch television are changing, shows produced for television remain a big part of most people's lives. Whether they are watched to pass the time, to learn, to disconnect from work or responsibilities, to laugh, or to feel our hearts beat faster, television remains a ubiquitous part of individual's lives. Some people might even argue that the ability to record or stream and binge-watch television shows increases the intensity of a viewer's relationship with television whether physically watching a television, a computer screen, or a phone screen. Research consistently confirms media viewing also serves to inform viewers' social lives—often as much as other social institutions such as family, school, and religious community (Ott 2010, 11). In television, viewers see themselves, who they might become; who they don't want to be; relationships or situations that they find or could find themselves in; and consequences that their favorite or despised characters face for the decisions they make.

In the United States, the television industry often lacks diversity in the representation of marginalized groups—for instance, women, people of color, poor people, and so on. Further, when characters from marginalized groups are depicted, the portrayals are often stereotyped, negative and/or one-dimensional (Croteau and Hoynes 2019). Advocates for diversity in television assert that the industry must create a space and a pipeline for more women, African Americans, Latinos, Asians, and other underrepresented groups into all aspects of television production. Yet, some research has shown that merely having a Black cast does not lead to success, as exampled the short-lived show "City of Angels" which ran for one and half seasons on CBS in 2000. However, it was later noted in interviews that the producers downplayed race using a colorblind philosophy, stating that race relations would not be a focus of the show (Warner 2012), which arguably could have been problematic in its creation. Successively, network television has seen tremendous strides for African Americans working in television production. Adamo (2010) cites five factors that facilitated these strides. The first was Fox network's late 1980s push to include sitcoms with African American casts, which was a success. Second, African American show creators who had long been working on shows as writers and in other roles, recognized their opportunity to reflect their changing cultural reality. Third, the introduction of UPN and WB networks in 1995 opened up spaces for new content especially as both channels launched using Fox's 1980s strategy. The fourth factor was the rise in satellite and cable television and fifth the popularity and success of hip hop culture which became America's youth culture and a mainstay of pop culture (4).

Although men dominated much of the media production industry, several African American women, such as Debbie Allen, Susan Fales-Hill, Winifred Hervey, Sara Finney Johnson, and Vida Spears were writing for, directing, and producing television shows in the 1980s (Dates 2005). These women opened the door for many other African American women. Among the African American women who have become wildly successful recently as showrunners are Issa Rae, Ava DuVernay, Shonda Rhimes, and Mara Brock Akil. Although Shonda Rhimes may be a more recognizable name for the average American household, Mara Brock Akil is a prolific showrunner who creates storylines featuring mostly Black casts and tackling topics with which most viewers—regardless of race—can identify. In particular, her show *The Game* serves as an excellent case study in audience reception because while it originally ran from 2006–2009 on the CW network, it was brought back with original episodes in 2011 because of the overwhelming demand on social media from fans who wanted more. Having a Black female producer is significant. For example, a study of the difference in *The Cosby Show* college-based sitcom spinoff, *A Different World*, found tremendous change when Debbie Allen took over as producer in the second season from Anne Beatts. The show received poor reviews under Beatts, who was white, as "it failed to mirror and comment on the lived experiences of Black college students in the United States" (Means Coleman 2012, 35). The author describes the myriad changes that Allen made to the show and concludes, "It was about inviting her audience to understand and experience Blackness" (Means Coleman 2012, 40).

THE GAME

After the success of her show *Girlfriends*, Brock Akil created *The Game*, a loosely related spin off on the CW network in 2006. *The Game* centered on six characters: couples Derwin and Melanie, Jason and Kelly, and mom and manager [referred to as a "momanager"] Tasha and her son Malik. The show began with Melanie, a medical school student at Johns Hopkins University, leaving school to follow and support her boyfriend Derwin, a football rookie recruit for the fictional San Diego Sabers. Shortly after moving to San Diego, Melanie is introduced to the Sunbeams—a group of girlfriends and wives of the Sabers. The leader, Kelly, is married to Jason, a top player. Malik is the star quarterback, who is single, and his momanager, Tasha, are major characters in the series. The episodes revolve around the football players, their partners, and the relationships and situations they navigate while trying to pursue money, happiness, success, and life balance. The series ran for three seasons until 2009 when it was canceled by the CW. Black Entertainment Television (BET) bought the rights to the show and aired it as reruns where it found new fans. In fact, high demand by fans led to a reboot with new seasons that ran from 2011–2015. When the fourth season debuted on BET, *The Game* broke the record for most-watched sitcom premiere in cable television's history with 7.7 million viewers. Additionally, a Viacom press release from two days after the debut provided astounding numbers for social media interaction. At one point *The Game*'s Facebook page reached 893 "likes" per minute and 750 comments per minute (Newswire 2011). The entire run of *The Game* consisted of 147 episodes, and throughout the years the show received twenty-five award nominations and won six NAACP Image Awards including Outstanding Comedy Series in 2013.

RESEARCH ON AFRICAN AMERICANS AND MEDIA

Some researchers attribute Herman Gray's *Watching Race: Television and the Struggle for Blackness* originally published in 1995 and then re-released with a new introduction in 2004 as setting the academic stage and providing a theoretical basis upon which to examine Black television shows (Smith-Shomade 2012, 2). There is a wide variety of research on Black representation in entertainment and news media, Black representations in entertainment media with majority Black casts, Black representation in news and sports, as well as work on Black opportunities in production spaces and their evolution, and audience research. Some of this work is found in journal articles, as chapters in academic books that are not specifically focused on race as well as ones that are, and complete academic books devoted to examining race in media.

UNDERSTANDING AUDIENCE RESEARCH

Two Theoretical Approaches

Observing and talking to audiences play a significant role in media studies research by providing insight into active audiences—how viewers interpret, understand, and use media in their private and social lives. Two of the main approaches to audience studies have been uses and gratifications and critical cultural studies (Croteau and Hoynes 2019). Uses and gratifications research focuses on *what* people are doing with media and *why* they are using media. Although some researchers use a qualitative approach by conducting focus groups or interviews, uses and gratifications research is often conducted with survey research, quantitatively. Critical cultural studies approaches focus on how viewers make meaning out of the media and how they interpret the media related to their social position (Croteau and Hoynes 2019). This can be accomplished by several research methods but is particularly well-suited to focus groups. Focus groups have a long history in academia as well as in marketing and political consulting, and because of the conversational style they often produce dynamic data and insights that would be less accessible with individual interviews or other qualitative methods as participants feed off each other's ideas to share related or contradictory ideas (Lindlof and Taylor 2019). Additionally, focus groups have been found to be particularly good for studying why people watch television (Adams 2000).

Stuart Hall (1973) introduced the encoding-decoding model to explain that media producers may have certain meanings and interpretations in mind, that are encoded, on the media text, and that viewers may decode messages using the intended or "preferred" reading, an "oppositional" reading, or a "negotiated" reading. Decoding is the way that viewers make sense of a film, television show, advertisement, or video using broad cultural codes; personal beliefs, values and experiences; and social location. To take a simple example, a television show might portray villains in darker clothes or darker makeup with serious expressions while protagonists smile more. This would be encoding on the production side. If audiences understand these roles as villain and protagonist, they have decoded the preferred reading. An oppositional reading might come from someone who thinks social circumstances are unfairly creating a villain out of someone who is good and noble and even see the protagonist as part of the reason why the "villain" is misunderstood, thereby opposing the encoded meaning. Negotiated readings, on the other hand, recognize the encoded message as legitimate, but bring their own interpretations into the equation. Perhaps they recognize the villain and protagonist but see aspects of the villain that can be redeemed or also recognize some evil in the protagonist. This study uses focus groups to examine how audiences make meaning using an encoding-decoding approach.

Audience Research

Several notable studies guide the understanding of audience research. The first widely cited research is Janice Radway's (1991) study of women readers of romance novels which cemented the idea of an active audience. The women in the study did not passively absorb the content of romance novels, but frequently used novel reading as a way to consciously disconnect from the demands of their daily life and escape to a world of personal meaning. The first significant study to test Hall's encoding-decoding model was David Morley's (Morley 1999) audience studies in the 1970s of the British news program *Nationwide*. Morley was interested in how different audiences interpreted ideological messages. Using eighteen different groups ranging in characteristics of gender, race, class, union membership, educational level, and political affiliation, Morley conducted focus group discussions. He found ample evidence of an active audience who negotiated and resisted meaning. Besides showing evidence for Hall's encoding-decoding model, Morley's studies showed that factors besides social class influenced audiences' readings.

Jhally and Lewis (1992) conducted a large qualitative study with fifty-two focus groups comprised of frequent or occasional viewers of *The Cosby Show* resulting in their term "Enlightened Racism" to compare the complexity of peoples' opinions of race when compounded with socioeconomic class (Jhally 1992, 10). To summarize:

> *The Cosby Show* leaves us with an ideological problem. It sustains and promotes the widespread assumption that a positive image of a black person is necessarily of an upper middle class black. This generated contradictory attitudes: first, it "proves that black people can make it in a predominantly white world, even though most black people have, on the reckoning, failed; second, it cultivates the illusion that economic success is as achievable for black people as for white people. This forces black Americans to buy into a system that handicaps them, without being able to explain (or accept) their persistently low levels of achievement. (Jhally 1992, 129)

Research has also examined *Beulah* and *Amos & Andy*, which were earlier and widely criticized shows with Black casts, which were condemned by the NAACP. While not a focus group study, Scott (2014) analyzed television interviews in which both Black and white viewers were asked what they thought about the show and reported that most people, regardless of race, enjoyed watching the show because it was funny and lighthearted. Race did not really play into their explanations at all. The author then continues to assert that Black performers in blackface used grotesque stereotypes to undermine racism—an oppositional reading, as a way to assert their humanity (Scott 2014).

Other recent audience research has focused on Black or mixed race audiences' perceptions of genres besides sitcom including sketch comedy (Perks 2012), reality television (A. Hall 2006), and film (Brown and Stanton 2014).

Perks (2012) conducted focus groups with viewers of the *Chappelle's Show* and found some nuances to the traditional encoding-decoding model when studying satire: a refusal of the decoding process, a focus on the text's resonance with reality, and an emphasis of the text's exaggeration of reality. A study of reality television found that there was much debate about the definition of reality television that viewers had a critical eye about it being reality— knowing that it was edited for drama as well as examining the reasons why people watched (A. Hall 2006). In a focus group study about Tyler Perry's films, researchers found that Perry's films get some things right and some things wrong when it comes to Black women. Specifically, he represents a wide range of Black women's experiences and the role of Black women in family cohesion, but the fact that the Madea character is played by a male complicates interpretations and college-age students found the female characters to be stereotypical "angry black women" (Brown and Stanton 2014).

Recent studies on perceptions of television shows found that viewers placed great importance on shows to which they could identify with and relate. One was a study of British viewers of the original British production of the sitcom *The Office*. Viewers identified with both the characters and certain situations and topics that they felt were uniquely British. In fact, several focus group participants had seen the American version of the show did not identify with it and felt that it was only about one liners and jokes (Bore 2009). Another study was conducted in Qatar among international students studying at the Education City Campus. The study examined the popularity of Turkish dramas among the Middle Eastern students and found that cultural proximity was a key factor in students' preference for these over American dramas. The findings indicated that seeing conservative values, familiar foods, and familiar family situations were among the most important reasons for the popularity of the shows (Berg 2017).

Besides audience research, much of the research examining Black female-led television shows have been critical studies with a feminist approach (Guerrero 2013; Dreher 2013; Wanzo 2013). In particular, Lewis (2012) examined Brock Akil's *Girlfriends* and *The Game* and their impact on dealing with Black women's health issues. The author presented Brock Akil's creative ownership and prioritization of women's health issues as a critique of hip hop's movement away from female artists to one in which "the roles that misogyny, homophobia, sexism, and materialism—staples of commercial hip hop . . . would play in the spread of HIV/AIDS among black women" (Lewis 2012, 159). Lewis argues that among the enduring legacies of *Girlfriends* and *The Game* are their positioning and location of Black women's experiences within rounded narratives of identity, sexuality, health, and authority (163). In understanding Brock Akil's effort to reconstruct Black womanhood for audiences and theoretical considerations within audience research, this study asks the following research question: How did viewers, especially young women, interpret and make meaning from *The Game*?

METHODOLOGY

The Participants

The study conducted three focus groups: one with current college students at a historically black university [HBCU] in the Southeast United States, one with adult women who had either watched the show while in college or after, and an online focus group using Facebook for women who expressed interest in participating but were unable to attend the scheduled focus group. Research refers to them as the class focus group, the adult focus group, and the online focus group. The class focus group had eight participants of whom seven were female and one was male. Seven identify as African American and one woman as African American and Hispanic. The participants were all born between 1993 and 1998, making them between twenty-one and twenty-six years old at the time of the study. The average age was twenty-three. The focus group was conducted in the classroom with other students observing and taking notes or helping with audiovisual equipment. The adult focus group had two female participants, one who identifies as an African American and Hispanic and the other who identifies as white. They were thirty-one and twenty-eight years old. The focus group was conducted in the evening in a conference room on campus. It was audio and video recorded.

The online Facebook focus group was created after several interested participants said that online would work better for them because of scheduling difficulties. Over a series of days, questions were posed to the group of women who consented, and they were tagged in the posts. The results were mixed. As with any focus group, some people participated more than others, but the transcript looks much more like people just answering questions than the typical conversational quality of a focus group. Yet, the data gathered was useful and is included in my analysis. A total of eight women participated in the online focus group. Five did not answer the demographic questions. The three who did all identify as African Americans and were between the age group of twenty-seven and thirty-three. Although the original Facebook post was public, most of the people who saw it were associated with me as the researcher and everyone who responded was a graduate of an HBCU in the Southeastern United States. The two additional members, who I was not acquainted with, were also college-educated women and identify as African Americans.

My Role as the Researcher

As mentioned, I knew all but two of the participants personally. All were either my current or former students. Due to the nature of the topic, I don't think that my role as professor to some of the students impacted their responses. The focus group was conducted with other students present, yet it is believed that having "an audience" did not substantially affect their responses. I identify as white, but I have been teaching and working at an HBCU for almost thirteen years. I do not think my race or my age substantially impacted the way participants answered. If anything, my race and age might have helped get more explanation if they thought they had to explain it to someone who might not know their standpoint. I had not been a fan or regular watcher of *The Game*; however, I recorded episodes and watched episodes through various seasons to acquaint myself with the characters. Although this may be viewed as a weakness, it could also be considered a strength because it encouraged participants to elaborate more if asked follow-up questions.

Procedure

The questions posed sought to understand how participants perceived the show, which characters they identified with or reacted strongly to, which plot lines or topics impacted them, how they talked to others about the show, and what other types of shows they had enjoyed at the same time. In comparison, research inquired about participants watching television shows created by Shonda Rhimes, another successful showrunner, and what differences they see between Brock Akil's work and Rhimes's work. The focus groups were semi-structured interviews, in which some questions were added as the discussion unfolded, and new topics arose. With the class focus group, participants were asked how they had learned about or been introduced to the show, and what role their parents had played in their viewing the show—because they likely were in early middle school when *The Game* originally aired. Members of the class focus group brought up how the show changed when it moved from CW to BET; therefore, the other focus groups were asked if they thought the show changed, and if so, how. Focus group audio recordings were transcribed and then used grounded theory procedure (Corbin 2015) by reading through all transcripts and taking notes on key words and phrases, then after a second reading identified themes and subthemes in the discussion.

ANALYSIS

The Game was Relatable

The key word that came up repeatedly in all focus groups was "relatable" or phrases such as "we could relate to" or "connected to us." In fact, this was mentioned sixteen times during the three focus groups. Throughout the seasons of *The Game*, in numerous interviews, Brock Akil discussed her goal to make characters and to address topics that were relatable. In an interview with *Urbanology* magazine after her keynote address at the 2015 Toronto Screenwriters Conference, she said, "I'm looking for original thought; I'm looking for honest, relatable truth" (Brock Akil as cited in Ramanuam 2015). So, it appears that this was a preferred reading of the encoded content. The key themes that centered around what made the show relatable were relationships and representation even though those were understood differently at the time by viewers who were in middle school when they watched versus participants who were in college. Participants also noted the originality of the show, but many described the show as less relatable after the new episodes began airing on BET.

Relationships

The participants in the focus groups discussed relationships in several ways. One was their own relationship with characters from the show, another revolved around the relationship problems they observed in the shows topics, and the third tied into family relationships such as different types of families, and in the case of younger viewers' discussions that occurred in their own families while watching the show.

Relationships with Characters

Almost all participants said that they could identify with a specific or a combination of the characters from the show. Most of the women said that they related to Melanie, but their reasons varied. One woman mentioned that Melanie was reserved in the beginning and "not about that drama," but that she got pulled into it by other people. Several women identified with Melanie's struggle to balance being a student with being a supportive partner to Derwin. Others mentioned that they identified with her because she came from a two-parent household with a lot of stability and support, but also high expectations for their futures. They all expressed how much they liked and admired the character of Tasha Mack not only because she was strong and did not hold back when she wanted to say something, but that she was also a genuinely good person. Fewer students mentioned her as someone with whom they identified. The male student, a current undergraduate female basketball player, and a former female student who played on the softball team in college all identified more with the male athletes. The softball player said:

> From an athletic standpoint, I would say I definitely identify more with the male athletes. When you come in as a freshman or new recruit, you sometimes

have to adjust with playing with more senior players or better competition. You may have left your school being the best athlete, but now you have to step up your game and adapt to the same game differently or on a bigger scale. This adds pressure to your game and other aspects of your life. All of the men on the show were the breadwinners of their families, so injuries and no play time meant less money. Ultimately, it becomes less of a 'fun game' and more of an intense job—where everything falls on you.

The male student identified with aspects of both Malik and Derwin. He said that

Malik was like someone that most of the guys want to be—like star quarterback, got all the endorsement deals, the money, you know, women chasing after him. But in reality, sometimes you feel like Derwin, because you feel overshadowed, like he wasn't the highest person picked. So, like, the person about trying to achieve better than his circumstances right now. I think I can relate to that.

The white female mentioned that she identified with Kelly some because of her "type A personality" but also Melanie because of her ability to empathize with others.

These comments and the ways that the participants identified with the characters illustrates the depth of their connection with *The Game*. While introducing Brock Akil in a video interview for a blog, the host refers to her as, "Everyone's favorite producer, their friend in their head" (Staff 2012). Referring to Brock Akil this way gives a nod to the mass communication theory of parasocial interaction, which proposes that viewers, particularly television viewers, create a one-sided psychological relationship with characters on television (Chandler 2016). Viewers, in this case, often feel quite certain that if they knew each other in real life, they would be good friends or somehow in a real relationship. This study does not explore parasocial interaction, but we can certainly say that these viewers adopted a preferred reading as they reported relating to the characters which was a stated intention of encoding by Brock Akil. We could also apply Fish's (1982) concept of interpretive communities in which people occupying similar social positions and experiences interpret texts similarly (173). In this case Mara Brock Akil is a college graduate. The focus group participants were all college students or college graduates, so they easily identified with characters who were trying to get ahead and create a better life under the ideological umbrella of capitalism emphasizing nice clothes, nice apartments or homes, nice cars, and other material wealth—a preferred reading increased their enjoyment of the show.

Romantic Relationships and Problems

The Game helped participants understand the complexity of romantic relationships and problems in romantic relationships. The male participant observed that *The Game* showed three types of relationships: the married couple, the single life, and a couple that's "just starting to come up and putting their life on hold for somebody else." The relationship topics that struck them most were cheating, making sacrifices, and that money does not equal happiness. Several participants reported that the cheating storyline between Derwin and Melanie made them "so sad." Another said that she was "so angry" with Derwin. Other students were upset with how controlling Jason was with Kelly and how "messy" their divorce got. Although most everyone related to Melanie, several were upset that she frequently used her decision to accompany Derwin to San Diego as leverage over him. One student sounded as though she was talking to Melanie as a personal friend when she explained,

> I understand you gave up a lot of stuff, but, girl, like, you gotta [*sic*] let go. We are here now. Either you're gonna [*sic*] stay or you don't. So, it was just frustrating and that's frustrating with people period. Like, once you make a decision and that's your decision, don't blame me for why you decided to come all the way out here to San Diego. You could've stayed where you were if you wanted to.

There is no reference for the encoded meaning that Brock Akil intended for these relationship issues. In fact, it could be argued that her goal was to allow fans to feel the emotions and make conclusions on their own. The nuanced readings of participants while varied still show a deep connection and analysis that they put into reading meaning into the show.

Family Relationships

The class focus group originated after it was discovered that many of the current students were fans of *The Game*. When asked how they had learned about the show or why the first began watching it, several participants of the class focus group noted that the CW network was airing a lot of shows at that time with mostly or all Black casts. One female student said that she was already watching *The Parkers* and *One on One* and she started watching *The Game* because it was a new show that was coming on after the others. Another student remarked that she watched during "family time" and said, "I guess we were young, like eight or nine." Others said that it was end of elementary school and beginning of middle school for them. While a couple other students said that they had never watched it on CW but had begun watching later when BET reran the seasons before airing new episodes.

Perhaps because of the younger age of this focus group's participants, they talked more about family relationships and what they learned from the show than the adult and online focus group participants did. The older participants linked the reasons why they identified with specific characters to similar family structures, while the class participants expressed that they learned more about different types of families. For example, in the online focus group, one woman said, "She [Melanie] comes from a two-parent household that has all these hopes and dreams for her to be a doctor and be successful in life. I came from a two-parent household until I was a teenager and my parents worked hard to provide the best life for me and had expectations for me to go to college, graduate and be successful in life." Another participant said that she identified with Tasha Mack because "I grew up with a single mom and watching Tasha try to adjust to the new life with Malik reminded me of parts of my childhood. When your child is advancing in ways that outgrow your poor circumstances, it's a beautiful thing, but it will still come with a price."

Whereas, in the class focus group with younger participants, one student felt that Malik meeting his father was an important topic and described Malik's mixed emotions as being relatable for people who grew up with only one parent in the household. Another participant said that she had gained insight into different types of families and family dynamics. The viewers who had been younger also talked about how the topics from the show led to discussions within their own families. One female participant said that she always had a television in her room and since her parents had given her that freedom, they talked to her about topics like pregnancy, relationships, and even Melanie's decision to move to San Diego. She commented, "Both my mom and my dad because it was like, 'this is the real world and sometimes these decisions come to you early.' We talked about stuff like that all the time." Another said that the conversations usually came up during commercial breaks and were often more admonishments than conversations. She said, "Like, 'you better not do that!'" When she said that, several other participants laughed and nodded in agreement.

The finding that the show led to family discussions for several participants follows recommendations from research on adolescent television viewing and sexual content (Collins, et al. 2017). Among the recommendations, they suggest that health care providers and policy makers should provide tools to help parents discuss the influence of media with their children (165). Although *The Game* did not show explicit sexual content, the topics of cheating and unwanted pregnancy contained implicit sexual content. Moreover, the negotiated readings of family relationships provide an excellent example of how viewers negotiate meaning when they are decoding.

Representation

The focus group participants from the three groups described *The Game* as relatable when it came to racial representation and sports. The show also represented a lesson or insight that most participants could learn from and apply to their own lives. This was sometimes explained as "insight" and seemed to show some kind of change in their viewpoint.

Racial Representation

None of the focus group participants mentioned race until I asked, "Imagine that you are talking to a friend who hasn't seen the show, what would you tell him or her about the show to convince them that they should be tuning in?" Among other answers to this question, one participant said, "It was nice to see a show that wasn't just an all-white cast." Another said, "It was like an all-black people sitcom." This comment generated some side talk about Kelly not being Black. Two participants then had an exchange that gave more insight into the importance of racial identification for them:

Participant 1: About the writer Mara Brock Akil, she was, like, big on black people on TV and stuff.
Participant 2: Hence, it's like *Girlfriends* was a group of four women who are well off or doing something with themselves and just showing their everyday lives. I think that's what connected us. You're just seeing these black people, I don't know . . . .
Participant 1: Living well.
Participant 2: Mostly well. It's just like not the whole entire show is terrible, like people struggling and probably like *Good Times*. [Others laugh at this] I'm not trying to be funny, but not like *Good Times*. I mean, they're going through trials and tribulations, but it seems like a little more normal.
Participant 1: Yeah.

Although race had not been mentioned up to this point in the focus groups, it was clearly an important aspect of what made *The Game* relatable to many participants along with seeing a representation of how educated Black women live. This is another topic that Brock Akil has discussed in interviews. In a 2016 article that appeared on *The Root* she is quoted saying, "I chose a way of turning my lens toward the things that I thought were missing in the land of not just television," Akil explains. "I didn't see myself," and that, Akil argued, is "more damaging, to be invisible to society. I wanted to paint in and fill in some of that negative space," Akil explained. "It's very damaging to the psyche when you don't see yourself" (Ozemebhoya Eromosele 2016).

The formation of ethnic identity is frequently explained using a model with three interconnected and mutually reinforcing dimensions: cognitive, behavioral, and affective. The cognitive dimension relates to knowledge that one has about the group. This is often originally learned from family and reinforced by community. The behavioral dimension provides members with cues, codes, and language that they identify with being members of the group. The affective dimension is the emotional side of the identity (Matsaganis and Katz 2011, 71). Matsaganis and Katz (2011) further assert that ethnic identity is dynamic—but changing over time and situations. They write, "Ethnic media can be an important platform for negotiating ethnic identity in different contexts" (72). It is also important to note and evaluate race as a negotiated meaning as not all participants mentioned it and some participants identified more with characters of opposite gender (in the case of athletes) and the one white participant reported that she identified with Melanie and Kelly based on aspects of their personalities, not race.

Representation of Athletes

Focus group participants also related to the representation of sports and athletes. At times, when discussing sports, they seemed to ignore the fact that this was a scripted television show about an imaginary team. When I asked them to describe the show assuming that I had never seen it, one participant in the online focus group wrote, "It's basically about the stress and struggles of relationships of NFL players and their families." Another participant wrote, "A behind the scenes look at the lives of professional athletes." In the class focus group, the male participant said, "The show really tries to show a representation of how the life really is for a professional athlete." In the adult focus group, one participant mentioned that she had dated an athlete in college, so she related to the show that way.

Representation of Self-Opening to Other Viewpoints

Overall, participants said that they could relate to the topics that came up in the episodes. However, this seemed to have been a more eye-opening experience for people who were younger when they watched the show. Many comments indicated a change in their viewpoint based on what they viewed. Often these insights were about issues in romantic relationships. One woman seemed almost resigned when she said that although she didn't agree with Melanie's sacrifices for Derwin, "It's something you have to do at the end of the day." The male student said that watching Kelly and Jason's breakup was hard, "Just because you got all the money and the fame, he had no peace in his house. He couldn't even sleep in his own bed," and concluded with "be careful who you're saying 'I do' to, cause it's just like people change later on down the road and you have to account for that." Some comments illustrated insight into characters' personal shortcomings. For instance, several participants from the class focus group expressed frustration with Derwin's decision-making. One woman said that Derwin was "just doing what everyone else was doing. He couldn't stay true to himself." Another woman expressed that she was always thinking, "Why aren't things going right for Derwin?" Another woman mentioned Derwin's relationship with religion and how that represented her own, and her friends' experiences. She said:

> Derwin, at the beginning, was all into his Christianity, and then as the season went on and he got involved with Janay, he kind of backed away from it. And when stuff started going down the drain for him, he tried to pick it back up. I think that is something that we can all relate to. When things are going good for you, you try to start out without it and you, kind of like, let it go and don't talk to Him as much. Then, when things get bad, you overly pray or overly need Him.

Participants in both the class and adult focus group seemed surprised and even a little disappointed in their interpretation that having money does not necessarily lead to happiness. One woman who watched the show as a young adolescent said, "They say money buys happiness, but, like, nobody on the show was happy. Like, Derwin had all these endorsements and Jason was the star quarterback. They were all at different levels and they all had money, but none of them were legitimately and truly happy. That's one thing, like, just be happy with yourself." Likewise, a participant who watched the show as a college student said, "Money plays a role—people associate that with happiness. They think that if they're dating an athlete or someone famous that everything is going to be great, but then there's that cheating or whatever."

The different meanings that participants ascribed to the show plotlines and situations that characters faced illustrates how they negotiated meaning. While Brock Akil's media interviews don't give answers regarding each episode's encoded meanings, she clearly succeeded in touching fans and making them think and in many cases rethink what they thought about relationships, religion, happiness, success, and money especially influencing younger viewers. As Briggs (2010) discusses, television discourses contribute to how audiences "imagine their futures and think about their pasts" (84). One participant summarized this idea when she responded to the first focus group item, "Assuming I have never seen *The Game*, tell me about it." She said, "I would describe it as a comedy that addresses those real issues that we face in life, that gives us a real blueprint on how people could address them and championing for people to pursue their career and championing for them to get out from under their husband's thumb and do their own thing."

The Game was an Original, then Unrelatable

Besides the ways that participants learned to navigate their own experiences, understand the complications of relationships, and see characters they identified with and aspired to be like, they also commented on the originality of *The Game* and the role they believed it played as a precursor of reality television to come. When asked specifically how *The Game* was different from other shows they enjoyed at the time, the male participant commented, "It focused on professional sports. We've always seen singers and artists, but not athletes." A female participant then commented, "It started with the Sunbeams and now we've got all these shows like *Real Housewives of Atlanta* and *Side Chicks of Charlotte*." Another female participant mentioned that it was the first show to really have multiple viewpoints—male and female characters. She recalled that most shows only featured female relationships and cited *Girlfriends* and *Eve*. Another participant mentioned that other shows featured teenagers, not adults, such as *Moesha* and *One on One*.

Three participants were not aware that the show had started on CW before later finding a home on BET. Two of these had begun watching the show from the beginning when BET reran the first season. The third watched the entire series after it had aired, watching all episodes on BET. But many of the participants who had enjoyed the show and had related to it on CW did not like the way the series changed when new episodes were created for BET.

Perhaps ironically, the racial identity of the show that they liked so much was exactly what they did not like when it switched to a network that focuses on Black entertainment. This part of the conversation began with the classroom focus group when one participant mentioned neutrally that the show changed with BET. Her words were "reinvented it," "did new stuff to it," and "brought new people on the show." Another student chimed in and said that the show became blacker. When asked to explain what that meant, she said, "ignorant, messy, more *Love & Hip Hop*-ish." She complained about characteristics of Jason's new love interest saying that she was "constantly neck popping." Later, she complained that the Jason and Kelly's daughter had "become disrespectful" and that "the new wife was all neck snapping, just extra." Another participant tried to explain it this way, "The topics from BET were more drama filled, like stereotypical what goes on in a Black family home—cheating, divorce, and when it was on CW, it was just like a little more diverse with the topics." With the mention of reality television, another participant noted that perhaps it was a change in writers rather than a change in channel that could explain the difference. She further explained that this was the time that reality TV was "popping up" and believed that the show had different competition. In fact, the first *Love & Hip Hop* did begin in 2009. However, there was not a big shift in writers. According to IMDB, the show had eight writers who worked throughout the years of both networks and then many writers who wrote for four or fewer episodes. In those cases, some wrote while on CW and some others wrote while on BET, and some contributed to a couple episodes on each channel (IMDB n.d.) Yet, the switch from broadcast television to cable television could explain some of the differences since cable is not confined to the same FCC regulations as broadcast channels. On broadcast television shows, certain words are prohibited if they might be considered offensive. While many cable shows self-censor, there is more leeway in terms of regulation. The philosophy behind this is that broadcast is over the airways and accessible to everyone while cable or satellite television is paid for and not accessible to everyone.

Due to the discussion in the classroom, the other focus group participants were asked whether they had noticed a change. One woman said that it became "over the top, unrealistic and not relatable." She gave the following example, "It got really sex, drugs, rock-n-roll, like a certain type of vibe where it was just too much of that. In every show you're going to have some of that, but when that just like becomes the premise—Malik always had like girls shaking their butts and that's cool for a couple episodes, but like not . . ." [unfinished thought].

Although *The Game* found new life on BET, many participants reported what could be considered an "oppositional" reading to it, where they felt that the show ventured into old, stereotypical portrayals of African Americans as having too many problems and lots of drama in their lives. In one interview, Brock Akil said that the BET episodes were going to "bring it hot" (Staff 2012). Unfortunately, it seems as though the issues and characters may have been too hot for fans of the show.

CONCLUSION

Ang's (1985) extensive research on audiences and soap opera enjoyment led to the distinction between "empirical realism" and "emotional realism." In empirical realism, respondents like to see their own worlds depicted realistically, recognizing the type of people and events that they themselves encounter despite the sensationalized events or personality traits in television. Emotional realism reflects the desire of viewers to see their inner lives, feelings, and emotions on the screens. These focus groups saw both empirical and emotional realism in their interpretations. They employed preferred, negotiated, and even oppositional readings in their readings. It may seem obvious, as fans that they incorporated preferred readings in their interpretations of *The Game*, particularly in how they related to the characters. The finding that several participants referred to it as a show that depicts what life is like for athletes, underscores the relatability of that aspect of the show. But the nuanced understandings and meanings of relationships and how one approaches situations in relationships illustrate the negotiated readings fans brought to their decoding of *The Game*. There was a noticeable difference between how younger fans and older fans related to the relationship situations. Younger fans claimed to have gained insight into the complex reality of relationships and talked about how their viewpoints changed. Older fans related relationship situations to their own experiences with their families. The aspect of racial representation was a negotiated reading as it was important for some participants, while others seemed to be more influenced by representation of athletes. Participants were also attuned to the ways that the show changed when it switched networks, many of them adopting an oppositional reading to the show and reporting that it became unrelatable. Nonetheless, Brock Akil's dedication to creating shows that feature Black casts resonates. Many of the focus group participants found *The Game* because they were already watching shows with characters that "looked like them" and could relate to them. The overwhelmingly success of *The Game* in terms of longevity, social media reaction, and award nominations lends support to the importance of promoting diverse voices in all aspects of television show production.

This study also confirms the continued social role that television plays in peoples' lives and the richness of conducting focus groups to gain a deeper understanding of how viewers make meaning of the media they consume. While surveys allow for more generalization and can be administered to large groups of people easily, they rarely, if ever, yield the depth of association that viewers create with characters and situations and how they apply these to their lives.

This study also yields insight and sets the stage for further research into how families view television together and how parents talk with their adolescent children about topic television show characters face. Participants in this study who were adolescents while watching the show recalled vividly when family discussion had occurred. Further research may also want to explore the relationship between social class and relatability. The study participants were all college students or college graduates. Being that *The Game* featured people living a middle class to wealthy life, they could relate to the idea of success or being on a path to success. It would be interesting to see how it impacted viewers who see themselves as struggling and perhaps not living a life that will look like the lives of the characters. Clearly the variety of Brock Akil's work resonates with fans—whether she is depicting girlfriends or couples, athletes or journalists. Her characters and the situations they face provide meaning to viewers.

REFERENCES

Adamo, Gregory. 2010. *African Americans in Television: Behind the Scenes*. New York: Peter Lang.

Ang, Ien. 1985. *Watching Dallas: Soap Opera and the Melodramatic Imagination*. London: Methuen.

Berg, Miriam. 2017. "The Importance of Cultural Proximity in the Success of Turkish Dramas in Qatar." *International Journal of Communication* 11: 3415–30.

Bird, S. Elizabeth. 2003. *The Audience in Everyday Life: Living in a Media World*. New York: Routledge.

Bore, Inger-Lise Klviknes. 2009. "Negotiating Generic Hybridity: Audience Engagement with "The Office". *Continuum: Journal of Media & Cultural Studies* 33–42.

Briggs, Matt. 2010. *Television, Audiences and Everyday Life*. New York: McGraw Hill.

Brown, Kennaria, Shannon Baldon, and Amber Stanton. 2014. "Getting it 'Right?' African American Women Reading Tyler Perry's Films." In *Interpreting Tyler Perry: Perspectives on Race, Class, Gender, and Sexuality*, edited by Jamel Santa Cruze and Ronald L. Jackson, II Bell, 240–53. New York: Taylor & Francis.

Chandler, Daniel and Rod Munday. 2016. *A Dictionary of Media and Communication*. Oxford: Oxford University Press.

Collins, Rebecca, Victor Strasburger, Jane Brown, Edward Donnerstein, Amanda Lenhart, and Monique Ward. 2017. "Sexual Media and Childhood Well-being and Health." *Pediatrics* 162–66.

Corbin, Juliet and Anselm Strauss. 2015. *Basic Qualitative Research: Techniques and Procedures for Developing Grounded Theory* (4th ed.). Boston: Sage.

Couldry, Nick, Sonia Livingstone, and Tim Markham. 2007. *Media Consumption and Public Engagement: Beyond the Presumption of Attention*. Basingstoke: Palgrave Macmillan.

Croteau, David and William Hoynes. 2019. *Media/Society: Technology, Industries, Content, and Users*. Thousand Oaks: Sage.

Dates, Jannette L. 2005. "Movin' on Up: Black Women Decisionmakers in Entertainment Television." *Journal of Popular Film and Television* XXXII, no. 2: 68–79.

Dreher, Kwakiutl. 2013. "'Scandal' and Black Women in Television." In *African Americans on Television: Race-ing for Ratings*, edited by J. David and Lisa A. Guerrero Leonard, 390–401. Santa Barbara: Praeger.

Fish, Stanley. 1982. *Is There a Text in This Class? The Authority of Interpretive Communities*. Cambridge, MA: Harvard University Press.

Guerrero, Lisa. 2013. "Single Black Female: Representing the Modern Black Woman in 'Living Single.'" In *African Americans on Television: Race-ing for Ratings*, edited by J. David and Lisa A. Guerrero Leonard, 177–90. Santa Barbara: Praeger.

Hall, Alice. 2006. "Viewers' Perceptions of Reality Programs." *Communication Quarterly* 191–211.

Hall, Stuart. 1973. "Encoding and Decoding in the Television Discourse." *Council of Europe Colloquy on "Training in the Critical Reading of Televisual Language"*. Leicester: Council & The Centre for Mass Communication Research, 1–21.

IMDB. Accessed February 5, 2019. https://www.imdb.com/title/tt0772137/fullcredits?ref_=tt_ql_1.

Jhally, Sut and Justin Lewis. 1992. *Enlightened Racism: The Cosby Show, Audiences, and the Myth of the American Dream*. Boulder: Westview Press.

Kellner, Douglas. 2015. "Cultural Studies, Multiculturalism, and Media Culture." In *Gender, Race, and Class in Media*, 4th Edition, edited by Gail Dines and Jean Humez, 7–19. Thousand Oaks: Sage.

Lewis, Nghana. 2012. "Prioritized: The Hip Hop (Re)Construction of Black Womanhood in 'Girlfriends' and 'The Game'." In *Watching while Black: Centering the Television of Black Audiences*, edited by Beretta Smith-Shomade, 157–71. New Brunswick: Rutgers University Press.

Lindlof, Thomas and Brian Taylor. 2019. *Qualitative Communication Research Methods*, 4th Ed. Thousand Oaks: Sage.

Matsaganis, Matthew, Vikki Katz, and Sandra Ball-Rokeach. 2011. *Understanding Ethnic Media: Producers, Consumers, and Societies*. Thousand Oaks: Sage.

Means Coleman, Robin and Andre M. Cavalcante. 2012. "Two Different Worlds: Television as a Producer's Medium." In *Watching While Black: Centering the Television of Black Audiences*, edited by Beretta Smith-Shomade, 33–48. New Brunswick: Rutgers University Press.

Morley, David. 1999. "The Nationwide Audience: Structure and Decoding." In *The Nationwide Television Studies*, edited by M. David and C. Brundson, 111–288. New York: Routledge.

Newswire, P. R. 2011. *Viacomm*. January 11. Accessed January 28, 2019. https://ir.viacom.com/news-releases/news-release-details/cable-debut-game-bet-ranks-1-ad-supported-scripted-series.

Ott, Brian and Robert Mack. 2010. *Critical Media Studies: An Introduction*. Oxford: Wiley-Blackwell.

Ozemebhoya Eromosele, Diana. 2016. *The Grapevine*. January 7. Accessed January 28, 2019. https://thegrapevine.theroot.com/this-mara-brock-akil-interview-begs-the-question-why-d-1790887662.

Perks, Lisa Glebatis. 2012. "Three Satiric Television Decoding Positions." *Communication Studies* 290–308.

Radway, Janice A. 1991. *Reading the Romance: Women, Patriarchy, and Popular Literature*, 2nd ed. Chapel Hill: University of North Carolina Press.

Ramanuam, Priya. 2015. *Urbanology Magazine*. Accessed January 28, 2019. https://urbanologymag.com/mara-brock-akil-making-relatable-tv/.

Scott, Mack. 2014. "From Blackface to Beulah: Subtle Subversion in Early Black Sitcoms." *Journal of Contemporary History* 743–69.

Smith-Shomade, Beretta. 2012. "Introduction: I See Black People." In *Watching while Black: Centering the Television of Black Audiences*, edited by Beretta Smith-Shomade, 2–15. New Brunswick: Rutgers University Press.

Staff. 2012. *Reality Wives*. May 7. Accessed January 28, 2019. http://realitywives.net/blogs/game-creator-mara-brock-akil-talks-100th-episode-bet-series.

Wanzo, Rebecca. 2013. "Can the Black Woman Shout? A Meditation on 'Real' and Utopian Depictions of African American Women on Scripted Television." In *African Americans on Television: Race-ing for Ratings*, edited by J. David and Lisa A. Guerrero Leonard, 373–89. Santa Barbara: Praeger.

Warner, Kristen. 2012. "A Black Cast Doesn't Make a Black Show: 'City of Angels' and the Plausible Deniability of Color-Blindness." In *Watching while Black: Centering the Television of Black Audiences*, edited by Beretta Smith-Shomade, 49–62. New Brunswick: Rutgers University Press.

Chapter 7

Race, Gender, and Participatory Dynamics

Facebook Representations of Being Mary Jane

Mia Moody-Ramirez

Being Mary Jane, one of Mara Brock Akil's most critically acclaimed television shows, documents Mary Jane Paul's life as a talented, Emmy-nominated anchor who has it all—beauty, material wealth, and a successful career. The show emphasizes what it perceives as a missing ingredient from her life—a husband and children of her own. Episodes of the show deal with a multitude of issues, including racism, police brutality, incarceration, sex trafficking, self-medication, racial profiling, and relationships. Throughout the four seasons of the show, Mary Jane posts sticky notes containing helpful quotes on windows and mirrors in her house, and true to the independent Black woman narrative, she spends much of her time solving the problems of others while disregarding her own troubles.

Being Mary Jane enjoyed widespread success throughout its four seasons. The television drama was consistently ranked as one of Black Entertainment Television's (BET) top-rated shows—averaging 2.6 million weekly viewers, 1.7 million of them were adults. *Being Mary Jane* was particularly popular among Black women, aged from eighteen to forty-nine. Of the 1.7 million adults in the age group, 1.1 million of them were Black women—which made it the number one scripted series on cable with its core audience (O'Connell 2015). *Being Mary Jane*'s social media presence is equally outstanding. The show garnered more than 1.7 million likes on Facebook, 99.9K followers, and 9,000-plus tweets on Twitter. Social networks are a useful tool for television executives as a platform to evaluate viewers' opinions on programs (Wallace 2015).

Despite the increasing number of empirical case studies on television shows and social networks, full-season analyses of different TV formats are still rare (Rossi and Giglietto 2016). In addition, because of the differences within the wide range of available social media platforms, it is impossible to generalize study findings across platforms (Giglietto, Fabio, Artieri, Gemini, and Orefice 2016). Therefore, continued research is important. To address these gaps in the literature, this chapter investigates the participatory dynamics of online audiences on Facebook during the 2017 fourth season of BET's *Being Mary Jane*. Using a Black Feminist lens, this chapter assesses patterns of social media audience interaction on Facebook. Specifically, it offers background and context of *Being Mary Jane*, a critical reflection on the show's characters and an analysis of the comments posted to BET's popular Facebook page for the show.

This chapter presents a literature review on social media audience interaction with an emphasis on Facebook. It provides details pertaining to *Being Mary Jane*, specifically, the fourth season of the television show. The research presents results of the Facebook analysis and provides a discussion of the findings and their limitations, while also suggesting some areas of future research. An analysis of this nature is important for several reasons. First, media provide historical content that scholars may use to analyze trends in mass media portrayals of gender and race. Consequently, it is essential to continually analyze and address perceptions of race and gender to offer insight and solutions to students, educators, and media/content producers who have the power to change representations in the future. Second, while traditionally communication has been top-down giving greater influence to elites, the web opens the possibility of horizontal communication without gatekeepers. It has long been understood and accepted that traditional media functions as the primary gatekeeper in disseminating information to the public. However, with the rise of user-generated content (UGC) and social media sites such as Facebook, Instagram, and Twitter, a varied group of gatekeepers emerge as numerous as those that use the medium. The growth of Facebook groups from a fringe activity to a significant communication source illustrates this evolution. Facebook's "groups" and "page" applications let like-minded individuals express their thoughts on topics in real time. As mass media continues to transform, the need to study group interactions in new media environments increases in importance. Scholars must continue to test all mass media theories, and existing media theories are the most efficient way to account for trends.

BLACK FEMINIST THEORY

The Black Feminist Movement developed in response to the Black Liberation Movement and the Women's Movement. Most women's movement writings equated "Black" with Black men and equated "woman" with white women (Collins 2000). As a result, Black women were an invisible group. The movement helped develop theory which could adequately address the way race, gender, and class were interconnected in their lives and to act to stop racist, sexist, and classist discrimination (Walker 1983). Therefore, Black feminist research and theory makes the experiences and perspectives of Black women central. By embracing a paradigm of race, class, and gender as interlocking systems of oppression, Black feminist thought (BFT) reconceptualizes the social relations of domination and resistance. Collins defined Black feminism, in *Black Feminist Thought (BFT)* (1991), as including "women who theorize the experiences and ideas shared by ordinary black women that provide a unique angle of vision on self, community and society." Black feminists contend that the liberation of Black women entails freedom for all people, since it would require the end of racism, sexism, and class oppression.

HISTORICAL REPRESENTATIONS OF BLACK WOMEN

Gender schema theory proposes that people look at the world through the lens of gender. Cultures tend to polarize men and women by organizing social life around mutually exclusive gender roles. There is no single feminist method of study, but feminist communication researchers have incorporated and transformed different methodologies (Krolokke and Sorensen 2006). What feminist-informed methods have in common is they put gender and gender-related concerns at the center of analysis and highlight notions of power in different ways. Research of mainstream media representations of persons of color illustrates ways such groups are portrayed as residing "below" the "dominant" group in society, placing white men at the top and Black women at the bottom (Hall, Evans, and Nixon 2013; hooks 1992; Tyree 2011; Wallace 2015).The literature on representations of Black women on television is diverse with most concluding that Black women are depicted in narrow stereotypical portrayals (hooks 1992; Tyree 2011). Early analyses found media deeply implicated in the patterns of discrimination operating against women, invisibility or gender stereotypes (Collins 2004; Hall, Evans, and Nixon 2013; hooks 1992; Wallace 2015). Studies have shown that while media and societal structures marginalize Black women, scholars add that mass media in general institutionalize white and male supremacist ideologies, which produce "specific images, representations of race, of blackness that support and maintain the oppression, exploitation, and overall domination of all black people" (hooks 1992, 2).

Collins examined class-based images of Black women that range from bitches and bad (Black) mothers to modern mammies, Black ladies, and educated bitches (Collins 2004). "The controlling image of the 'bitch' constitutes one representation that depicts Black women as aggressive, loud, rude, and pushy" (123). In general, stereotypes of Black women have demonstrated the difficulties they have in forming positive relationships with men. The Black woman is either too educated and independent to need or want a man, or she is desperate and lost without a man (Moody 2013). As such, portrayals pit her against women of other races in the battle to maintain a healthy relationship with the opposite sex. Hence, she becomes frustrated and "angry." Dichotomous representations of Black women depict them either as unintelligent or extremely educated and ambitious, or listless, attractive, or ugly. In another example, the sexually promiscuous Black woman, also known as the "oversexed-black-Jezebel," is an extreme opposite of the "Mammy," who is nurturing and passive. In some instances, even positive representations have negative undertones. Likewise, the independent woman who is successful and intelligent is the extreme opposite of the "welfare cheat" who is lazy and dependent on public assistance. The "independent Black woman" archetype is overachieving and financially successful on one hand, and narcissistic and overbearing on the other. The definition of an "Independent Woman" in the *Urban Dictionary*, a predominantly African American written and defined website, states, "A woman who pays her own bills, buys her own things, and does not allow a man to affect her stability or self-confidence. She supports herself on her own entirely and is proud to be able to do so."

These representations of Black women fit a historical narrative that incorporates negative viewpoints of their perceived roles in society. Traditionally, the myth of the Black Superwoman essentially consisted of stereotypes deeply rooted in the enslavement period of Black people. The idea that although "lazy," Black women are able to do more physical labor than the average woman while consistently sacrificing themselves for others, have no emotion and are really just men. These characterizations led to an ideal of female beauty in the United States that "puts a premium on lightness and softness mythically associated with white women, and downplays the rich stylistic manners associated with black women" (West 2001).

Black Women in Television

Black women have appeared in television shows since the 1950s. The 1950 ABC sitcom, *Beulah*, started as a CBS radio show, was the first network show to feature a Black actress in a leading role. In the television show, Beulah is a maid who has a knack for fixing her employers' problems. NBC's 1968 sitcom, *Julia*, broke ground for being the first network show to feature a Black actress in a non-stereotypical role. Diahann Carroll plays a widowed nurse raising her young son. Several years later, ABC's *Get Christie Love!* stared Teresa Graves as Christie Love, a female police detective who goes undercover to try to thwart a drug ring (Dates and Barlow 1993; Nittle 2018). In another analysis, the researcher noted that NBC's *Homicide: Life on the Street* provided the venue for African American women to portray ordinary and powerful storylines beginning in 1993 (Mascaro 2005). However, while Black women were making strides in their roles on the TV show, none had reached the prominence of the men on the show. *Homicide* was a step in the right direction.

More recently, several researchers have looked at representations of Black women in modern shows such as *Being Mary Jane* and *Scandal*, concluding the shows have both positive and negative implications. In examining post-racial resistance of Black women in the media Joseph (2018) notes that while Mary Jane is flawed and less than perfect, her girlfriends are supportive and loyal: "Women of color hold a "mirror to her face," "lift her up," and "call her out." A loyal social media following watch the show week after week. Chanel (2016) analyzed episodes of *Scandal* through the use of the Black female tropes identified by various scholars and African-centered paradigms such as post-traumatic slave syndrome. The research concluded *Scandal*'s celebration of Olivia Pope, the Black mistress of the white U.S. president, concurrently objectifies Black women and keeps Blacks in a state of psychological slavery. In a similar study, the researcher discusses how Shonda Rhimes' characters such as Olivia Pope in *Scandal* manage to succeed against the odds (Cartier 2014). She highlights the politics of "crossing over" and how Rhimes' characters triumph where other characters have failed. The study encouraged scholars to "get beyond hackneyed debates about whether any of their screen images are 'helping or hurting' black popular culture," in order to "more fully discern the nuances of how black media representations continue to recycle and recirculate the disparities between black male and female subjectivities" (Cartier 2014). An analysis of *Being Mary Jane* viewers Facebook posts offers the opportunity to continue this vein of research.

FACEBOOK PRESENCE

Social network sites (SNSs) are web-based services that allow individuals to construct a public or semipublic profile within a bounded system. Facebook is the biggest key player in social networking. It has grown steadily since its inception. Because of the convergence between mass and social media, audience interaction with TV content has reached an unprecedented level both in terms of volume and visibility (Rossi and Giglietto 2016). Facebook's functionality is driven by the personal profiles of individual users, which are tied to the real-world identities. Facebook is also noteworthy as several scholars have found that users connected to social networks may be more honest in their online representations (Toma, Hancock, and Ellison 2008; Walther and Parks 2002). Engagement on a secondary device while watching television is becoming a widespread phenomenon. While in 2009, 57 percent of U.S. Internet consumers declared that they watched TV while simultaneously browsing the web at least once a month in 2013, 43 percent of U.S. tablet owners and 43 percent of U.S. smartphone owners said they used their device while watching TV every day (Nielsen 2019).

The widespread use of digital platforms such as Facebook, Twitter, and YouTube have encouraged changes in how people consume television content. Audiences constantly watch, share, and remix the content aired by TV networks (Rossi and Giglietto 2016). Social television has grown in the new media environment because of the evolution imposed by the combination of social networks, second screens, and television (Quintas-Froufe and Gonzalez-Neira 2014).

Facebook-related studies have fallen into one of three categories: activism, Facebook hate groups and uses, and gratification. Very few have focused on full season of television shows. Scholars have studied the use of social media by audiences defined by gender, race, and ethnicity. Such studies, which are labeled social TV or second screen, have increased in recent years (Giglietto et al. 2016). The focus of articles on this topic is often restricted to Twitter. For instance, in their article titled *Trending Topics: A Cultural Analysis of Being Mary Jane and Black Women's Engagement on Twitter*, Harris and Saxton Coleman (2018) concentrate on Mary Jane's struggles during the show's first and second seasons, then analyze tweets posted during these seasons. This article builds on the literature with an analysis of how Facebook is used as a second screen to communicate and comment on *Being Mary Jane*.

TEXTUAL ANALYSIS OF BEING MARY JANE FACEBOOK POSTS

This study builds on the existing research to date by closely reading comments posted to the *Being Mary Jane* Facebook page to better understand the dynamics between audience communication and the television drama. Based on the review of the literature, this chapter addresses the following questions: (1) What dominant themes of gender and race emerge in fourth season episodes of *Being Mary Jane*? (2) What critical issues do Facebook users address in *Being Mary Jane* Facebook content? (3) What are the specific moments in *Being Mary Jane* that catalyze audience engagement?

Critical analyses often look at a text within its historical and social context or by comparing various representations of a cultural group. The interpretive analysis approach outlines culture as a narrative or storytelling process in which particular "texts" or "cultural artifacts" consciously or unconsciously link to larger stories in the society. Analysis focuses on how the media support and reproduce dominant ideologies about difference and culture. Inserting texts into the system of culture within which they are produced and distributed can help elucidate features and effects of the texts that textual analysis alone might miss or downplay. Context is often measured through textual analysis, which seeks to get beneath the surface and help researchers outline culture as a narrative in which particular texts consciously or unconsciously link themselves to larger stories at play in the society.

To get a sense of the *Being Mary Jane* Facebook presence, Facebook posts shared by the BET network fan page during the fourth season were analyzed. This period was chosen because the fourth season was the last full season of the program. *Being Mary Jane* ended in 2017. Facebook posts were collected throughout the entire Season 4, allowing for a comprehensive analysis of the online communicative patterns that took place between *Being Mary Jane* executives who posted Facebook content and audience members who experienced it. The study provides insights into how TV networks and audiences approach an online means of communication using Facebook.

Season Four Overview

For the first three seasons, *Being Mary Jane* was produced by creator Mara Brock Akil, along with her husband Salim Akil. In 2015, Brock Akil announced the two were stepping down to take on a new venture with Warner Bros. They remained as *Being Mary Jane*'s executive producers. *Being Mary Jane*'s Season 4 was broken into parts with ten episodes airing from January 10, 2017, to March 21, 2017, and ten episodes airing from July 18, 2017, to September 19, 2017. The first ten episodes have "getting" in the title, while the second ten have "feeling" in the title. The season centers on Mary Jane's career move to New York City, her relationships with two different men, racism, and job woes. The original air dates and BET's synopses are provided in table 7.1.

Being Mary Jane Facebook Groups

At the time of this analysis, nine Facebook groups existed with the title "Being Mary Jane" in them. Their number of followers and themes are listed in table 7.2. The number of followers ranged from 1.7 million to 122. Themes ranged from the TV storyline to favorite quotes. Strictly fan pages also existed to demonstrate support for Mary Jane or the show in general.

The most popular Facebook page, *Being Mary Jane*, hosted by BET, has 1.7 million likes on Facebook and 99.9K followers. BET executives

Table 7.1 *Being Mary Jane* Season 4 Episodes, Original Air Dates and BET's Synopses

Episode Title	Episode Number	BET Synopsis of Episode
Getting Nekkid	Episode 1 of Season 4	Mary Jane starts fresh with a brand-new job on a hot show in New York City. But she is also determined to take care of some more . . . personal needs.
Getting Naked	Episode 2 of Season 4	Mary Jane's dream job starts to become a bit of a nightmare when she finds herself competing with her idol. Niecy tries to bring order to her life.
Getting Real	Episode 3 of Season 4	Mary Jane goes viral after airing a disastrous but wildly entertaining interview. Back at home, she and Lee decide to get just a little bit kinky.
Getting Schooled	Episode 4 of Season 4	Despite being less than thrilled with her new gig, Mary Jane pursues a hot-button story with huge potential. Kara hits it off with a baseball player.
Getting Served	Episode 5 of Season 4	PJ and Mary Jane get homesick. Back in Atlanta, local celebrity Niecy lands in trouble after creating a spectacle during an expensive night out.
Getting Home	Episode 6 of Season 4	Mary Jane heads back to Atlanta to cover a big story for work. But a night at her family's house gets awkward when a surprise guest arrives.
Getting Judged	Episode 7 of Season 4	After getting a bit closer to Lee's family than she expected, Mary Jane finds herself dealing with a leaked story about behind-the-scenes drama.
Getting Risky	Episode 8 of Season 4	Mary Jane gets anxious about Lee's ex. At work, the unlikely duo Justin and Mary Jane live dangerously and do some investigating.
Getting Serious	Episode 9 of Season 4	Mary Jane tries to wrap her head around Lee's response to Zoe's ultimatum. Justin pitches a cushy story idea to Ronda, but not all is at it seems.
Getting It	Episode 10 of Season 4	As her fortieth birthday approaches, Mary Jane gets in on Justin's dicey plan to hopefully take care of Ronda once and for all.
Feeling Raw	Episode 11 of Season 4	Distrustful of Justin after Kara's firing, Mary Jane tries to make it work with Lee, but resisting Justin is undermining her performance in the coveted co-anchor spot of the morning show.
Feeling Conflicted	Episode 12 of Season 4	Since Kara is having a tough time in arbitration with her wrongful termination claim, Mary Jane and Justin decide not to confess that they're seeing each other.
Feeling Exposed	Episode 13 of Season 4	Kara's discovery that Mary Jane is sleeping with Justin sends their friendship into a tailspin and upsets the power dynamic at the studio. Sensing there's more to Mary Jane's breakup with Lee, Helen sends Niecy to New York to "check-in" on MJ. Little does she know, Niecy has other plans to meet up with a match from a dating app.

(Continued)

Table 7.1 (Continued)

Episode Title	Episode Number	BET Synopsis of Episode
Feeling Friendless	Episode 14 of Season 4	Feeling alienated, Mary Jane allows her own party to be transformed into a media event. Meanwhile, Niecy returns to Atlanta invigorated and ready to set her dreams in motion; and Patrick becomes a mentor to a rowdy activist.
Feeling Hashtagged	Episode 15 of Season 4	Mary Jane and Justin's relationship goes viral. Meanwhile, Frank, an old family friend of Helen and Paul's, stirs long-forgotten memories of a love triangle that clouded the early years of their marriage.
Feeling Ambushed	Episode 16 of Season 4	Mary Jane and Justin's relationship is tested when their notoriety on social media leads to discoveries about his past; and Kara makes her own discovery about the girlfriend of one of Orlando's teammates.
Feeling Lost	Episode 17 of Season 4	Word of Lee's brimming success and new girlfriend throws Mary Jane's already tenuous relationship with Justin into doubt. In other events, Kara meets Orlando's young attractive mother.
Feeling Destined	Episode 18 of Season 4	After learning that Paul and Helen are getting a divorce, the Paterson family struggles to cope with the imminent changes.
Feeling Seen	Episode 19 of Season 4	Mary Jane uncovers information about Justin's past that spin their love into a new phase. Meanwhile, Kara and Justin are forced to take down a dark horse who has entered the race for the executive producer slot.
Feeling Tested	Episode 20 of Season 4	After learning she has a say in who replaces Garrett, Kara or Justin, Mary Jane questions whether Justin's overtures are motivated by his desire to get her vote. Kara helps Orlando in his transition from athlete to broadcaster.

Credit: M. Moody-Ramirez.

encourage participatory online viewership by actively using their official Facebook profile to engage audiences. The page includes video clips, photos, and posts from the fans of the show. Many of the Facebook posts highlight each week's show—often asking questions related to the show. Posts offer teasers about upcoming episodes and ask questions after they air such as these: "Should Paul have kicked his wife Helen out the house?" "Black women are they destined to be alone?" and "Was Lee wrong to write a pilot about his relationship with Mary Jane?"

Table 7.2 Being Mary Jane Themed Facebook Groups

Facebook Page Title	Number of Followers	Theme
1. Being Mary Jane	1.7M like this	TV Show As Mary Jane juggles life, work, and commitments to family, how far is she willing to go to find the missing pieces from her life as a single Black female?
2. Being Mary Jane Quotes	4K like this	TV Show Favorite Quotes from Being Mary Jane
3. Being Mary Jane Fans	2.8K like this	TV Show A fan page dedicated to the new original drama on BET, Being Mary Jane. We're here routing for you MJ Paul!
4. BEING MARY JANE Fanatics	1.2K like this	TV Show This page is for all the fans of *Being Mary Jane* who just want to vent, rant, taunt, and simply chat about the series
7. Being Mary Jane—Viewing Party	12K like this	TV Show This is a friendly place to watch BET's *Being Mary Jane* as a group, discuss, talk smack, and have fun!
8. Being a Mary Jane Fan	122 like this	Community This page is for fans of the show, *Being Mary Jane*. We are in no way affiliated with the show, its creators or BET.
9. Being Mary Jane Season 3	250 like this	TV Show *Being Mary Jane* Season 3 Full Online Stream HD Quality

Credit: M. Moody-Ramirez.

Facebook Post Themes

An analysis of the most common words in Facebook posts in the sample helped tease out the prevalent themes in the *Being Mary Jane* Facebook posts (table 7.3). In particular, the posts emphasized job dynamics, relationships,

Table 7.3 Frequency and Top Words of *Being Mary Jane* Season 4

Word	Occurrences	Frequency (%)	Rank
Justin	56	2.3	1
love	30	1.3	3
Lee	30	1.3	3
Kara	27	1.1	5
man	19	0.8	8
men	18	0.8	8

Credit: M. Moody-Ramirez.

and double standards for men and women. The relationship theme ranked highest on the list, as much of the show emphasizes Mary Jane's relationships with men, relatives, colleagues, and friends. As such, the majority of the Facebook content in our sample emphasizes some element of relationships, dating, and sexuality.

#TeamLee or #TeamJustin

The first half of Season 4 highlights Mary Jane's relationship with Lee (Chiké Okonkwo), a British comedian who treats her well and makes her laugh. This seemingly normal relationship is interrupted by Lee's ex-wife who wants to have a baby with him, and the relationship Mary Jane develops with Justin, a coworker during the second half of the season. As expected Mary Jane's peaceful relationship with Lee dissolves mid-Season 4, when she leaves Lee in favor of a less stable relationship with Justin. Justin's name was one of the most common words mentioned in *Being Mary Jane* Season 4 Facebook content with fifty-six references (table 3). While not as common, Lee's name was also mentioned at a high rate—thirty times. Facebook users debated who would be a better match for Mary Jane, ethical considerations and Mary Jane's decision-making skills.

With encouragement from the show's producers, Facebook users often used hashtags #TeamLee or #TeamJustin to indicate their support for beau over the other. Themes of trust, looks, and compatibility emerged in many of the posts. For instance, in once post, a Facebook user stated, "I don't like MJ with Justin. He can NOT be trusted!! But how is your secret romance only gonna last one episode?!?!? Bring back Lee!!! #TeamLee" (BET Being Mary Jane Facebook Account, 2017). Questioning Mary Jane's decision-making skills, another Facebook user posted, "For a character who's supposed to be intelligent & well educated, Mary Jane always seems to make knee jerk, dumbass decisions . . . smh." In another Facebook post, a user stated, "I think Lee was the perfect man for her. He catered to her particular kind of Crazy. Justin is a beautiful fantasy" (BET Being Mary Jane Facebook Account, 2017).

Being Mary Jane has garnered attention, much of it positive, for the portrayal of Mary Jane as a successful journalist. However, the show has also been criticized for the behaviors of its stars and its reinforcement of negative racial stereotypes. These include the sexually promiscuous Black woman—the "oversexed-black-Jezebel" as well as the overachieving "Black Lady"—who emasculates the Black males in her life. The fourth season begins with Mary Jane coming clean to her boyfriend Lee about her rendezvous with Justin in the newsroom. "You're obviously still that broken girl I met on the first night," Lee told her. Likewise, Justin responded negatively after learning that Mary Jane broke up with Lee in order to be with him: "Look, we had sex. Once. And we both agreed that it was a mistake. This isn't love. I have a girlfriend, and I'm not going to ruin the relationship for . . . I'm not going to blow up my world on a whim, OK? And you shouldn't want me to" (Being Mary Jane, 2017). Facebook users highlighted Mary Jane's search for happiness and her many failed relationships with men. Facebook comments during Season 4 frequently referred to Mary Jane as "ho" for her relationship choices and decisions to sleep with various men (Being Mary Jane, 2017).

A subplot that surfaced in Season 4 was the revelation that Mary Jane's mother had an affair with Frank, a man she had been in love with for years. It was also revealed that he was the father of Mary Jane's older brother. Throughout the first few seasons, her mother (Margaret Avery) battled lupus; her brother (Richard Brooks) dealt with a drug addiction; and her young niece (Raven Goodwin) had two babies by two different men. Viewers discussed the lunacy of reconnecting with a many forty years later. One person questioned the sincerity of Frank. "A man walks back into your life after 40+ years and just like that u pick up where u left off. Really??!! Why couldn't the writers just keep this beautiful black couple with 3 kids and grandchildren together and in a solid marriage? Since that's not going to happen I hope he divorces her and moves on with his life." Other viewers paralleled Mary Jane's life with her mother's. One viewer stated, "Now that we know more of Helen's back story, Mary Jane is starting to make more sense . . . ." The affair is noteworthy, as in early seasons, viewers saw the representation of a strong male and female relationship in Mary Jane's parents. And while the relationships of their children are flawed, we see love exemplified in the love they have for their grandchildren and children.

Independence/Sexuality

As mentioned in the review of the literature, representations of the independent black woman are often dichotomous: the black woman is either too educated and independent to need or want a man, or she is desperate and lost without a man. Themes of independence and sexuality were highlighted in many of the Facebook posts in our sample. Mary Jane is a single, Black, woman in her forties, and the stereotype of the independent Black women is inevitable. Viewers highlight the difficulty Black women have building meaningful relationships with men. One viewer stated, "I think our biggest downfall is this strong independent crap. Look what is doesn't need to be explained or said a million times . . . ." Another Facebook user wrote,

> The writer's goal is to write authentic stories that viewers can identify with and difficulty with relationships. Women 40 older or under can relate to Mj quest to

be happy with who makes her happy. Women can also relate to loving a man but being in Love with another. I totally hate this season they have made Mary Jane into a total sorry to say hoe. She changed from being a classy, independent diva (who was hurt but still believed in love), to a confused, vulnerable woman that finds joy in sleeping around. (BET Being Mary Jane Facebook Account, 2019)

Similarly, double standards for men and women were also discussed. Facebook users stated that it is OK for men to have multiple partners, but it is not OK for women. One Facebook user stated, "Women aren't supposed to date more than one guy at a time, even when she isn't sleeping with them, because it just doesn't look right! But men can date as many as they wish, because that's just what men are supposed to do. smh!" (BET Being Mary Jane Facebook Account, 2019).

Mary Jane & Kara

Facebook users stated the women on the show—Mary Jane and Kara—were too quick to sleep with men. Viewers encouraged her to settle down and to stop being "stupid" about relationships with men. The idea that Mary Jane was being too promiscuous was also emphasized. Viewers pondered why brilliant Black women were often depicted as being sexually loose. In one post, a Facebook user stated, "In my opinion, Mary Jane is too quick in sleeping with men when she only known them for a second. Why don't she give relationships some time to flourish then she can be able to see what she wants and doesn't want in a man. The biggest mistake she mad[e]." Earlier seasons of *Being Mary Jane* reflect a healthy relationship between Mary Jane and Kara, best friends who work at the same TV station. The two support one another and offer sound advice during difficult periods. This positive dynamic between the two took a twist during Season 4 when Mary Jane is charged with voting for Kara or Justin for a position at the TV station. In response to this storyline, Facebook posts discussed job dynamics and Mary Jane's decision to hire her boyfriend or best friend. Facebook users unanimously agreed Kara was a true friend that Mary Jane should not risk losing. Facebook users sympathized with Mary Jane who was faced with choosing her boyfriend, Justin, or best friend, Kara, for producer's position. They lamented having to make such a decision. Facebook posts include, "Kara is a True friend, the one you call when you are happy or in trouble. Im happy now bcoz she found a way to accept Mj and relationship. #truefriend (*sic*)" (BET Being Mary Jane Facebook Account, 2019).

Another Facebook user stated, "Ok this would be a very difficult decisions between Kara and Justin . . . but were missing one important factor in Justin has 30 MILLION!! While Kara is supporting children and I think Justin is a thrill seeker he loves his job for the power. Now I do see where Justin is opening up to MJ more its cute and he always says WE!! Love it" (BET Being Mary Jane Facebook Account, 2019).

Representations of Race

Being Mary Jane is not afraid to tackle tough race-related issues. Leading up to Season 4, the show confronted how Mary Jane, a primetime news anchor, is still subject to blatant racism. In one episode, Mary Jane experiences a racist rant after taking a parking spot from a white man, who proceeds to call her a "Black bitch," and then tells her she looks like an "ugly black monkey." In another episode, the head of SNC dismisses Mary Jane's issues at work by saying, "I just don't know why people get so sensitive over this stuff. They have the president, NBA, Jay Z and Beyoncé. Carnival Cruise and American Express are run by black people. What is Mary Jane upset about? . . . Just do the damn job and shut up" (Being Mary Jane, 2017).

In the final episode of Season 3, the epidemic of police brutality against Black women is addressed. In this episode, Mary Jane's twenty-one-year-old niece gets pulled over by two police officers as she was taking her new car for a drive with her two young children in tow. When the police officer asked for her driver's license and registration, Niecey asked him why she was pulled over. He eventually admitted that he'd pulled her over because her "music was too loud" to which she immediately became annoyed and argumentative and attempts to roll up her window. The officer attempted to reach into her car before opening her door and yanking her out, which caused her to resist. The officer continued the forceful arrest and the scene ended abruptly just as one of Mary Jane's newsroom reporters was shown showing her a video of her niece being manhandled by the police. Facebook users sounded off to show support for Niecy who up until this season has been depicted as an irresponsible teen mother of two children. Many advocated for her to receive a second chance to prove herself. The storyline of police brutality continued into Season 4 during which Mary Jane's brother, Patrick, organized Black Lives Matter rallies after Niecy's altercation with the police. One question that arose in connection with Patrick's civil rights efforts is this: "Does a person's sexuality or gender matter, when they are fighting for the rights of black people?" Facebook users responded that race and sexuality don't matter, but it is important to emphasize Black people. For instance, one Facebook user responded, "No it shouldn't matter all lives matter homosexuals bisexual gay lesbian shouldn't matter with black lives matter looking for the same thing." Another user responded, "No, it doesn't! I am an African American woman who loves my people first! I am proactive for my people because we haven't been fairly given privileges as our Caucasian neighbors." Taking a different stance, another Facebook user chimed in, "No but that person shouldn't merge the two. I'm taking real issue with the homosexual community merging their flag with RBG or every time they talk about issues that face black America they always steer the conversation to homosexual or trans rights. Sorry but black America is constantly being pushed to the back while others thrive" (BET Being Mary Jane Facebook Account, 2019).

Workforce Racism

Other instances in which the issue of race were addressed on *Being Mary Jane* Season 4 included workforce issues. In particular, this occurs when Mary Jane navigates a strained relationship with her coworker Dani (Victoria Staley), a new hire at *Good Day USA*, who has some strongly misguided political opinions about people of color. Dani is hired based on a controversial appearance on Mary Jane's show and her looks—she is young, blonde, and traditionally attractive based on conventional standards of beauty. In one episode, Mary Jane overhears Dani implying that Justin—a *Good Day USA* producer who is light skinned with green eyes—is smart because he might have a white parent. In response to Dani's presumption, Mary Jane explodes. The tirade ended with, "Shut the hell up, you ill-mannered, overprivileged, undereducated simpleton" (BET Being Mary Jane Facebook Account, 2019). Mary Jane is later forced to apologize in front of the entire newsroom to prevent any negative press. By hiring Dani, and overlooking her racism, the network created an unhealthy work environment.

Viewer response to this storyline was mixed. Many viewers indicated they sympathized with Mary Jane, and had experienced similar situations at work. One Facebook user responded, "Today's episode is for all black women who work in corporate America. This is exactly how white people act with subliminal messages, privilege and entitlement." Other Facebook users indicated a deep dislike for Dani for trying to sabotage Mary Jane and her deep-seated privilege based on her skin color, hair, and facial features. Viewers discussed her youth, inexperience, and wealth. One person responded, "MJ's new broadcast buddy, the young Ann Coulter that lives at home and is still on her parents health insurance, thanks to the ACA which she rails against on her YouTube Channel." Indicating diversity in the show's viewers, others supported Dani. One viewer responded, "Justified?!?!?! How was she justified?!?! She was being honest and all she said was this is what I always thought, that people with lighter skin and colored eyes are probably biracial, she probably did not have any racism or malice or hatred in her heart." Viewers also indicated they used to love the show; however, they were growing weary of the show's content. One person responded, "I've watched every season. I've been watching this season. All I hear is racist comments. The new episode has a girl wearing a make America great again hat. So who you vote for now makes you racist? I'm just done with the racial comments. This show just lost a fan" (BET Being Mary Jane Facebook Account, 2019).

CONCLUSION

Using a Black Feminist lens, this analysis of *Being Mary Jane* addresses gaps in the literature on the participatory dynamics of online audiences on Facebook during the 2017 fourth season of BET's *Being Mary Jane*. It builds on the literature of critical scholars who have analyzed representations of Black women in television shows such as *Beulah, Get Christie Love, Julia, Scandal, and How to Get Away with Murder*. Findings indicate historical stereotypes of African American women are still prevalent (while not as strong). As with other television shows featuring Black women, study findings reveal *Being Mary Jane* simultaneously embodies and critiques specific race/gender tropes, and race is frequently explored in the narrative of Black women. Mary Jane depicts an African American woman who is highly successful in her career, but struggles to find balance with her social life—particularly in having a husband and child. However, the television show also offers an indication of cultural progress with regard to Black female representation. Mary Jane is praised for her success as a Black news anchor and for frequently tackling tough issues such as racial profiling and workforce racism.

It is evident that viewers bonded with members of the cast and shared in their joys and pain—particularly Mary Jane. The Facebook pages featured in this analysis primarily focused on the show as a whole, the individual cast members, most especially Mary Jane's relationships with men. Fans expressed annoyance with Mary Jane's constant search for happiness and failed relationships with men. In particular, audience response to the show during Season 4 highlighted Mary Jane's weaknesses when it comes to men, as viewers frequently lamented her relationship with two different men. Facebook users showed support for either one man or the other, and encouraged Mary Jane to choose one and not string them both along. It is also apparent that current media representations of Black women are linked to historical and contemporary realities. Viewers perceived her failed relationships as reinforcing negative stereotypes of Black women. The stereotype of the "independent black woman" in particular depicts the Black woman as a narcissistic, overachieving, financially successful woman who emasculates Black males in her life. Facebook users expressed disappointment in this representation of Mary Jane, indicating that they wanted to see less of the "Jezebel" stereotype in the season's line up, which often featured Mary Jane sleeping around.

Findings also have implications for future television shows featuring Black actors. While viewers expressed joy in having someone to look up to on television, they displayed disappointment in some of the stereotypes that were illustrated on the show. Facebook users expressed a strong desire to see Mary Jane in a successful role in which she had a well-rounded life that includes a successful career and a sustainable relationship with a significant other. They emphasized that Mary Jane's character often illustrates that women cannot have it all. In other words, they have to give up something in order to succeed. While this show is a step in the right direction, and presents a progressive portrayal of a black women, viewers emphasized they wanted more. Facebook users honed in on this aspect of the show and frequently commented about her failed relationships with men. Future shows must continue to tackle tough issues while featuring Black women in positive roles. A happy medium must be reached if we are to continue making progress in the representations of Black women.

BIBLIOGRAPHY

"BET Being Mary Jane - Facebook Home." Accessed March 13, 2019. https://www.facebook.com/BeingMaryJane/.

Benedict, Helen. 1997. "Virgin or Vamp: How the Press Covers Sex Crimes." In L. Flanders (Ed.). *Real Majority, Media Minority*. Monroe, Maine: Common Courage Press, 115–18.

Boylorn, Robin. 2008. "As Seen on TV: An Autoethnographic Reflection on Race and Reality Television." *Critical Studies in Media Communication* 25(4): 413–33. doi:10.1080/15295030802327758.

Cartier, Nina. 2014. "Black Women On-Screen as Future Texts: A New Look at Black Pop Culture Representations." *Cinema Journal* 53(4): 150–57.

Chaney, Cassandra. 2016. "Chains of Psychological Enslavement: Olivia Pope and the Celebration of the Black Mistress in ABC's Scandal." *Africology: The Journal of Pan African Studies* 9(3): 126–53.

Collins, Patricia Hill. 2000. *Black Feminist Thought: Knowledge, Consciousness, and the Politics of Empowerment*, revised 10th anniversary edition. New York: Routledge.

_____. 2004. *Black Sexual Politics: African Americans, Gender and the New Racism*. New York: Routledge.

_____. 2009. *Black Feminist Thought: Knowledge, Consciousness, and the Politics of Empowerment* (3rd ed.). New York: Routledge.

Dates, Jannette, and William Barlow. 1993. *Split Image: African-Americans in the Mass Media* (2nd ed.). Washington, DC: Howard University Press.

Entman, Robert M. 1991. "Symposium Framing U.S. Coverage of International News: Contrasts in Narratives of the KAL and Iran Air Incidents." *Journal of Communication* 41 (4): 6–27.

Erigha, Maryann. January 2, 2015. "Shonda Rhimes, Scandal, and the Politics of Crossing Over." *The Black Scholar* 45 (1): 10–15.

Giglietto, Fabio, Giovanni Boccia Artieri, Laura Gemini, and Mario Orefice. January 2016. "Understanding Engagement and Willingness to Speak Up in Social Television: A Full-Season, Cross-Genre Analysis of TV Audience Participation on Twitter." *International Journal of Communication* 10: 2460–80.

Hall, Stuart, Jessica Evans, and Sean Nixon, eds. 2013. *Representation: Cultural Representations and Signifying Practices* (2nd ed.). Los Angeles: Milton Keynes; United Kingdom: Sage Publications Ltd.

Harris, Felicia L., and Loren Saxton Coleman. January 2, 2018. "Trending Topics: A Cultural Analysis of Being Mary Jane and Black Women's Engagement on Twitter." *The Black Scholar* 48 (1): 43–55.

hooks, bell. 1992. *Black Looks: Race and Representation*. Boston, MA: South End Press.

Jacobson, Susan. July 1, 2013. "Does Audience Participation on Facebook Influence the News Agenda? A Case Study of the Rachel Maddow Show." *Journal of Broadcasting & Electronic Media* 57(3): 338–55.

Joseph, Ralina L. 2018. *Postracial Resistance: Black Women, Media, and the Uses of Strategic Ambiguity*. New York: NYU Press.

KrolØkke, Charlotte, and Anne Scott SØrensen. 2006. *Gender Communication Theories & Analyses: From Silence to Performance*. Thousand Oaks, California: Sage.

Marilyn, Yarbrough with Crystal Bennett. 2000. "Mammy Sapphire Jezebel and their Sisters." *The Journal of Gender, Race & Justice*: 626–57.

Mascaro, Thomas A. July 1, 2005. "Shades of Black on Homicide: Life on the Street." *Journal of Popular Film and Television* 33 (2): 56–67. https://doi.org/10.1080/01956051.2005.10662063.

Moody-Ramirez, Mia. 2011. "A Rhetorical Analysis of the Meaning of the 'Independent Woman' in the Lyrics and Videos of Male and Female Rappers." *American Communication Journal* 1 (13): 16.

Moody-Ramirez, Mia, and Jannette Dates. 2013. *The Obamas and Mass Media: Race, Gender, Religion, and Politics*. New York: Palgrave Pivot.

Nielsen Report. 2009. *Three Screen Report Media Consumption and Multi-Tasking Continue to Increase Across TV, Internet, and Mobile*. http://www.nielsen.com/us/en/insights/news/2009/three-screen-report-media-consumption-and-multi-tasking-continue-to-increase.

Nielsen Report. 2013. *The Cross-Platform Report: A Look Across Screens*. https://www.nielsen.com/us/en/insights/reports/2013/the-cross-platform-report--a-look-across-screens.html.

Nittle, Nadra K. 2018. "Network Television Shows Starring Black Women You Should Check Out." *ThoughtCo*. Retrieved from https://www.thoughtco.com/network-television-shows-starring-black-women-2834722.

O'Connell, Michael. April 17, 2015. "TV Ratings: 'Being Mary Jane' Wraps Sophomore Run, Still No. 1 on BET." *The Hollywood Reporter*. https://www.hollywoodreporter.com/live-feed/tv-ratings-being-mary-jane-789558.

Quintas-Froufe, Natalia, and Ana González-Neira. July 2014. "Active Audiences: Social Audience Participation in Television." *Audiencias Activas: Participación de La Audiencia Social En La Televisión* 22 (43): 83–90.

Rossi, Luca, and Fabio Giglietto. June 2016. "Twitter Use During TV: A Full-Season Analysis of #serviziopubblico Hashtag." *Journal of Broadcasting & Electronic Media* 60 (2): 331–46.

Toma, Catalina L., Jeffrey T. Hancock, and Nicole B. Ellison. August 2008. "Separating Fact from Fiction: An Examination of Deceptive Self-Presentation in Online Dating Profiles." *Personality and Social Psychology Bulletin* 34 (8): 1023–36.

Tyree, Tia. October 1, 2011. "African American Stereotypes in Reality Television." *Howard Journal of Communications* 22 (4): 394–13.

Walker, Alice. 1983. *In Search of Our Mothers' Gardens: Womanist Prose*. San Diego: Harcourt Brace Jovanovich.

Wallace, Michele. 2015. *Black Macho and the Myth of the Superwoman* (3rd ed.). New York: Verso.

Walther, Joseph B., and M. R. Parks. 2002. *Cues Filtered Out, Cues Filtered In: Computer-Mediated Communication and Relationships*. Thousand Oaks, CA: Sage.

West, Cornell. 2001. *Race Matters*. Boston: Beacon Press.

Chapter 8

Social TV and Stereotypes

The Social Construction of #BeingMaryJane on Twitter

Morgan W. Smalls

The stereotypical portrayals of Black women in media have the ability to create real-life consequences as their safety is compromised, bodies objectified, and narratives pushed to the margin (hooks 1992; Collins 2000). In turn, misrepresentations, a lack of representation, and a scarcity of positive representations of Black women on television create unhealthy implications for Black young girls and women (Bogle 2001; Cheers 2018; Dates and Barlow 1993; Tyree 2011). These media portrayals are not only regulated to the television screen but also watched via the internet on various hand-held or alternative devices, such as cell phones, and laptops from which programming is viewed. In addition, "these new forms of viewing are heavily linked with social media, which extends the viewing experience, enabling a viewer to engage in conversation with other forms of interaction with his or her social networks" (Wohn and Na 2011, 2). With the evolution of television viewing and increased social media usage, these images also infiltrate social media spaces as conversations surrounding the shows entering the digital world.

Being Mary Jane is an American drama series that focuses on the main character, Mary Jane Paul, played by actress Gabrielle Union. Union's character is a thirty-eight-year-old fashionable, attractive, and successful news anchor in Atlanta, Georgia. Mary Jane, born into an African American family as Pauletta Patterson, is the middle child and only girl of her parents, who have been married for decades. Despite her physical attractiveness, nice car, beautiful home, and professional accolades at Satellite News Channel (SNC), she has yet to achieve her ultimate goal: to get married, have a family, and be just as successful in her personal life as she is in her professional life. The show centers on Mary Jane's quest to have it all (The Futon Critic 2013).

Being Mary Jane continued a recent trend in television where the lead role, such as *Scandal* (ABC), *How to Get Away with Murder* (ABC), *Empire* (FOX), and *Blackish* (ABC), is played by an African American woman, and the series is either created, directed, or produced by an African American. All of these shows have been nominated and received numerous awards since their creation (Nielson 2015). Created by Mara Brock Akil, *Being Mary Jane* aired on Black Entertainment Television (BET) and was executive produced by Brock Akil and her husband, Salim Akil (Andreeva 2016). Brock Akil as creator and executive producer is significant as the research suggests that "the African American story must be told to viewers from the African American perspective rather than always through a filter of (admittedly, very often, quite sympathetic) whites who, nevertheless, usually have a different perspective and objective" (Dates and Barlow 1993, 316). The mission statement of BET states, "BET Networks is the pre-eminent entertainment brand serving African Americans and consumers of Black culture globally" (BET Networks n.d.). Show programming bolsters this mission and *Being Mary Jane* is no exception as Stephen Hill, former president of Programming at BET, stated that the show "is full of characters and stories about which BET viewers are passionate" (Andreeva 2016, par 4). Moreover, as the show's creator, executive producers and main cast are all women or men of color, it is believed that *Being Mary Jane* would present insight into Black womanhood and Black experiences.

One of the important features of *Being Mary Jane* is that the show successfully integrated television and social media. For example, during the 90-minute pilot, *Being Mary Jane* was "the highest-rated show on cable and the second-highest-rated program on all of TV" for the age group of eighteen to forty-nine, while the official hashtag, #beingmaryjane trended No. 1 in the United States and worldwide during the premiere telecast (Moraes 2014). Social television is a way in which audiences can engage in digital spaces in a one-directional or interactive manner with each other while viewing *Being Mary Jane*. Social television, watching television alongside audience interaction through an additional device, such as a tablet or computer has increased in popularity (Doughty, Rowland, and Lawson 2012). One way to understand viewer insight into the character Mary Jane Paul is to analyze how viewers engage online while watching television. Specifically, social television enables the viewers of *Being Mary Jane* to define, discuss, and share ideas of Black womanhood, as it relates to the main character Mary Jane Paul. Walsh (2014) opined, "Live-tweeting television (and recapping and commenting after an episode) is a way for fans to participate in the show itself: to insert themselves into the game of television via technology" (11).

One way viewers engage in social television is through the use of Twitter as viewers use it to discuss their immediate responses to television shows. In fact, viewers are encouraged to use the hashtag #BeingMaryJane while watching the show. As a microblogging platform designed "to give everyone the power to create and share ideas and information instantly, without barriers" (Fox 2014), Twitter has become an instant "'watercooler' in the cloud" where viewers can participate in social television (Walsh 2014). Harrington, Highfield, and Bruns (2013) note that "Twitter is a very rich stream of data to produce both qualitative and quantitative research that is useful for scholars, marketers, and researchers alike. Consequently, it is no surprise that Twitter's popularity and influence on world events have made it a hot topic for social media research" (Kenett, Morstatter, Stanley, and Liu 2014, 1) and can be useful in understanding how viewers make sense of the show and the main character, Mary Jane Paul.

The inherent and live audience built within the Twitter platform, combined with "the enforced brevity of microblog postings" (Goh and Lee 2011, 433) and "rapid communication and information diffusion" (Kenett et al. 2014, 2), makes Twitter have a unique and universal appeal. The use of Twitter is prevalent in the African American communities. According to the Pew Research Report, in the United States, "23% of all [adult] internet users use Twitter; [this equates to] 20% of the entire adult population" (Duggan 2015, 14). Of those who use Twitter, over one-fourth of the users are Black; this equates to 28 percent of Twitter users (Duggan 2015). A consumer report noted, "Twitter was the third-most used app among African American households earning $100,000 or more, spending nearly two hours and about 13 sessions on the mobile Twitter app per month" (Nielson 2015, par. 9). Furthermore, the "#BlackTwitter phenomenon has become a platform full of cultural humor, entertainment, breaking news and trends" and television shows are regularly trending topics on Twitter (Nielson 2015, par. 6). This is important because as *Being Mary Jane* is catered to the African American community, it is plausible that Twitter could be a chosen platform to use for this powerful community (Nielson 2015).

Through social television use, viewers of the show also engage in concurrent social media postings about Mary Jane Paul, which has the opportunity to create perceptions of Black women that extend beyond each episode of the show. Since its pilot on July 2, 2013, it has aired for four seasons (fifty-two episodes) and has become a topic of conversation in the Twittersphere. This conversation has the potential to influence the lived experiences of Black women by altering the ways in which they are perceived or treated in digital and physical spaces. In addition, what distinguishes *Being Mary Jane* from other current popular shows featuring Black women is that, although it airs during prime time, it is not shown on a major broadcast network. Furthermore, there are little to no studies on *Being Mary Jane*, and none that specifically focus on the way that Mary Jane Paul is socially constructed online, which further justifies its investigation.

PURPOSE OF THE RESEARCH

The purpose of this study was to analyze how perceptions of Black womanhood were portrayed in *Being Mary Jane* and discussed online by identifying themes within the discourse surrounding the show on Twitter. As such, it is important to interrogate the discourse on social media surrounding television shows that focus on Black women in that it can lend insights on how Black women are objectified, marginalized, and presented in narratives that create a negative and myopic perception of Black women. Black women's experiences have been studied multiple times in the field of Communication Studies, Africana Studies, and Gender Studies. Researchers note that Black women have a unique experience that is distinguished from other women in America (Collins 2000; hooks 1992). Black women are faced with challenges and discrimination associated with being a woman and being of color. For that reason, how Black women are portrayed on television screens and constructed in digital spaces can influence how they are perceived and treated in physical settings. This, in turn, impacts the lived experiences of Black women and can also influence the identity formation and construction of self as well as social interactions Black women have with others.

This research question creates a foundation for the discovery of how users are socially constructing Mary Jane Paul and expressing themselves in reaction to the show. Furthermore, it helps uncover how and if Mary Jane is constructed in similar or contradictory ways than on television. This study seeks to analyze how the main character in *Being Mary Jane* is portrayed by answering the following question: How is Mary Jane Paul socially constructed on Twitter?

THEORETICAL FRAMEWORK

This study utilizes the social construction of reality theory (Berger and Luckmann 1966) and uses and gratifications theory (Miller 2005). These two theories work together to understand how viewers construct the main character of the show, while also providing insight into the reasons viewers utilize Twitter while watching the show. Social construction of reality theory operates under the assumption that knowledge is a cultural product shaped by social context and history. In turn, each person's perception of reality is created not only through their interactions with others but also by the "media-generated images" they encounter (Williams and Tyree 2015, 50). On Twitter, users socially construct their perception of *Being Mary Jane* and the character of Mary Jane Paul. Uses and gratifications theory aids in understanding why and how audiences selectively engage and react to media (Miller 2005). Specifically, it is useful in understanding the reasons viewers use Twitter to discuss the show. Uses and gratifications theory operates under the assumption that those who participate in social television while viewing the show receive benefits or gratification from their use. Hence these theoretical frameworks are ideal in interrogating viewer's responses to the main character via Twitter.

Social construction of reality theory is suitable to use, because this theory is relevant in understanding how social media users interpret, construct, and respond to the television character Mary Jane Paul. Recently, social construction of reality theory has been utilized by Weiland and Dunbar (2016) in studying the perceptions of reality television by analyzing tweets about the show. They conducted a case study and collected tweets to better understand viewers' perceptions of reality television and uncovered five themes: excitement for the show, relationships, conflict, emotional connection, and favorite characters (Weiland and Dunbar 2016). Similarly, yet more specifically, this study seeks to understand how Twitter users perceive the character Mary Jane and the way in which the construction diverges or converges from stereotypical portrayals of African American women. This operates on the stance that Black media stereotypes are commonly socially constructed images that are selective, partial, one-dimensional, and distorted in their portrayal of African Americans (Dates and Barlow 1993). The understanding of the world is inclusive of the way viewers ingest, dissect, and engage with the images seen on television, and the way those images are discussed on social media.

Reality is socially constructed, historically situated, and contextually framed (Williams and Tyree 2015). Therefore, a person's knowledge and awareness of self and others is the amalgamation of all those factors. As reality is socially constructed, Black women have their own set of experiences navigating their reality, and within it, oppression and resistance to interlocking systems of racism, sexism, and classism. As Collins (1989) noted, "A subordinate group not only experiences a different reality than a group that rules, but a subordinate group may interpret that reality differently" (748). This would be valuable at looking at the way the character of Mary Jane is socially constructed, as well as the themes that emerge, because it places emphasis on race, class, and gender, which could influence how she is constructed and the themes that emerge from the discourse on Twitter.

Uses and gratifications theory is based on the assumption that consumers of media are active audiences who have their own motivations for selecting, investing, participating, and using media. Different audience members may watch the same show, listen to the same radio station, or gather and disseminate information on the same social media platform, all for disparate reasons (Miller 2005). Uses and gratifications theory takes into consideration the agency and multiplicity of the audience. Miller (2005) argues that even within one medium (i.e., television) and for one person a variety of gratifications—information, personal identity, integration and social interaction, entertainment—are being served. However, media does not always and consistently satisfy the needs of its audiences.

The four gratification categories are information, personal identity, integration and social interaction, and entertainment (Miller 2005). They are useful in understanding how *Being Mary Jane* viewers that participate in social television via Twitter are seeking and potentially fulfilling a need by their engagement. Miller explains information that includes "satisfying curiosity and general interest" and "finding out about relevant events and conditions in immediate surroundings, society, and the world." Personal identity includes "finding reinforcement for personal values, finding models of behavior, identifying with valued others (in the media) and gaining insight into one's self." Integration and social interaction includes "gaining insight into circumstances of others: social empathy; identifying with others and gaining a sense of belonging; enabling one to connect with family, friends and society," and entertainment includes "escaping, or being diverted from, problems; emotional release; relaxing" (Miller 2005, 258). All these aspects are useful, because they help the researcher understand the ways in which viewers use social television to express their ability to socially construct Mary Jane in ways that they are able to relate to, identify with, praise, or belittle.

The connection between uses and gratifications and social television has been researched by multiple scholars (Whiting and Williams 2013; Wohn and Na 2011). Wohn and Na (2011) used the theory to explore what types of messages people share with others while they are watching television and how those messages correspond to the context of the program they are watching. They found that Twitter bridges the gap between television viewing and social network sites and "while not designed as a television discussion forum service *per se*, Twitter is an ideal venue to view how people express their uses and gratifications of their television viewing behavior" (Wohn and Na, 3). In addition, Whiting and Williams' (2013) exploratory study showed how uses and gratifications theory is highly relevant to understanding social media usage among society. Their study found ten uses and gratifications for using social media: "social interaction, information seeking, pass time, entertainment, relaxation, communicatory utility, convenience utility, expression of opinion, information sharing, and surveillance/knowledge about others" (Whiting and Williams 2013, 362). This is relevant as it indicates how social media, specifically Twitter, is a platform on which television viewers can tweet to communicate about, express their opinion, and interact with others while engaging in social television.

Female Stereotypes in the Media

In order to understand the characterization of Mary Jane Paul, it is necessary to historically situate the depictions of African Americans. Stereotypes in mass media have been documented by scholars from multiple disciplines, such as mass communications, social psychology, and popular culture (Seiter 1986). Historically, stereotypes of African Americans were used in film and television to entertain by stressing Negro inferiority (Bogle 2001). Bogle (2001) noted the earliest character types of the coon, tragic mulatto, mammy, and violent black buck were all "merely filmic reproductions of black stereotypes that had existed since the days of slavery and were already popularized in American life and arts" (4). These stereotypes have continued into present day, as bell hooks noted the insidious nature of African American representation when she observed that magazines, books, television, films as well as photographs contain "images of black people that reinforce and reinscribe white supremacy" (hooks 1992, 1). Indeed, the present day characterizations of Black people can be "frightening when we consider many of these images created over a century ago still haunt us" (Jackson 2006, 26).

The portrayal of African American women continues this depiction of projecting not only racial inferiority but also gender inferiority. Collins (2011) highlights the underrepresentation and negative portrayals of women, across a range of media and settings. Wood (1994) believes this lack of representation creates a false standard that favors men and renders women "unimportant or invisible" and found that the portrayal of men and women in newscasts, primetime television and children's programming "reflect and sustain socially endorsed views of gender" (31). The projection of limited definitions of masculinity or femininity within the media perpetuates unrealistic, stereotypical, and limiting perceptions (Wood 1994, 31). Combined with limited presence in media, when people of color are shown, it is often in a stereotypical manner or in supporting roles (Wood 1994; Collins 2011). In discussing the presence of minorities in media, Wood (1994) notes that "minorities are even less visible than women, with African Americans appearing only rarely and other ethnic minorities being virtually nonexistent" (32). This study investigates perceptions of the African American woman, who embodies two marginalized groups in one body, and necessitates the understanding how being both of color and woman is represented in media.

The dominance and longevity of long-standing Black female caricatures in American popular culture such as the Mammy, Sapphire, and Jezebel figures as well as the perceptions that are associated with them have been documented (Thompson 2009; West 1995). Thompson (2009) describes how "[t]he happy, maternal Mammy, who cares for white families, and the hot-tempered Sapphire, who berates black children and emasculates man, generate misperception of black women as unattractive and asexual" (3). In contrast, she explains the "Jezebel, the compulsively sexual temptress, fuels beliefs about black immorality and justifies sexual abuses" (Thompson 2009, 3). Tyree and Jones (2015) suggest there is a continuum in the positive and negative implications that come with those portrayals.

Chaney and Robertson (2016) argue these stereotypes have not disappeared; instead, they have been dynamic and reconfiguring to fit modern time. In addition to the long-standing images, there are contemporary versions of the gendered stereotypes that are attributed to African American women, which include, but are not limited to: "diva, gold digger, freak, dyke, gangster B., sister savior, earth mother, and baby mama" (Tyree and Jones 2015, 59). In fact, "scholars have identified several tropes that have been attached to Black women in the media, namely: (1) The Mammy; (2) The Matriarch; (3) The Welfare Mother; (4) The Lady; (5) The Jezebel (aka 'Hoochie'); (6) The Diva; (7) The Golddigger; and (8) The Freak" (Chaney and Robertson 2016, 8). This work does not seek to provide an in-depth analysis of each stereotype but to historically situate the depictions of African American women in television.

Race Representation via Television

Research has examined African American women's limited depictions on television. Tyree (2011) investigated if and how the characters on ten reality television shows fulfilled particular African American stereotypes. Her findings indicated each show contained at least one participant who fit into stereotypical characters, including the angry Black woman, hoochie, and hood rat (394). Evans (2014) analyzed *Scandal*'s Olivia Pope character and argued "Pope's education, confidence, and boldness help to confront the lack of complex African American female characters, while her affair with the president simultaneously reinforced negative stereotypes regarding African American women's sexuality" (2). Chaney and Robertson (2016) found Pope's character to be an amalgamation of Hill-Collins' (1997) Matriarch, Jezebel, and Lady tropes despite being professionally and financially successful.

The increased creation of television shows with minority women could create a perception that stereotypes of African American women are being challenged; however, studies have shown stereotypes of Black women persist in television shows such as *Scandal* (King 2015), *Ugly Betty* (Kretsedemas 2010), and reality television (Tyree 2011). Although studies have focused on representations of Black women in television (King 2015; Kretsedemas 2010; Tyree 2011) and popular culture (Muhammad and Arthur 2015) using qualitative methods, none have also focused on how that representation in television is transferred online in the public space of Twitter.

Black Women's Representation in Social Television

A 2016 report by Edward Jones noted that the past few decades have seen an evolution of the multimedia entertainment market from a limited number of national and local broadcast channels, to more pay-TV channels via cable and satellite delivery, and multiple options for watching video content on any device via the internet (Heger, Olson, and Deidrich 2016). This combined with an increase in social media platforms, such as Facebook, YouTube, Instagram, SnapChat, and Twitter, have led to an integrated viewing experience. When television and Twitter are examined, studies have looked at the way networks are formed while watching shows (Doughty, Rowland, and Lawson 2012) the potential benefits to advertisers (Walsh 2014), motivations for tweeting (Schirra, Sun and Bentley 2014) and types of content (Wohn and Na 2011), and the communication activities users engage in while on Twitter (Buschow, Schneider and Ueberheide 2014). Studies have not examined the manner in which the characters in the television show are portrayed and discussed online.

Social media has also been used to better understand the representation of women on television. Social media platforms create a pseudocommunal experience of watching a television show and using social networking sites (Wohn and Na 2011). For example, Everett (2015) explored *Scandal* fans' collective intelligence, obsessive tweeting while viewing, and how participatory and interactive experiences and engagements have become an unparalleled game changer in the transformed firmament of network television production and consumption (34). González (2014) investigated *Scandal*'s use of Twitter in its success and popularity by not only the viewers but also the cast as a marketing tool. These studies make it clear that Twitter is a television-viewing tool that allows for shared meaning-making and learning.

METHODOLOGY

This study employed a textual analysis to analyze the tweets posted during the first episode of *Being Mary Jane*. A textual analysis is a method often used to investigate the overt and implied meanings within text. Fursich (2009) defines a textual analysis as "a type of qualitative analysis that, beyond the manifest content of media, focuses on the underlying ideological and cultural assumptions of the text" (240). Marshall and Rossman (2016) indicated that textual analysis is one of the methods typically useful for research that focuses on language and communication. Moreover, this method is helpful to media research because of its ability to interrogate audience's interpretations of media content (Fursich 2009). In relation to social media, textual analysis has been a tool used to examine tweets. Because Twitter is a microblog that is text-based, it is ideal to use textual analysis methods to investigate (Marwick 2013).

Sample

This study used a systematic purposive sampling process to collect data. Purposive sampling is a technique used to produce a sample that can be logically assumed to be representative of the population (Lavrakas 2008). In this process, the researcher uses subjective methods to decide which elements should be included in the sample (Lavrakas 2008). To collect data, the researcher used Twitter to collect the "top" tweets that surfaced on the premiere date of January 7, 2014, from 8pm to 12:30am EST. The premiere episode was titled "Storm Advisory," and was released months after the pilot, which aired on July 2, 2013. Twitter has an advanced search system that allows the user to tailor his or her search results. The search for tweets used the hashtag #BeingMaryJane during the designated timeframe; from that list, the search was narrowed down to the top tweets. Twitter's "top" tweets are selected through an algorithm to produce the most relevant tweets based on popularity, keywords, and other factors.

Collected top tweets and quoted tweets with the hashtag #BeingMaryJane resulted in over 200 pages of tweets with an average of fifteen tweets per page. To ensure that all tweets during the four-hour timeframe were considered, the tweets were divided per hour and selected by using the first 160 tweets that fit sample criteria. Only tweets that constructed or described the viewers' reaction to the character of Mary Jane Paul in the first episode were a part of the sample. These tweets covered first and repeat watchers, DVR viewers, and were cross-sectional among the time zones.

Analytical Procedure

Once the sample was identified, data collected and textual analysis completed, a thematic analysis was conducted. The thematic analysis sought to understand how Mary Jane was socially constructed within the show and how that diverged, converged, or reimagined historical stereotypes of Black women on television. Furthermore, it also sought to understand viewers' reactions to the current ways in which *Being Mary Jane* continues a larger conversation about the increase of Black women characters on television.

The researcher first watched the show to contextualize the tweets. The researcher then went through various rounds of analysis to understand which themes emerged from the data. Guided by Clarke and Braun's (2013) six phases of a thematic analysis, the researcher became familiar with the data, analyzed/coded the data, searched for themes, reviewed them, defined/named themes, and wrote findings. In similar fashion, Weiland and Dunbar (2016) employed a thematic analysis reviewing tweets from viewers participating in social television while watching reality television shows to gather viewers' perception of reality television. In the analysis, only replies that discussed the show and specifically characterized Mary Jane were counted. Various rounds of analysis were conducted to understand which themes emerged from the data. First, data was collected, and tweets organized, which included the sifting and removing tweets that did not fit the requirements. After the data was in a manageable size, the data was read multiple times to generate possible categories and themes. Throughout the analysis, the data incorporated tools for reflexivity, such as journaling to capture thoughts and reflections associated with the analysis process. Pseudonyms, at times, will be used for the Twitter handles of those users quoted within the chapter.

FINDINGS AND DISCUSSION

Three themes emerged that helped understand how Mary Jane was socially constructed in ways that aligned with stereotypical representations of Black women: the Jezebel, relatability, and infidelity. The themes centered on an overarching conversation concerning the ways in which *Being Mary Jane* portrayed Mary Jane as a Jezebel but extended to a larger conversation on whether current television shows, such as *Being Mary Jane*, continue to perpetuate a detrimental narrative that portrays Black women in a negative light.

The analysis showed that Mary Jane was constructed as a modern-day Jezebel, also termed a "thot, ho, side chick," and other derogatory terms that insinuate Mary Jane prioritizes her sexual satisfaction over aligning with societal norms and honoring marital vows. Thot is an acronym for "That Ho Over There" (Tyree and Kirby 2017). The second theme centered on the ways Twitter users related to Mary Jane's personality or her actions. Mary Jane was a relatable persona for many viewers based on the authenticity and realness of the character. The third theme highlighted the way television shows starring Black female leads were negatively portraying Black women and the larger implication of having programs in which the main storylines include infidelity and adultery. Viewers expressed disappointment in her knowingly having sex with a married man. Furthermore, Twitter users discussed the larger societal implications of having television programs that glamorize infidelity and adultery, regardless of race.

Mary Jane Paul was socially constructed by viewers on Twitter in ways that align with stereotypes of Black women. Although *Being Mary Jane* had a Black female lead, minority cast, and was created and produced by Mara

Brock Akil, Twitter users constructed Mary Jane as a modern-day Jezebel and likened her to modern terms of that stereotype, including freak, sexual siren, or "ho." For example, one user tweeted "Sooo she's a homewrecker #BeingMaryJane" (Chenelle 2014). After watching the episode another person summarized the show as such: "Like I said an hr ago #BeingMaryJane is about a successful side chick trying to find love in another woman's man" (BLAZEL 2014). This characterization is prompted when Mary Jane knowingly has sexual relations with a married man, Andre, which is defined by a different Twitter user as ". . . a thot move . . ." (Ambz 2014). In alignment with that interpretation, another viewer concurred by also identifying her actions as the "thot move she [Mary Jane] pulled" (interlude 2014). In line with the denigrating description, another user observed the actress "Gabrielle Union on TV lookin' like a sideline bop" (ChillWave 2014). These tweets showcased in contemporary language, the way in which Twitter users viewed Mary Jane Paul as a Jezebel. Yet, the tweets also demonstrated a very limited view of Mary Jane that focused primarily on her act of indiscretion, while completely ignoring the culpability of Andre (the married man), the context of the events leading up to her having sex with him or the humanity of her character. In the actual episode, Mary Jane saw Andre enter the gym, and upon recognizing him she immediately stopped exercising and went to the locker room to take a shower, change, and leave. He followed her into the ladies' locker room, where men are not allowed. In her towel and shower cap, she sees him approaching and sarcastically states, "Oh this day just keeps getting better. Are you out of your mind?" They have a brief conversation, in which she tearfully lamented how she was embarrassed and ashamed, because he did not tell her that he was married, and their relationship was based off untruths. She stated, "You made me break one of my rules, Andre. I don't have many but sleeping with a married man is definitely on the list." She then goes on to reflect, "Oh my God! If my friends knew, if my family knew. This isn't me." Andre apologized, says he did not plan it, and it is clear that she is not emotionally stable and at that point, heartbroken. She tearfully asked him "why?" and he apologized again, wiped her tears, and kissed her. After his apology, Mary Jane proceeds to engage in consensual, passionate sex with Andre in the gym shower.

Tweets, such as the following, provide some context to the situation, yet still label the character's action: "Comfort sex. Never prosperous. Comfort sex with a cheating man who isn't even your man . . . treacherous. #BeingMaryJane" (Danica 2014). Mary Jane's decision to have sex with Andre was not as simplistic as the "thot move" some tweets suggested. Her actions may be reminiscent of a Jezebel, but her motivation is different. In addition, often Jezebels act from a place of power. Cheers (2018) asserts the Jezebel stereotype depicts African American women not only as lascivious and lewd but also as predatorily promiscuous. Mary Jane appears broken and disenchanted. This is noted when Faye tweeted "Nooo Mary Jane you have to be stronger than that [emoji] not the married guy with the family . . . #BeingMaryJane" (2014). For example, in response to the shower scene where Mary Jane engaged in sex with Andre one Twitter user observed her brokenness and tweeted, "He took advantage of her vulnerability #beingmaryjane" (Ash 2014).

In recognizing the complication of the situation, some removed the blame from Mary Jane, while still labeling her a Jezebel in examples such as this: "Its not her fault she didnt mean to be a home #wrecker #BeingMaryJane" (The Real J-Spitta 2014). However, this perspective was not tweeted as often in the construction of her character, which mostly aligned with the Jezebel narrative. Mary Jane's morality, judge of character, intellect, and standards were all diminished based on her indiscretion with Andre in comments such as, "MJ sure does not act like a relatively famous news anchor. Ooh the messiness of life. #BeingMaryJane" (Tyne 2014). The tweets also demonstrate how patriarchy works to remove the blame from Andre. The onus is placed on Mary Jane to have high standards and consistently act in alignment with those standards. Viewers chastised Mary Jane for having sex with Andre, as she was constructed as a person that was not supposed to "fall for it" or engage in "comfort sex." One tweet noted, "She wasn't suppose to fall for that in the gym" (Lysss 2014). In fact while viewing the shower scene, viewers requested that Mary Jane not engage with Andre and "please don't be a homewrecker" (Slimmmm 2014). Andre was rarely indicted as the one married, and Mary Jane was the one held to a higher standard. This is reminiscent of Wood's (1994) research that showcases the double standard in the portrayals of men and women. In one tweet, a user entered the conversation and reminded the Twitterverse, "I see a lot of ya'll mad at Mary but don't forget about that trifling ass MARRIED man. #BeingMaryJane" (Mosley 2014). In the tweets, it was observed that although Mary Jane was shown as successful, smart, talented, and beautiful, that was not enough to keep her from being called a "whore," "ho," "side chick," or "homewrecker." Rarely did users mention the culpability of or disappointment in anyone besides Mary Jane.

A deeper analysis of the tweets exemplifies bell hooks' assertion that more representation of Blacks or other marginalized groups in film does not equate to diversity of roles or a change in the archaic representation of them; inclusion in television or film does not mean positive representation (Squires 2013). In addition, assuming a show on a television network that caters to Black audiences has a responsibility to assure the images that are portrayed differ from mainstream television shows is fallacious. In sum, this aligned with what Wood (1994) explained when she stated, "While more African Americans are appearing in primetime television, they are too often cast in stereotypical roles" (32).

The Risk of Relatability to Mary Jane Paul

Despite the portrayal of Mary Jane as a Jezebel, Twitter users also constructed the character as very relatable, despite her flaws. In discussing relatability, one person notes, "Believe it or not guys, Gabs character on #BeingMaryJane is one that most black women can relate to. Sorry she's not Claire Huxtable" (Pablo 2014). This showcases the understanding that *Being Mary Jane* is not in alignment with a more acceptable television representation of Black women; however, her lack of alignment does not negate her relatability to the Twitter users. Often viewers of the show expressed the personal connection they had with Mary Jane's character in tweets. For example, one user wrote, "#BeingMaryJane is a Mirror of my life! . . . lots of females can relate to #MaryJane" (Fukwat_uthink 2014). Others enjoyed and related to the realness of the character, even her flaws, and tweeted, "Bitches swear they so holy man smh #BeingMaryJane is real af! Every woman and most women can't be all holier than art thou and say no" (James 2014).

In their relatability, users were able to understand the moral ambiguity and complexity of the character and dissect the ways in which they could relate to Mary Jane. Tweets such as "There are many sides to Mary Jane. Being single I can see some of myself in the character . . . #BeingMaryJane" (Izastar 2014) or "#BeingMaryJane speaks to me on so many levels! I feel every woman can relate to this show in some way" (INDIA 2014) explored the ways in which viewers constructed how they identified with aspects of the character. However, tweets also suggested that audiences, at times, viewed it as a negative to be relatable in any way to Mary Jane: "If another ninja says I'm #BeingMaryJane I'm going to scream. I am not lonely and desperate. Well . . . at least not all the time . . . ." (Chick 2014). It should be noted that less than 4 percent of the tweets explicitly rejected any potential connection to Mary Jane Paul's character in tweets such as: "You know single professional black women are not this effin scattered. Or desperate. We can be messy yes but not this #beingmaryjane" (McClary 2014), while more than 10 percent of the tweets, even in their disagreement with the character's action, noted the fact they there were still elements to which they could relate.

These examples showed that even when a viewer did not fully identify with Mary Jane, the viewer was able point out positive aspects of her charcter. Viewers identified desires for certain features of her life, but also showed disappointment in some of Mary Jane's decisions. For example, "Can I have her clothes, car, job and house please tho? She can keep that married D" (Yan 2014). This showed that viewers were more likely to only identify with the more positive aspects of her character. Viewers' comments rarely openly related to their perceived negative behavior of Mary Jane, such as adultery. Research found that no tweet within the analysis showed a user explicitly identifying with participating in infidelity and adultery.

The problem with relatability in combination with negative stereotyping is that, at times, it does not allow viewers to see beyond the stereotypical portrayal of Mary Jane, and by extension is associated with Black womanhood. If Twitter users are constructing the character online in a way that is in alignment with African American female stereotypes, then the portrayal of Mary Jane is not open to alternative or negotiated readings that challenge those stereotypes of Black women. If the interpretation of Mary Jane's character is limited to binaries of representation, then it continues to perpetuate the narrative that has been used to oppress African American women while upholding the hegemony and patriarchy associated with whiteness in America. By nature of Mary Jane's decision to engage with Andre, Black women are still reduced to their sexual choices, despite the ways in which Mary Jane defies other negative stereotypes. Furthermore, this characterization has the capacity to limit the way in which Tweeters live their own lives or the type of relationships they expect. The first step in critiquing the images itself is understanding if and in what way viewers are constructing Mary Jane and then relating to her. There was relatability with the Mary Jane character, but the audience was very clear in the ways in which they chose to relate to her, either in a general manner, but never explicitly in the adulterous manner.

Mary Jane Paul versus Olivia Pope

The third theme was infidelity and adultery and the larger implications to the African American community in terms of influence with images of women like Mary Jane on television. In comparing the main character of *Being Mary Jane* to similar shows (i.e., *Scandal*) with a Black female lead, many Tweeters discussed the larger trend of how they feel Black women are negatively portrayed on current television shows. About 13 percent of the tweets provided a comparison of Mary Jane Paul to *Scandal*'s Olivia Pope. Viewers asked, "Can I please see a Black woman play a lead role where she's not sleeping with a married man? #BeingMaryJane #Scandal" (Williams 2014). Other tweets focused on the dominance of adultery being shown on television and the affront that is to the sanctity of marriage. Tweets were also concerned with the societal impact these portrayals can have on viewers. Viewers' immediate comparison of Mary Jane to *Scandal*'s Olivia Pope highlights viewers' understanding of how professional Black women are being negatively portrayed on television. Mary Jane is a successful television news reporter that seems to have everything going for herself. She, like Olivia Pope, is powerful and successful in her career, yet both women's personal dating lives are in shambles. Each woman's reality is in stark contrast to the notion that a woman can have it all: a great career, nice family, and children. Twitter users noted how in these two shows it appears as if that is not a possibility for Black women. As a part of that discussion, comments such as "We got another #OliviaPope on our hands. #MaryJane knowingly sleeps with a married man. Forgive her FATHER for she is a WHORE #BeingMaryJane" (Maurice 2014) were tweeted. Furthermore, some tweets also questioned the implications of this show on younger generations. "Ok, #BeingMaryJane and #Scandal is teaching young girls that beautiful, successful, black women are just side whores. #Noteanoshade #fact" (Bridges-Mathieu 2014).

Twitter users were also having internal conflicts with the show's mixed messaging. "I'm conflicted #scandal and #BeingMaryJane selling me the be a black woman who is strong but a side chick . . . need to evaluate my life" (MaSibanda 2014); "That scene was so wrong but it definitely made me feel some type of way. Can't wait for next week! #BeingMaryJane" (Wright 2014); "between #scandal &+ #beingmaryjane, idk who's better off, the wives or the sides . . . love looks deeper on the cheating side lol" (Jayy 2014). Paradoxically, some tweets highlighted a sense of fear for those in marriages as well as advice for married women to be aware of how these shows are giving hope to single women, looking to take their man. As one user said, "First #LoveAndHipHop Then #Scandal Now #BeingMaryJane Im Telling Yall Side Hoes Taking Over The World One Show At A Time #WifeysBeware" (BigBellySmoothBoy 2014). This was echoed by one viewer's observation that there is "way too much glorification of the jump off on TV these days . . . giving these broads hope. #Scandal #BeingMaryJane #WordsFromaWife" (Zil 2014). Twitter users felt that the show painted a perception that there are women actively plotting and planning to take a married man; however, that narrative is inconsistent with what actually occurred on the first episode. Mary Jane did not know Andre was married when she began the relationship; he was not honest about his marital status and Mary Jane developed feelings for him. Therefore, Mary Jane did not seek a married man; she met a married man, who was not honest about his marital status.

The discussion on Twitter regarding the implications of *Being Mary Jane* were particularly important, because they extended beyond the show and branched out to an online community discussion as viewers voiced their critiques on Black female roles shown on television. Although Twitter users acknowledged the increase in African American women on television shows, they were still concerned about the type of images being portrayed. For example, one user wrote, "Excited about the resurgence of AA TV shows! Concerned they depict Black women as smart, successful & philandering. #BeingMaryJane #Scandal" (Farrelly 2014). Evans (2014) asserted a similar conclusion when stating, "Although Olivia Pope is not a perfect representation of politically active African American women, her character offers a fine starting point for a minority group that at this point has not been represented in a rectified manner" (11).

CONCLUSION

In analyzing tweets during the first episode of the series *Being Mary Jane* three themes were found. The themes showcased viewers' perception of Mary Jane Paul as a modern-day Jezebel, their conflicting relatability to the character and viewers' disappointment with her choice to participate in an affair. These themes indicate an overall concern of the implications of negative portrayals of African American women on television. Tweets suggested the viewers were concerned that Black women leads on network television, regardless of their character's perceived success, were negatively portrayed and could have lasting effects on young viewers. One of the issues with stereotyping is that it does not necessarily relate to or reflect the lived experiences of Black women. This has damaging ramifications for not just women of color, but all women. This study's findings aligned with current research about the use of reoccurring and popular stereotypes on television when portraying African American women.

When *Being Mary Jane* debuted it was one of the few shows with a minority cast and lead, yet show depictions did not fully deviate far from popular culture representations of Black women on television. Social construction of Mary Jane on Twitter was in alignment with the previous and historically discouraging stereotypes of Black women in that viewer tweets highlighted their consciousness of a reoccurring trend of showing successful Black women with Jezebel-esque flaws, questioning whether more representation means more of the same negative stereotypes.

It is necessary, however, to be cognizant of the current limitations as a critical view must be taken to understand and even challenge the ownership structures and powers that decide when, how, and what type of representations of Black women are acceptable to enter mainstream media. While viewers acknowledged that certain positive aspects of Mary Jane's character were relatable, Twitter users also felt like her adultery was glorified and glamorized in the first episode of the show. As exampled in both *Being Mary Jane* and *Scandal*, successful Black women engaged in affairs with married men which could be interpreted as commonplace. To combat this, Higgins (2016) asserted that viewers must start demanding movies and television series that allow us to view Black women in all their glory. "I am all for art imitating life, but what about roles that represent and showcase positive characterizations of black women?" (par. 14).

LIMITATIONS AND FUTURE RESEARCH

Some limitations to the study include it only used one social media platform, the pilot episode of the show, and a small sample of tweets in its analysis. Looking at multiple social media platforms could allow for a more extensive analysis and also would allow for the researcher to discover if the characterization of Mary Jane Paul and the themes that emerge diverge or converge on different platforms. Looking at a larger sample of tweets from the timeframe could also lead to more findings. Furthermore, this study focused on one episode of *Being Mary Jane* and did not take into consideration the racial and gender differences from the tweets, which may have changed the findings of the study. A future study could investigate more episodes and seasons of the show to examine character growth. As a researcher, steps were taken to ensure the reliability of the data and reflexivity was used throughout the selection and analysis of tweets. However, incorporating more quantitative research or taking a mixed method approach may be helpful in the future.

Future studies may want to consider how African American males and other racial groups are portrayed on this television series as well. Furthermore, when looking at Twitter, studies may want to investigate if and how gender plays a role in the current findings of this study. By this, the author suggests examining gender in social constructions of Mary Jane Paul. Lastly, a deeper comparative analysis of this and other shows that have Black female writers and actors, such as *Scandal* and *Insecure*, could be beneficial in understanding this phenomenon better.

In sum, this study sought to analyze the ways in which Twitter users wrote about their reactions and perceptions of the main character, Mary Jane Paul in *Being Mary Jane*. Through a textual analysis and thematic analysis, it was found that despite the positive and relatable aspects of the character Mary Jane, her choice to engage in an affair, and Jezebel stereotyping lead to a negative social construction on Twitter, and beyond.

REFERENCES

Ambz (@PINKfantasyyy). *Twitter Post*. January 8, 2014, 11:03 PM. https://twitter.com/PINKfantasyyy/status/420767788849176576.

Andreeva, Nellie. 2016. "'Being Mary Jane': Will Packer Joins As EP, Erica Shelton Kodish Named Showrunner." *Deadline Hollywood,* May 23, 2016. http://deadline

.com/2016/05/being-mary-jane-will-packer-producer-erica-shelton-kodish-show runner-1201761333/.

Ash (@s0ulsearching_). *Twitter Post*. January 8, 2014, 11:04 PM. https://twitter.com/s0ulsearching_/status/420767826555584513.

Being Mary Jane. Season 1, episode 1, "Storm Advisory." Directed by Salim Akil. Written by Mara Brock-Akil, Jessica Mecklenburg, and Devon Greggory. Aired January 7, 2014, on BET.

Berger, Peter L., and Thomas Luckmann. 1966. *The Social Construction of Reality: A Treatise in the Sociology of Knowledge*. New York: Penguin Group.

BET. 2016. Being Mary Jane. Retrieved October 31, 2016, from http://www.bet.com/shows/being-mary-jane.html.

BET Networks. n.d. "BET Networks Corporate Mission Statement." Accessed November 5, 2017. https://betcareers.viacom.com/about.html.

BigBellySmoothBoy (@MarloMFU4Weez). *Twitter Post*. January 7, 2014, 11:04 PM. https://twitter.com/MarloMFU4Weez/status/420767873725124608.

BLAZEL PROMO PAGE (@BLAZELPROMO). *Twitter Post*. January 7, 2014, 11:02 PM. https://twitter.com/BLAZELPROMO/status/420767475341754368.

Bogle, Donald. 2001. *Toms, Coons, Mulattoes, Mammies, and Bucks: An Interpretive History of Blacks in American Films*. New York: The Continuum International Publishing Group, Incorporated.

Bridges – Mathieu, S. (@Shacklesoff). *Twitter Post*. January 8, 2014, 12:05 AM. https://twitter.com/Shacklesoff/status/420783321866448896.

Buschow, Christopher, Beate Schneider, and Simon Ueberheide. 2014. "Tweeting Television: Exploring Communication Activities on Twitter While Watching TV." *Communications – European Journal of Communication Research* 39, no. 2: 129–49. https://www.researchgate.net/publication/260243840_Tweeting_television_Exploring_communication_activities_on_Twitter_while_watching_TV.

Chaney, Cassandra, and Ray V. Robertson. June 2016. "Chains of Psychological Enslavement: Olivia Pope and the Celebration of the Black Mistress in ABC's Scandal." *Africology: The Journal of Pan African Studies* 9, no. 3: 126–53. http://www.jpanafrican.org/docs/vol9no3/9.3-11-Chaney-Ray.pdf.

Cheers, Imani. 2018. *The Evolution of Black Women in Television: Mammies, Matriarchs and Mistresses*. New York: Routledge.

Chenelle (@BlackBeauty0529). *Twitter Post*. January 7, 2014, 11:03 PM. https://twitter.com/BlackBeauty0529/status/420767616127762432.

Chick, That (@that_chick911). *Twitter Post*. January 8 2014, 12:14 AM. https://twitter.com/that_chick911/status/420785444154900480.

ChillWave (@MellifluousVibe). *Twitter Post*. January 7, 2014, 11:03 PM. https://twitter.com/MellifluousVibe/status/420767800316006400.

Clarke, Victoria, and Virginia Braun. 2013. "Teaching Thematic Analysis: Overcoming Challenges and Developing Strategies for Effective Learning." *The Psychologist* 26, no. 2 (February): 120–23. http://thepsychologist.bps.org.uk/volume-26/edition-2/methods-teaching-thematic-analysis.

Collins, Patricia Hill. 1989. "The Social Construction of Black Feminist Thought." *Signs* 14, no. 4 (Summer): 745–73. https://www.jstor.org/stable/3174683.

Collins, Rebecca L. 2011. "Content Analysis of Gender Roles in Media: Where Are We Now and Where Should We Go?" *Sex Roles* 64, nos. 3–4 (January): 290–98. doi:10.1007/s11199-010-9929-5.

Collins, Patricia Hill. 2000. *Black Feminist Thought: Knowledge, Consciousness and the Politics of Empowerment.* New York: Routledge.

Danica, Princess (@beingPrincessD). *Twitter Post.* January 8, 2014, 12:00 AM. Comfort sex. https://twitter.com/beingPrincessD/status/420782142444933120.

Dates, Jannette, and William Barlow. 1993. *Split Image: African Americans in the Mass Media.* District of Columbia: Howard University Press.

Doughty, Mark, Duncan Rowland, and Shaun Lawson. 2012. "Who is on Your Sofa?: TV Audience Communities and Second Screen Social Networks." *EuroITV Proceedings of the 10th European Conference on Interactive TV and Video* (July): doi:10.1145/2325616.2325635.

Duggan, Maeve. 2015. *Mobile Messaging and Social Media 2015.* Washington, DC: Pew Research Center (August 19, 2015). http://www.pewinternet.org/2015/08/19/mobile-messaging-and-social-media-2015/.

Evans, Lydia. 2014. "Representations of African American Political Women in Scandal." *Pepperdine Journal of Communication Research* 2, no. 4: 1–14. Retrieved from http://digitalcommons.pepperdine.edu/pjcr/vol2/iss1/4.

Everett, Anna. 2015. "Scandalicious." *The Black Scholar* 45, no. 1: 34–43. doi:10.1080/00064246.2014.997602.

Farrelly, Nanyamka (@_nanyamka). *Twitter Post.* January 7, 2014, 8:03 PM. https://twitter.com/_nanyamka/status/420767794545037312.

Fox, Justin. 2014. "Why Twitter's Mission Statement Matters." *Harvard Business Review,* November 13, 2014. https://hbr.org/2014/11/why-twitters-mission-statement-matters.

Fukwat_uthink (@P1nky_Duh). *Twitter Post.* January 7, 2014, 11:03 PM. https://twitter.com/P1nky_Duh/status/420767626655064065.

Fursich, Elfriede. 2009. "In Defense of Textual Analysis: Restoring a Challenged Method for Journalism and Media Studies." *Journalism Studies* 10, no. 2: 238–52. doi:10.1080/14616700802374050.

Goh, Dion Hoe-Lian, and Chei Sian Lee. 2011. "An Analysis of Tweets in Response to the Death of Michael Jackson." *Aslib Proceedings: New Information Perspectives* 63, no. 5: 432–44. doi:10.1108/00012531111164941.

González, Pedro A. 2014. "The Role of Social Media in the Success of the Sitcom "Scandal": First Come Twitter . . . and Then the Show." *Research Gate.* Retrieved from https://www.researchgate.net/publication/265612924_The_role_of_social_media_in_the_success_of_the_Sitcom_Scandal_First_come_Twitter_and_then_the_show.

Harrington, Stephen, Tim Highfield, and Axel Bruns. 2013. "More Than a Backchannel: Twitter and Television." *Journal of Audience and Reception Studies* 10, no. 1 (May): 405–9. http://www.participations.org/Volume%2010/Issue%201/30%20Harrington%20et%20al%2010.1.pdf.

Heger, D., J. Olson, and R. Diedrich. 2016. *From Static to Streaming: The Evolution of tv Entertainment* (Research Report RES-10071A-A). Retrieved from Edward Jones website https://www.edwardjones.com/images/RES-10071-A.pdf.

Higgins, Jonathan P. "Why Hollywood's Portrayal of Black Women Is Problematic." *The Root*. N.p., November 24, 2016. Web. November 26, 2016.

hooks, bell. 1989. *Talking Back: Thinking Feminist, Thinking Black*. Boston: South End Press.

hooks, bell. 1992. *Black Looks: Race and Representation*. Boston: South End Press.

I N D I A (@SincerlyIndo_). *Twitter Post*. January 7, 2014, 11:04 PM. https://twitter.com/SincerlyIndo_/status/420767941404422144.

interlude, K. (@PluzSizeBeauty_). *Twitter Post*. January 7, 2014, 11:03 PM. https://twitter.com/PluzSizeBeauty_/status/420767670989234176.

Izastar, Mimi (@Sassykiss79). *Twitter Post*. January 7, 2014, 11:03 PM. https://twitter.com/Sassykiss79/status/420767792066224128.

Jackson II, Ronald L. 2006. *Scripting the Black Masculine Body: Identity, Discourse, and Racial Politics in Popular Media*. Albany, NY: State University of New York Press.

James, T'keyah (@NunBut_GORGEOUS). *Twitter Post*. January 7, 2014, 11:03 PM. https://twitter.com/NunBut_GORGEOUS/status/420767710650191872.

Jayy, K (@KindaSortaJade). January 8, 2014. *between #scandal &+ #beingmaryjane, idk who's better off, the wives or the sides .. love looks deeper on the cheating side lol [Tweet]*. Retrieved from https://twitter.com/KindaSortaJade/status/420767524444450816.

Kenett, Dror Y., Fred Morstatter, H. Eugene Stanley, and Huan Liu. July 2014. "Discovering Social Events Through Online Attention." *Plos One* 9, no. 7: 1–7. doi:10.1371/journal.pone.0102001.

King, Kendall. 2015. "Do African-American Female Stereotypes Still Exist in Television? A Descriptive Character Analysis of Olivia Pope." *Elon Journal of Undergraduate Research in Communications* 6, no. 2: 1v5. https://www.inquiriesjournal.com/a?id=1361.

Kretsedemas, Philip. June 2010. ""But She's Not Black!": Viewer Interpretations of "Angry Black Women" on Prime Time TV." *Journal of African American Studies* 14, no. 2: 149–70. doi:10.1007/s12111-009-9116-3.

Lavrakas, Paul J. 2008. *Encyclopedia of Survey Research Methods*. Thousand Oaks: Sage Publications, Inc.

Lysss (@tenomamor). *Twitter Post*. January 7, 2014, 8:07 PM. https://twitter.com/__LoveeeT/status/420768623788326912.

MaSibanda (@nokidizzle). *Twitter Post*. January 8, 2014, 12:18 AM. https://twitter.com/nokidizzle/status/420786546846220289.

Marshall, Catherine, and Gretchen B. Rossman. 2016. *Designing Qualitative Research (sixth edition)*. Los Angeles: Sage Publications.

Marwick, Alice E. 2013. "Ethnographic and Qualitative Research on Twitter." In *Twitter and Society*, edited by Katrin Weller, Axel Bruns, Jean Burgess, Merja Mahrt, and Cornelius Puschmann, 109–122. New York: Peter Lang.

Maurice, Alexis (@_alexisMAURICE). *Twitter Post*. January 7, 2014, 11:02 PM. https://twitter.com/_alexisMAURICE/status/420767545164308481.

McClary, Robin C. (@celestemc). *Twitter Post*. January 7, 2014, 11:02 PM. https://twitter.com/celestemc/status/420767559613284353.

Miller, Katherine. 2005. *Communication Theories: Perspectives, Processes, and Contexts. Second Edition.* New York: McGraw-Hill.

Moraes, Lisa de. 2014. "BET's 'Being Mary Jane' Series Debut Cumes 5 Million Viewers." *Deadline,* January 8, 2014. https://deadline.com/2014/01/bets-being-mary-jane-series-debut-cumes-5-million-viewers-660781/.

Mosley, Nina (@TheMonaLisaa). *Twitter Post.* January 2014, TIME. https://twitter.com/TheMonaLisaa/status/420767474670632960.

Muhammad, Gholnescar E., and Sherell A. McArthur. 2015. "'Styled By Their Perceptions': Black Adolescent Girls Interpret Reinterpretation of Black females in Popular Culture." *Multicultural Perspectives* 17, no. 3: 133–40. doi:10.1080/1521 0960.2015.1048340.

Nielson. September 30, 2015. "Black Influence Goes Mainstream in the U.S." Retrieved November 20, 2016, from http://www.nielsen.com/us/en/insights/news/2015/black-influence-goes-mainstream-in-the-us.html.

Pablo, Petty (@torisneaux). *Twitter Post.* January 7, 2014, 11:04 PM. https://twitter.com/thePHAmemonster/status/420767958428688385.

Schirra, Steven, Huan Sun, and Frank Bentley. 2014. "Together Alone: Motivations for Live-tweeting a Television Series." In *Proceedings of the 2014 Association for Computing Machinery (ACM) Conference on Computer-Human Interaction (CHI)* (2441–2450). New York, NY: ACM Press. https://www.researchgate.net/publication/266655621_Together_alone_Motivations_for_live-tweeting_a_television_series.

Seiter, Ellen. June 1986. "Stereotypes and the Media: A Re-evaluation." *Journal of Communication* 36, no. 2: 14–26. doi:10.1111/j.1460-2466.1986.tb01420.x.

Slimmmm (@itsME_Slim). *Twitter Post.* January 7, 2014, 8:03PM. https://twitter.com/itsME_Slim/status/420767723652521984.

Squires, Catherine R. 2013. *Bell hooks: A Critical Introduction to Media and Communication Theory.* New York: Peter Lang Publishing, Inc.

The Futon Critic. 2013. "BET Networks' First Original Scripted Series "Being Mary Jane" Starring Gabrielle Union Premieres on Tuesday, January 7, 2014 at 10 P.M. ET/PT." *The Futon Critic,* October 24, 2013. http://www.thefutoncritic.com/news/2013/10/24/bet-networks-first-original-scripted-series-being-mary-jane-starring-gabrielle-union-premieres-on-tuesday-january-7-2014-at-10-pm-et-pt-664210/20131024bet01/#2QPxGX87IpwOLkt1.99.

The Real J-Spitta (@JSpitta3). *Twitter Post.* January 7, 2014, 8:03 PM https://twitter.com/JSpitta3/status/420767633357537280.

Thompson, Lisa B. 2009. *Beyond the Black Lady: Sexuality and the New African American Middle Class.* Urbana: University of Illinois Press.

Tyne (@TyneElaine). *Twitter Post.* January 7, 2014, 11:03 PM. https://twitter.com/TyneElaine/status/420767749317853185.

Tyree, Tia. November 2011. "African American Stereotypes in Reality Television." *Howard Journal of Communications* 22, no. 4: 394–413. doi:10.1080/1646175.2011.617217.

Tyree, Tia, and Michelle Jones. 2015. "The Adored Woman in Rap: An Analysis of the Presence of Philogyny in Rap Music." *Women's Studies* 44, no. 1 (February): 54–83. doi:10.1080/00497878.2014.971217.

Tyree, Tia, and Morgan Kirby. 2017. "#THOTsBeLike: The Construction of the THOT Female Sexual Stereotype in Social Media." In *Social Media Culture and Identity,* edited by Kehbuma Langmia and Tia Tyree, 3–25. Lanham: Lexington Books.

Walsh, Katie. 2014. "What Does Twitter Really Offer TV Audiences, and At What Cost?" *Spectator* 34, no. 2 (Fall): 11–15. http://search.proquest.com/.

Weiland, Scott J. and Kaitlyn Dunbar. 2016. "What's Real About Reality Television?" *Journal of Mass Communication & Journalism* 6, no. 3. doi: 10.4172/2165-7912.1000308.

West, Carolyn M. 1995. "Mammy, Sapphire, and Jezebel: Historical Images of Black Women and Their Implications for Psychotherapy." *Psychotherapy Theory Research & Practice* 32, no. 3 (Fall): 458–66. doi:10.1037/0033-3204.32.3.458.

Whiting, Anita, and David Williams. 2013. "Why People Use Social Media: A Uses and Gratifications Approach." *Qualitative Market Research: An International Journal* 16, no. 4: 362–69. doi:10.1108/QMR-06-2013-0041.

Williams, B. M. (@Ms_BMWilliams). *Twitter Post.* January 8, 2014. https://twitter.com/Ms_BMWilliams/status/420767920466051072.

Williams, Melvin L., and Tia Tyree. 2015. "The Un-Quiet Queen: An Analysis of Rapper Nicki Minaj in the Fame Comic Book." In *Feminist Theory and Pop Culture,* edited by A. Trier-Bieniek, 49–64. Boston: Sense Publishers.

Wood, Julia T. 1994. *Gendered Media: The Influence of Media on Views of Gender.* Belmont: Wadsworth Publishing.

Wohn, D.Yvette, and Eun-Kyung Na. March 2011. "Tweeting About tv: Sharing Television Viewing Experiences Via Social Media Message Streams." *First Monday* 16, no. 3: 1–13. Retrieved from http://firstmonday.org/article/view/3368/2779.

Wright, Ashonte' (@ashontewright). *Twitter Post.* January 7, 2014, 11:03PM. https://twitter.com/ashontewright/status/420767604915990529.

Yan (@neeki876). *Twitter Post.* January 7, 2014.

Zil (@OnlyZil). *Twitter Post.* January 7, 2014, 11:04 PM. https://twitter.com/OnlyZil/status/420767959146328064.

Chapter 9

@MaraAkil

An Analysis of Mara's Balance of Life, Family, and Production on Instagram

Candace P. Parrish

The life of a major entertainment screenwriter and producer can presumably be quite hectic—especially for a writer and producer with multiple top-rated shows. Mara Brock Akil—the creator of shows like *The Game* and *Being Mary Jane*—may have quite a popular body of work; however, her personal life remains under the radar. This chapter serves as an analysis of the star producer's personal Instagram account and provides more insight on how Mara balances and represents her career, relationships with family and friends, and life in general. The social media platform of Instagram was used as a method to obtain content to analyze due to the social networks visual nature—providing a consistent amount of visual and textual data for analysis. Mara's Instagram account is also one of her most utilized social media platforms. Findings from this chapter help shape the narrative of self-representation and performance of prominent African American women in Hollywood, such as Mara, on a social platform.

ENTERTAINMENT'S SOCIAL MEDIA ADVANTAGE

In the entertainment industry, social media plays a critical role in communicating and promoting for shows, productions, behind the scenes content, and celebrities themselves. One of the most popular benefits the entertainment industry has gained from the evolution of social media is the ability to engage and communicate directly with target audiences and fans (Saha 2018). More specifically, music artists, actors and actresses, producers and designers have the opportunity of two-way communication in which they can share and receive immediate information from their followers (Saha 2018; Snow 2015; Winslett 2017). "Given the opportunity to communicate and promote shows and productions, it makes sense that producers would harness social media platforms to expand their reach and build anticipation for airing or upcoming shows or movies" (Snow 2015; Winslett 2017). However, an interesting dynamic occurs when members of the entertainment industry utilize personal social media platforms for production promotion and as a method of transparency in communicating their lives and personalities to fans (Kim and Song 2016; Snow 2015). The discussion of how producers and creators showcase their lives, in conjunction with their public work, on social media is a topic area which is lacking within scholarly discussion. In the case of this specific research, the Instagram page of Mara Brock Akil, the renowned director of several classic African-American, love-centered shows, was analyzed to explore how she balances communication and visualization of her life, work, family, and friends.

MARA'S WORK

Mara Brock Akil is a well-known writer and producer in entertainment and television. She has a writing and production catalogue that spans over twenty years (Internet Movie Database (IMDB) 2018). Brock Akil has won five television and social awards for her writing and producing and has additionally been nominated for other awards related to her work (IMDB 2018). Her portfolio includes shows like *Girlfriends* (2000–2008), *The Game* (2006–2015), *Being Mary Jane* (2013–2018), *Black Lightning* (2018), and her most recent production *LOVE IS___* (2018) (IMDB 2018). To date, analyses of Brock Akil have been centrally focused on her writing and production of Black people and Black women's lifestyle for mainstream television (Lewis 2012; Squires 2014, 188). Although, some critics have compartmentalized several of her shows as "spin-offs" from popular white shows, many feel her portrayal of issues concerning Black women are timely and honorable (Lewis 2012; Squires 2014, 188).

Extant research highlights the positive effect these shows potentially have as the Black writers are able to write scripts that directly speak to lifestyle, health, and social issues concerning women of color (Dates 2005, 68–78; Lewis 2012; Squires 2014, 188). Additionally, casting for shows like these affirm the storylines created as there is a physical mix of representation of women, like in Brock Akil's show *Girlfriends* (Dates 2005, 68–78). However, perspectives and tone of discussion about her work may vary by race and gender. In an article by Steele (2018, 112–27), the author highlights comments made by Black men on a blog site that express disdain for the perceived promiscuity of the lead star Mary Jane of the series *Being Mary Jane*. The article also highlights the push back expressed by blog readers who felt the storyline of *Being Mary Jane* had more layers than just sexuality and should be commended for its holistic approach for representing possible lifestyles of contemporary Black women (Steele 2018, 112–27). Further, it is safe to say that Brock Akil wrote and produced a provocative array of shows that helped stimulate discussion of Black experiences and their portrayal in mainstream television and entertainment.

PORTRAYAL OF MARA'S PERSONAL LIFE

Until recently, Brock Akil generally provided limited glimpses into her private life. On her Instagram page, she occasionally shares pictures of and comments about her children (sons), husband, Salim Akil, and other family and friends. However, the launch of her new series, titled *LOVE IS___*, on the Oprah Winfrey Network (OWN) provides fans and viewers with a glimpse of Brock Akil's personal life (Holmes 2018; N'Duka 2018). In an interview by Holmes (2018), Brock Akil shared that the storyline of *LOVE IS___* was loosely based upon the story of her and her husband's relationship. Further explaining the reason for sharing the storyline of their relationship, Mara shared: "The pilot sort of nails a lot but as the season of courtship goes on, we manipulate some of the facts so that Nuri and Yasir can be aBrock Akilssadors for this idea that *love is* achievable if you define it for yourself" (Holmes 2018). This new path of expressing personal experiences is rather new for Brock Akil's and has generated a lot of buzz from viewers, fans, and various people in the industry as she stepped away from her traditional format of fictional writing and production (Tillet 2018; N'Duka 2018).

Beyond *LOVE IS___* there are limited occurrences where she actively shares moments of her life outside of her social media. For this reason, this research will examine the social media platform she most engages, Instagram, to find connections and create deeper context to how Brock Akil communicates and visualizes her life, family, and work with fans, peers, and the world.

RESEARCH QUESTIONS

RQ1: How does Mara Brock Akil communicate and visualize her life, including relationships with family and friends, on her Instagram account?
RQ2: How does Mara Brock Akil communicate and visualize work, production and societal views on her Instagram account?

METHODOLOGY

Qualitative Research

Analysis of Brock Akil's social media is a topic that has not been well-explored in communication or entertainment research. Thus, qualitative research was employed as it houses a host of methods that are great for exploring new and uncharted phenomenon, events, or circumstances (Berg 2009; Corbin and Strauss 2014; Jansson-Boyd 2015; Lindof & Taylor 2011). Qualitative research is great when utilized to explore and generate context to human behavior as it is naturally a study of the lived experienced (Berg 2009; Corbin and Strauss 2014; Jansson-Boyd 2015; Lindof & Taylor 2011). When strategically used, this type of research can generate a wealth of data surrounding the topic at hand. Specifically for this analysis, qualitative research was the necessary route for exploration to bring context to the way Brock Akil communicates about her herself, family, friends, and work on social media.

Qualitative Content Analysis

The qualitative research method of content analysis was used during this research to help review, discover, and create context to the way Brock Akil communicates about her life on social media. Qualitative content analysis is a method whereby researchers systematically review various forms of content (whether visuals or text) for new or reinforced meanings or connections about an event, incident, or person (Berg 2009). The content analysis method, in qualitative research, is primarily a textual analysis, however, the process has and can include quantitative components and variables (Berg 2009; Miles et al. 2014).

Data Collection

The data for this analysis on Brock Akil's social media was collected from the producer's Instagram page. At the time of this analysis, Brock Akil had over two thousand Instagram posts. In order to give equal opportunity for various types of content to surface, a random number generator was used to determine the frequency at which each post for analysis would be collected. The random number generator provide the number four, thus, every fourth post from Brock Akil's Instagram was chosen until saturation in content was achieved. The concept of saturation in qualitative research pertains to the point when repetition is noticed in data and themes and is a signal for the researcher to cease data collection (Carlsen & Glenton 2011, 1–10; Fusch and Ness 2015, 1408–16). In total, seventy posts from Brock Akil's Instagram page were analyzed for greater context and meaning. The posts selected ranged in date from November 27, 2017 to November 1, 2018.

Data Analysis

Analysis of Brock Akil's Instagram posts were guided by the Grounded Theory Approach. The Grounded Theory Approach is a theory used for qualitative data analysis that is aimed at allowing the content to show categories, themes, and connections in data (Corbin & Strauss 2014; Denzin & Lincoln 2000; Jansson-Boyd 2015; Lindof & Taylor 2011). The Grounded Theory Approach is inductive by nature and has several different coding components (Corbin & Strauss 2014; Denzin & Lincoln 2000; Jansson-Boyd 2015; Lindof & Taylor 2011). Of the components of the theory open coding, axial coding, in-vivo coding, and constant comparison methods were employed. The data were first coded line-by-line (and visual-by-visual) for categories and concepts, further refining emerging ideas and outcomes (Denzin & Lincoln 2000). During analysis, open coding was used to gain a general understanding of the data and to create substantive categories and themes (Corbin & Strauss 2014). In-vivo coding was then utilized to appoint codes to clusters of relating information, categories, and themes (Corbin & Strauss 2014). The analysis method of axial coding was used to comb back through the data and create and finalize connections between those prior determined categories and themes to assure they are representative of the data (Berg 2009; Corbin & Strauss 2014; Lindof & Taylor 2011). There were seventy Instagram posts that were analyzed in total.

Instagram

The visual social media platform of Instagram was used to communicate a compilation of visual and textual content (DeMers 2017; Moreau 2018). Instagram, now owned by Facebook, is one of the highest utilized social media platforms (DeMers 2017; Moreau 2018). Entertainers, artist, and producers are especially active on the social media platform as it often serves as a direct way of communicating about their life and work directly to their fans and audiences (Kim and Song 2016; Snow 2015). Brock Akil's Instagram account was specifically used for analysis as it provides a balance of visual and textual content about her life, family, and work—which this research analysis explored to gain greater context.

RESULTS

The analysis of Brock Akil's Instagram account yielded various results relating to how the renowned television producer uses the social media platform of Instagram for communication about her life, family, friends, and work. The following results are presented by reoccurring themes and correlations from the analysis related to each research question.

RQ1: How does Mara Brock Akil communicate and visualize her life, including relationships with family and friends, on her Instagram account?

During analysis of Brock Akil's Instagram posts, the following themes relating to the portrayal of her life and relationships with family and friends emerged: selfies and profile photos, nostalgic posts about sons, paying homage to Black women and friends, and highlighting loved ones.

Selfies and Profile Photos

Selfies have become a staple form of visual communication on personal social media accounts in the past decade. Not surprising, there were several selfies and self-portraits posted on Brock Akil's Instagram page. A few were "off guard" photos where she seemed to be in the middle of laughter or gazing into the distance. Most of these types of photos were intentional selfies or self-portraits that featured her smiling and gazing right into the camera. One post featured Brock Akil stylishly posing in a leather (or leather-like), ankle-length dress with white ankle boots. The caption for this post read: "*LOVE IS___* Feeling beautiful . . . it's appreciated when a girl gets some extra help to make her appear like she hopes to be seen. A heart full of thanks to my #beautyteam for my @adcolor talk last Friday night . . . ." A follow-up post from the same event that was analyzed featured Brock Akil laughing onstage while seated as a panelist. The post read: "*LOVE IS___* ADCOLOR . . . and a smile. My big smile was capture at #ADColor last Friday . . . #InTheLandOfColor #LivingMyBestLife."

Nostalgic Posts About Sons

A few of the posts on Brock Akil's account featured moments with her family, more specifically her sons. Of the Instagram posts examined, Brock Akil's sons were posted and communicated about in a positive light, usually reflecting on their growth. As their mother, Brock Akil many times spoke about the persons they were becoming and her nostalgia for the babies they once were. One post, which featured her older son in a Halloween costume, read: "*LOVE IS___* This beautiful boy behind the Friday the 13th mask. It's hard to believe he was once a #lioncub."

Paying Homage to Black Women and Friends

During this analysis, it was apparent that Brock Akil has deep appreciation for the strides her fellow and preceding Black women have made. There were several posts where she celebrated the life and accomplishments of Black women in the entertainment and production arenas. Several posts were of her friend and business partner Oprah Winfrey. These posts were either a celebration of birthdays or promotion of Oprah's new endeavors/movies. In addition, Brock Akil often posted about other women in the industry, whether it was someone acting in one of her series or Black women who paved the way for her success. One post was a photo of Ntozake Shange, whereby Brock Akil wrote about the director/producers passing and successes: "Blast the horns—an iconic storyteller who cared about making the visible invisible is coming home . . . I honor this brave women who wrote unapologetically about Black women's humanity between the axis of our joy and pain."

Highlighting Loved Ones

Brock Akil has shared a few posts relating to her family and friends. Sometimes the posts appeared as isolated posted not related to work. Other times the posts intertwined personal relationships with work and production. One example is of a post dedicated to her husband that featured a photo of the two behind a sign related to *Black Lightning* being inducted into Comic Con. The caption reads: "VISIONARY OF BLACK LIGHTNING// Met this cutie in study hall . . . We go together now. Gonna keep this one cause he's real cute, he's real smart, and I can see he's going places!!" In another post Brock Akil highlighted friendship, as she shared a selfie-style photo of two of her friends and herself celebrating a friend's birthday. The post reads: "*LOVE IS___* My Girlfriends! I've been riding with these talented and beautiful women for 25 years . . . we've celebrated weddings, births, surviving the Grand Canyon, scholarships, professorships, TV shows, movie premieres, and of course birthdays . . . HAPPY BIRTHDAY GINA!!! I love you . . . Today was a good day." This post's caption also intertwined Brock Akil's personal life with work as the captions starts with the series title "*LOVE IS___*."

RQ2: How does Mara Brock Akil communicate and visualize work and production and societal views on her Instagram account?

Analysis of Brock Akil's Instagram communication methods revealed the following themes related to portrayals of her work and production and societal views: show promotion, *LOVE IS___* campaign, comradery, and political expression.

Show Promotion

Given that Brock Akil leads a public life as a celebrity producer, the majority of her social media content was dedicated to promoting her various shows and productions. Of the posts analyzed, Brock Akil was very active in posting during times when her shows were either about to launch or on-air. A large amount of the posts analyzed where related to or showcasing information about the 2018 release of *LOVE IS___*, her latest show that appeared on OWN. The highest second cluster of posts was dedicated to the show *Black Lightning*, which is a series based on a comic book superhero. The types of posts relating to her shows ranged from posts about show times, season finales, and press appearances for show promotion, and so on.

LOVE IS___ Campaign

Brock Akil dedicated and intertwined a significant amount of post captions to the new series she produced called *LOVE IS___*. There were many posts, as evidences in various parts of this results section, that began with *LOVE IS___*. These posts ranged from professional to personal. The theme seemed to begin as a promotional tactic for the new love-centered series, however, may have been adopted by Brock Akil as a personal motto and method of recognizing and the many forms of "love" exemplified in her love, life, work, and relationships.

Comradery

In the analysis of Brock Akil's communication and visualization of her working relationships, she exemplified a great deal of comradery for and among her collaborators across all projects. In one post, Brock Akil used a combination of a picture from the *LOVE IS___* advertising and added a message of thanks to the writers of the show for their dedication and creative excellence in finishing the writing for Season 1. Several of the posts analyzed were dedicated to specific members of the casts. A post dedicated to cast member Kadeem Hardison read: "*LOVE IS___* KADEEM HARDISON! A stellar talent!! I prayed for you . . . God answered my prayer and exceed my hopes and dreams. Your complexity! Your drive for excellence! Your love! Is simply legendary . . . Take a bow."

Political Expression

There were several posts that Brock Akil included on her Instagram that served as political expressions and thoughts. Brock Akil even intertwined her work with communication about various political actions such as voting. In one post, Brock Akil provided a graphic photo featuring *Black Lightning* (one of her series' superheroes) and the national dates by state for voter registration deadlines. This post read: "REGISTER TO VOTE// And be your own #SuperHero. [IMPORTANT: For 10/9 Deadlines you can still register online just make sure it is stamped with 10/9. You have until midnight.]" In another post, Brock Akil added a photo of Dr. Christine Blasey Ford and wrote the note, "I believe her . . . I thank her." Brock Akil also posted an image of Colin Kaepernick and cited him as a "real superhero" in the caption of the post.

DISCUSSION

Upon analysis of Brock Akil's Instagram account, it is clear that she intentionally displays a well-rounded amount of textual and visual content regarding her life, work, relationship, and political views. One of the most prominent findings is the high frequency in which Brock Akil intertwines promotion of the *LOVE IS___* series with her personal life. Based on this analysis, Brock Akil communicated about this particular show the most and repeatedly used language from the show in personal posts. Given the inspiration for the show, it is clear why there would be a great emotional connections to this particular production.

As previously mentioned, the storyline from the show was derived from her personal love story with her husband, Salim (Holmes 2018; N'Duka 2018). Of the posts analyzed, Brock Akil gave great attention to promotion through posting multiple and varied types of social mediated content for *LOVE IS___* alone. Prior to the show, she dedicated several posts to displaying the casts members, writers, and producers. In addition, she shared a good amount of photos from the press tour with the main stars of the show. Prior to the show's release she conducted a multiday, multi-post countdown to airing. The discussions around the posts were less strategically worded and more so communicated like a genuine and heartfelt enthusiasm for sharing her love story. Even beyond direct promotion of the show, Brock Akil repeatedly used the title of the show as an opening statement comment supporting the photos posted. In fact, a very large amount of her comments (associated with photos shared) began with the phrase *LOVE IS___* and continued with varying perceptions of love based upon the subject and context of the photo shared.

During the time frame of the entire set of Instagram posts analyzed, Brock Akil's coproduced show *Black Lightning* (with husband Salim) was also airing. Although on a smaller scale than *LOVE IS___*, Brock Akil did have a few posts relating to promotion of the show and also intertwined some of her relational and real-world thoughts with the essence of the show. Discussion around these post were often less emotionally charged and more strategic in marketing nature. As with *LOVE IS___*, there were posts promoting show times and expressing gratitude for cast members. However, it appeared that the essence of the show dictated the context of information she shared about the show. In one post, which is mentioned above, Brock Akil posted a photo of she and her husband Salim attending Comic Con, where they provided a brief and straightforward expression of how they met and are still together. Given the very detailed and deep posts she shared around *LOVE IS___*, it is imaginable that if this photo were geared toward the romantic series, rather than the superhero series, Brock Akil might have been likely to give a more emotional and elaborative post.

In terms of Brock Akil's portrayal of relationships with friends and family, she seemed to communicate how appreciative she was of these relationships. The posts she shared about her family were often nostalgic or "throwback" photos. Regarding her sons and husband, she communicated about fond memories they shared via the type of visuals and captions posted. The instances when Brock Akil shared anticipation of future events were related to work and production. Her family life was kept a bit more private with only updates and comments about present and past experiences. Regarding friends, the lines between coworkers and friends seemed to cross paths often. It appears that Brock Akil celebrates having friend or family-like relationships with coworkers and that many of her closest friends are people she met in the industry at some point. She dedicated several posts toward showcasing their talents, accomplishments, and endeavors. There were several posts promoting and/or highlighting Oprah Winfrey, which combined the essence gratitude and admiration in the supporting captions. Brock Akil also posted and commented about the strides and advancements of Black women past and present. Further, it appears that the sisterhood and comradery that she infuses in her storylines (from *Girlfriends* to *Being Mary Jane*) might actually be a part of her tenants for maintaining personal relationships.

Lastly, Brock Akil was not opposed to sharing her views on several political and social topics and occurrences. There were a handful of post that communicated her stances on justice, election practices, and solidarity. In one instance, Brock Akil intertwined the promotion for the *Black Lightning* show and voting in the elections of 2018. The post had *Black Lightning* centered around two list of dates for voter registration deadlines by state and in her caption she insinuated that you could be your own superhero by voting. Just like with *LOVE IS___*, Brock Akil found a way to combine her real-world thoughts and beliefs into promotion of her current productions. Further alluding to the idea that she may feel her creations are relatively close to real-world experiences and/or lifestyles (or at least close enough to continuously include in thoughts about real-world happenings). As prior mentioned, Brock Akil has been noted to write and produce content that realistically reflects and resembles the lives of Black people and Black women specifically (Lewis 2012; Squires 2014, 188).

For celebrity producers like Brock Akil, Instagram has proven helpful in communicating the deeper thoughts and feelings about shows to fans and audiences. This idea is consistent with prior literature that presents social media as a perfect opportunity for more direct and effective communication, advertising, and marketing (Kim and Song 2016; Snow 2015). Brock Akil has even more of an advantage with using Instagram for communicating with fans and audiences as she is a great and strategic writer. As evidenced by her Instagram, she has the ability to create a more realistic narrative and storyline that conveniently compliments her broadcasted productions. Thus, many of her 207,000 Instagram followers have a community on her page in which they can bounce between the series and her posts/comments for an expanded experience with each show's brand.

CONCLUSION

As social media continues to widen the range of digital engagement for entertainment artist, writers, producers, and marketers there are many possibilities for extended engagement that are yet uncovered. Brock Akil may have knowingly or unknowingly tapped into these opportunities by continuing to showcase the essence of her shows within the narrative of her posts about life, family, friends, and work. As evidenced by Brock Akil's Instagram account, she has shared a wide range of content relative to her life and work experiences and relationships. These occurrences and posts have helped to provide more context to her life (as a mother, wife, and friend), work, and beliefs and viewpoints. Coincidentally, her engagement and communication on social media has most likely raised her social profile and the notoriety of her shows. By using social media, in this case Instagram, Brock Akil successfully created a community for continued engagement with her broadcast productions and complimenting narrative that reveals connections between her personal and professional life.

REFERENCES

Berg, Bruce L. 2009. *Qualitative Research Methods*. Boston, MA: Pearson Education Inc, 2009.

Carlsen, Benedicte and Claire Glenton. 2011. "What about N? A Methodological Study of Sample-size Reporting in Focus Group Studies." *BMC Medical Research Methodology* 11(26): 1–10.

Corbin, Juliet and Anselm Strauss. 2014. *Basics of Qualitative Research: Techniques and Procedures for Developing Grounded Theory* (Fourth ed.). Thousand Oaks, CA: Sage Publications, Inc.

Dates, Jannette. 2005. "Movin' on Up: Black Women Decision Makers In Entertainment Television." *Journal of Popular Film & Television* 33: 68–79.

DeMers, Jayson. 2017. *Why Instagram Is The Top Social Platform For Engagement (And How To Use It)*. https://www.forbes.com/sites/jaysondemers/2017/03/28/why-instagram-is-the-top-social-platform-for-engagement-and-how-to-use-it/#2a4bd0ca36bd.

Denzin, Norman and Yvonna Lincoln. 2000. *Grounded Theory: Objectivist and Constructivist Methods Handbook of Qualitative Research*. Thousand Oaks, CA: Sage Publications, Inc.

Fusch, P. and L. Ness. 2015. "Are We There Yet? Data Saturation in Qualitative Research." *The Qualitative Report* 20: 1408–16.

Holmes, M. 2018. *Why Mara Brock Akil and Salim Akil Shared Their Love Story in 'Love Is___'*. https://variety.com/2018/scene/news/love-is-premiere-mara-brock-akil-salim-akil-own-1202843117/.

Internet Movie Database (IMDB). 2018. *Mara Brock Akil*. https://www.imdb.com/name/nm0015327/.

Jansson-Boyd, Cathrine V. "Karen E. 2015. Dill (Ed.), The Oxford Handbook of Media Psychology." *Psychology Learning & Teaching* 14, no. 1: 90–91.

Kim, Jihyun and Hayeon Song. 2016. "Celebrity's Self-disclosure on Twitter and Parasocial Relationships: A Mediating Role of Social Presence." *Computers in Human Behavior* 62, no. C: 570–77.

Lewis, Nghana. 2012. "Prioritized: The Hip Hop (Re)Construction of Black Womanhood in *Girlfriends* and *The Game*." In *Watching While Black: Centering the Television of Black Audiences*, edited by Beretta E. Smith-Shomade, Eric Pierson, Robin Means Coleman, and Andre Cavalcante et al. New Brunswick, NJ: Rutgers University Press.

Lindof, Bryan C. and Thomas R. Taylor. 2011. *Qualitative Communication Research Methods* (3rd Ed.). Thousand Oaks, CA: Sage Publishing.

Miles, Matthew, Michael Huberman, and Johnny Saldana. 2014. *Qualitative Data Analysis: A Method Sourcebook*. Thousand Oaks, California: Sage Publications, Inc.

Moreau, Elise. 2018. *Everyone's Using This App Called Instagram . . .* https://www.lifewire.com/what-is- instagram-3486316.

N'Duka, Amanda. 2018. *'Love Is___' Creator Mara Brock Akil Talks How Series Was Inspired By Black Females*. https://deadline.com/2018/06/love-is-own-mara-brock-akil-salim-akil-american-black-film-festival-1202412030/.

Saha, Malay. 2018. *How Social Media Has Changed the Entertainment Experience*. https://socialnomics.net/2017/04/28/how-social-media-has-changed-the-entertainment-experience/.

Snow, Sarah. 2015. "How Celebrities Use Social Media [INFOGRAPHIC]." *Social Media Today*, October 27, 2015. https://www.socialmediatoday.com/social-networks/sarah-snow/2015-10-27/how-celebrities-use-social-media-infographic.

Squires, Catherine R. 2014. "Watching While Black: Centering the Television of Black Audiences." *Cinema Journal* 53: 188.

Steele, Catherine Knight. 2018. "Black Bloggers and Their Varied Publics: The Everyday Politics of Black Discourse Online." *Television & New Media* 19: 112–27.

Tillet, Salamishah. 2018. *The Black Sitcom Steps Out of the '90s and Gets Real*. https://www.nytimes.com/2018/06/15/arts/television/love-is-mara-brock-akil-black-sitcom.html.

Winslett, Ryan. 2017. *The Convergence of Social Media and Entertainment*. https://www.cision.com/us/2013/08/the-convergence-of-social-media-and-entertainment/.

Afterword

What Representations and Racial Messages Television Teaches Our Children

Ronald L. Jackson II

Televisual representations of Black lives by Black directors have always sought to reflect the complexity of what it means to be an African American. Although this act of reflecting life and its intricacies may seem like an ordinary task for any director, it is redoubled for an African American director who must consider the all too frequent caricatures of Black life on the big and small screen. As I have written in a previous volume on the Black masculine body the uneven media portrayals of a pathologized blackness have left audiences with a one-dimensional, lackluster snapshot that does nothing more than reinstate the epistemic violence, which accompanies popular media stereotypes about marginalized people. The cementing of these plastic inscriptions is extremely difficult to dissolve; yet the work of directors like Mara Brock Akil have been successful in doing this work.

In fact, as this brilliant volume *Being Mara* shows the work of representing Black love, joy, pleasure, and pain was never meant to be groundbreaking. It was only about establishing the normalcy of Black life. Brock Akil does it with piercing accuracy in every one of her richly authentic TV shows about Black women. Audiences are treated to a glimpse of Black women they rarely get to see, a glimpse that shows confident, Black female characters navigating worlds where they are simultaneously presented as strong and nurturing, deftly motivated and yet relaxed and joyful, and sometimes anxious in relationships but often assured in their careers. With Brock Akil's work we get to experience, as a TV audience, a pleasant escape from TV's usual stereotypical ratched image of a Black woman fed to us by shows like the *Housewives of Atlanta* series. Perhaps what is most refreshing about Brock Akil's consistent televisual representations, no matter whether in *Girlfriends*, *Being Mary Jane*, *Love Is ___*, *Black Lightning*, *The Game*, or any of the other shows were she has written a few episodes such as on *Moesha*, or the

Jamie Foxx Show, there is a deliberate set of narratives about Black characters being respected and valued for their strength while also living satisfying lives. Naturally we get the conflicted side of the characters as well, the ones that are not always able to avert hurting themselves or others. These are the normalizing and authentic portrayals, but Brock Akil seems to work hard to offer scripts that release audiences from the kind of daily, toxic, paralyzing dialogue that often accompanies other TV shows where the resolution leaves audiences even more depressed than they were before the show started. Viewing audiences for a TV show are akin to students at a university. Without an audience viewing the content the creative narratives have nowhere to go. The bottom line is TV scripts are in search of an audience.

Over the years of my life I have become especially careful about what I consume on television. I treat it as a diet. I am not interested in consuming pathological blackness. I get enough of that already. I have had a steady diet of it most of my life. In fact, it is difficult to reach adulthood and not have seen plastic edifices erected to celebrate the mammy, jezebel, sapphire, buck, mammy, coon, uncle tom, and tragic mulatto. Even when I wasn't paying close attention to the TV shows I watched these representations were slipped into my proverbial "cereal" as a child. I am reminded of the mammy image in *Tom and Jerry*, and the picaninny images in *The Little Rascals*. I was hopelessly introduced to images and representations that had become their own pedagogy about blackness. Certainly they taught non-Black people about the tragically inescapable condition of Black people as non-intellectual, incapacitated, often passive, sometimes sassy, but almost always sexually deviant, criminal minded, and impoverished. When I was old enough to understand what I had been watching I changed my diet. When I began to study the inherent tensions in TV narratives about Black life I realized something had to change, but that it needed to start with me and my household.

As a young parent, I committed myself to being an example of what I wanted for my children. My wife and I made a concerted effort to raise our children showing them what a healthy, successful, loving lifestyle looks like, so that if they ever saw something toxic elsewhere, including on television, they would know it to be another version of a lifestyle they did not have to live. Although the first examples we wanted to set as parents started at home, we were well aware that our children, like all others, pick up another set of images in various media.

My wife and I decided to become intentional about introducing our daughter and son to productive TV portrayals of Blackness. We wanted them to embrace a healthy pattern of self-care, self-worth, self-love, and self-confidence, and to see that reflected in real life and on screen. I wanted my daughter to know that it is possible to experience a positive, healthy, and godly love from another human being. I wanted her to know she could find that in her own community. I wanted to show her through my example of the way I love her mom that this kind of love is real, and not just something fictive she could only find on television. I also wanted her to understand that she is beautiful and deserving of love, and that anything antithetic to love ought to be rejected. I wanted to cultivate for her a lifestyle where she was surrounded by success. We wanted our kids to be around our own family and friends' families that were raising their children likewise.

We were keen to instill similar notions of pride and self-efficacy for my son. We focused less on him recognizing himself as beautiful, and more on him making choices that would not limit his opportunities. To say it plainly, we did not want him to "drink the kool-aid" about Black males being innately incapacitated, incompetent, inarticulate, ineludibly sexual deviants, derelicts, and dangers to society. We wanted him to see the pathological representations for what they were, sociopolitically motivated plastic inscriptions about Blackness that had become so distantly foreign that even Black people could barely recognize them. We wanted him to be cautious but not inhibited. We felt caution was warranted in a society that has seen countless instances of fatal brutality against Black males for doing nothing more than being in the wrong place at the wrong time as was the case with Trayvon Martin, or playing music loudly as with Jordan Davis, or for holding a toy gun on a park bench like Tamir Rice. We wanted him to understand that even the televisual narratives about Black males insinuate that Black males are perennially poor choice makers. We wanted him to understand that did not have to be the case with him.

My wife and I wanted my daughter and son both to know that they were amazing, beautiful, normal human beings whose productive possibilities were endless, whose success in life would always be well within reach, and whose cultural heritage puts them in direct lineage with kings and queens. We wanted them to understand their regality from day one. We wanted their sense of self-efficacy to never intersect with a mindset of poverty, nihilism, and despair. Television was a tool we used to help accomplish this set of objectives.

TV shows like those produced by Mara Brock Akil were exactly what I wanted my children to see. As they have grown older and are able to make their own viewing choices, my children clearly recognize healthy images about Blackness and resist pathological ones, which ultimately reject their normalcy and tell toxic narratives. My now adult daughter has fallen in love with *Love Is ___* and *Being Mary Jane* because of the empowering stories about women they tell.

A fair and balanced range of images of Black lives is the most any community can hope for from any writer, director, or producer. In Mara Brock Akil's work we see a range of representations of Black women and men. It would be unrealistic to have only positive images of any given community. We TV viewers all recognize that there is malady and success in every culture. Even the most culturally conscious media consumer would probably agree that the stories about despair can offer an uplifting commentary about the struggle to achieve success and healthy alternatives in one's life. That plot twist is part of the formula for most scripts. The challenge marginalized groups have experienced watching televisual representations of Black life has been the imbalanced, mostly pejorative stories about that render the Black community bereft of anything worth celebrating, perhaps other than athletic prowess or hip hop music.

There has been quite a renaissance of hit TV shows and films produced, directed, and/or written by Black people within the last twenty-five years. Julie Dash, Spike Lee, Tim Reid, Charles Dutton, Charles Burnett, and John Singleton are no longer the sole producers of healthy narratives about Black life. We now have Mara Brock Akil, Shonda Rhimes, Ava DuVernay, Ryan Coogler, Amma Asante, F. Gary Gray, Gina Prince-Bythewood, Antoine Fuqua, Kasi Lemmons, Jordan Peele, Darnell Martin, Lee Daniels, Malcolm Lee, Troy Byer, Kenya Barris, Tim Story, George Tilman, Jr., Charles Stone, Barry Jenkins, Justin Simien, Paris Barclay, Cheo Hodari Coker, and Steve McQueen to name a few. The fact that we have such a plethora of Black directors and producers telling their own stories means we have more options. The result has largely been more authentic and positive portrayals of blackness.

We must continue to celebrate producers and directors like Mara Brock Akil when they present us with productive narratives that allow Black people to be seen as normal, successful, and positive. It is important for ourselves, our community, and perhaps most importantly our children.

Index

#BlackGirlMagic, x, 13

Akil, Salim, x, 5, 89–90, 103, 106, 139, 154, 179
audience reception, 6, 7, 112
audience studies, 114–15
authenticity, 1, 6, 163;
    authentic, 2–3, 7, 17, 68, 70, 74, 144, 191–92, 194

Barlow, William, 68, 70,137, 153–54, 157.
    See also Split Image: African Americans in the Mass Media
Being Mary Jane, x, 1, 4, 6–7, 13, 44, 47–49, 53–57, 59, 61–62, 64, 67–68, 70, 72–73, 83, 133–34, 137–48, 153–56, 158, 161–63, 166 –70, 177–79, 193
BET. See Black Entertainment Television
Black Entertainment Television (BET), 1–2, 7, 15, 47, 67, 113, 118–19, 122, 126–27, 133–34
Black feminist, 7, 30–31, 52;
    scholarship, 52;
    studies, 52
Black feminist thought, 6, 16–17, 21, 44, 68, 70;
    epistemology, 35, 83
Black Lightning, 5–6, 49, 178, 183–86, 191
Black women's standpoint, 71
Black women's talk, 71–72, 83;
    ethic of caring, 7, 71, 78;
    personal accountability, 115, 117, 123, 124, 129

Collins, Patricia Hill, 6, 16.
    See also Black feminist thought
colorism, 19, 24–25, 97
controlling images, 6, 14, 16, 34–35, 43–44, 68;
    bad black mother, 41;
    black lady, 6, 34–37, 43–44, 51, 61–62, 143;
    breeder, 34;
    diva, 145,160;
    educated black bitch, 51, 59, 61–62;
    freak, 34, 160, 164;
    gold digger, 34–35, 38–40, 43–44, 89, 160;
    Jezebel, 7, 16, 29, 34, 44, 48, 51, 136, 143, 148, 159–60, 163–66, 169–70, 192;
    Mammy, 16, 29, 48, 51, 95, 97, 136, 159–60, 192;
    mule, 34;

Sapphire, 16, 29, 37, 38, 41, 43, 69, 159, 192;
Super Strong Black Woman/ Superwoman, 34–35, 41, 44, 136;
THOT, 163–64;
welfare mother, 34
counter-hegemonic, 7, 97–98, 106
critical discourse analysis, 90, 94–95
CW, 5, 15, 33, 112–13, 118, 121, 126–27

Dates, Jannette, 68, 70,137, 153–54, 157.
   See also Split Image: African Americans in the Mass Media
DuVernay, Ava, 4, 112, 194

encoding-decoding, 114–16

Facebook, 7, 113, 117, 133–34, 137–39, 141–49, 161, 181
femininity, 7, 37, 51, 159
focus groups, 114–19, 123, 127–28
Foucault, Michel, 95–96
friendship, 3, 6–7, 14–15, 23, 44, 67–69, 73, 75, 82–83, 183

The Game, x, 2, 7, 13, 15, 44, 49, 70, 83, 111–13, 117–23, 125–28, 177, 191
gender schema theory, 136
Girlfriends, ix, 2–3, 6, 13–20, 22, 29, 31, 33–35, 43–44, 48–49, 70, 83, 112, 116, 123, 126, 178, 186, 193
Grounded Theory Approach, 181.
   See also grounded theory procedure
grounded theory procedure, 118

Hall, Stuart, 94, 114

identity, 6, 13, 16, 19, 21, 23–27, 29, 31, 99, 116, 124, 126, 156, 158
identity performance, 49
ideological analysis, 72
Insecure, 4, 170.
   See also Rae, Issa
Instagram, 5, 7, 134, 161, 177–85, 187
intersectionality, 14–17, 19–21, 27, 30

The Jamie Foxx Show, ix, 2, 13, 33, 191
Julia, x, 67, 69, 136, 148

Living Single, ix, 14, 69, 88
Love Is ____, x, 5, 7, 49, 70, 83, 87–91, 97–99, 102–6

marriage, 3, 15, 19, 36–38, 41–42, 55, 63, 75, 79–80, 88–89, 104, 144, 167–69
Mary Jane Paul, ix, 1, 44, 47, 50, 60, 133, 153–57, 159, 162–64, 166–67, 170
masculinity, 51, 104
media literacy, 90, 92, 106
media ownership. *See* ownership
Moesha, ix, 2, 13, 126

Olivia Pope, 2, 137, 160, 167, 169.
   See also Scandal
oppression, 16–18, 20, 22, 29–30, 70–71, 135, 157.
   See also Black feminist thought
Oprah Winfrey Network (OWN), ix, 5, 90, 103, 179, 184
OWN. *See* Oprah Winfrey Network
ownership, ix, x, 116, 169

patriarchal, patriarchy, 17, 44, 68, 88, 102,104, 165, 167

qualitative content analysis, 94, 180
Queen Sugar, 4.
   See also DuVernay, Ava

Rae, Issa, ix, 4, 112
The Real Housewives of Atlanta, 67, 69
relatability, 128, 163, 166–67, 169
representation, 3, 14, 30, 47–48, 111, 113, 119, 123, 134–37, 144, 148–49, 153, 163, 165, 167, 169, 178;

of athletes, 125, 128;
authenticity in, 1, 83;
Black womanhood and, 6, 47, 61–62;
framing and media, 91, 93, 102, 108;
gender and, 7, 101–2;
hip hop feminism and, 52;
intersectional, 90–91;
masculinity and Black manhood, 104;
ownership and, ix, x;
racial, 95, 97–98, 123, 128, 146,160;
respectability politics and, 53;
of self-opening, 124;
sisterhood, 67;
television, x, 68–69, 160–61, 166, 191–94;
visual, x, 92–93;
respectability, 6, 47–52, 55, 59–64;
respectability politics, 48–50, 52–53, 60
Rhimes, Shonda, 2, 13, 112, 118, 137, 194

safe spaces, 71, 80.
See also Black feminist thought
Scandal, 1, 67, 137, 148, 153, 160–61, 167–70.
See also Rhimes, Shonda
semiotics, 92
Sex and the City, ix, 14
sexuality, 3, 6, 15, 19, 26–27, 37, 47–52, 59–62, 102, 116, 143–44, 146, 160, 179

showrunner, ix, 1, 3–4, 7–8, 91, 96–97, 112, 118
sisterhood, 6, 13, 15–16, 19–23, 25–27, 29–31, 67, 71–72, 78–80, 186
SnapChat, 161
social construction of reality theory, 156–57
social media, 4, 7, 48, 67, 88–89, 112–13, 128, 133–34, 137–38, 153–58, 161, 170, 177–82, 184, 187
social network sites, 137
social television, 138, 154–55, 157–58, 161, 163
South Central, ix, 13, 33
Split Image: African Americans in the Mass Media, 68

textual analysis, 138–39, 161–62, 170, 180
thematic analysis, 6, 35, 49, 53, 162–63, 170
Twitter, 7, 102, 133–34, 138, 153–58, 160–70

Union, Gabrielle. See Mary Jane Paul
UPN, 14–15, 33, 112
uses and gratifications, 114, 156–58

voice, x, 2, 4, 6–7, 16–18, 21, 25, 29–31, 70–72, 128

WB, 112
Winfrey, Oprah, ix, 183, 186

About the Contributors

Imani M. Cheers, PhD, is an award-winning digital storyteller, director, producer and filmmaker. As a professor of practice, Dr. Cheers uses a variety of mediums including video, photography, television, and film to document and discuss issues impacting and involving people of the African Diaspora. Her scholarly focus is on the intersection of women/girls, technology, health, conflict, agriculture and the effects of climate change in sub-Saharan Africa. Dr. Cheers is also an expert on diversity in Hollywood, specifically the representation of Black women in television and film.

Dr. Cheers is the cocreator and managing editor of Newsroom U, an innovative, immersive multimedia journalism initiative for high school and college students. She is also the executive director for the Global Media Project, an international storytelling program. Before joining SMPA, Dr. Cheers was director of educational resources and a multimedia producer for the PBS NewsHour, a producer/writer at Howard University Television and a multimedia producer at Newsweek.com.

Kandace L. Harris, PhD, is the special assistant to the president and an associate professor of mass communication and media studies at Shaw University. Dr. Harris' honors include being department chair at Johnson C. Smith University, Shaw University, and Clark Atlanta University; the 2012 recipient of the Shaw University Excellence in Academic Teaching Award; a 2014 Who's Who in Black Atlanta "Leader in Academia"; and the 2016 recipient of the Rex Crawley Outstanding Service Award from the National Communication Association's Black Caucus. She most recently authored "Follow Me on Instagram": "Best Self" Identity Construction and Gaze through Hashtag Activism and Selfie Self-Love" in *Women of Color and Social Media Multitasking Blogs, Timelines, Feeds, and Community*.

About the Contributors

Tina M. Harris, PhD, is the Douglas L. Manship, Sr Dori J. Maynard Chair in Race, Media and Cultural Literacy at Louisiana State University in Baton Rouge. Among her responsibilities, Harris actively mentors junior faculty, graduate and undergraduate students navigate academe. Harris' research expertise is on interracial communication, interracial dating, race relations, racial representations of African Americans in film and television, race and ethnic group disparities in health, genetics and religious frameworks, and Christian identity and communication. She is a nationally renowned interracial communication scholar and has co-authored the leading textbook *Interracial Communication: Theory to Practice* (2015; Sage) with African American communication scholar Mark P. Orbe of Western Michigan.

Natasha R. Howard, PhD, earned her doctorate in mass communications and media studies, with a graduate certificate in women's studies, from Howard University in 2012. Currently she is an assistant professor of communication at the Community College of Baltimore County. She is a coeditor of the book *Black Women and Popular Culture: The Conversation Continues* (2014). Dr. Howard has published and presented on her areas of specialization that include hip hop culture, media effects, and representations of the intersections of race, gender, and sexuality in mass media. Outside of the academy, she is also a freelance writer and journalist.

Ronald L. Jackson, II, PhD, is a professor of communication at the University of Cincinnati. Dr. Ronald L. Jackson II is one of the leading communication and identity scholars in the nation. He is author of fourteen books including *Scripting the Black Masculine Body in Popular Media, Interpreting Tyler Perry* (with Jamel Bell) and the 2014 Comic-Con Eisner Award finalist *Black Comics: Politics of Race and Representation* (with Sheena Howard; Bloomsbury). Professor Jackson is the immediate past president of the National Communication Association.

Mia Moody-Ramirez, PhD, is the director of graduate studies, director of American studies and an associate professor of journalism, public relations and new media in the Baylor University College of Arts and Sciences. Her research emphasizes mass media representations of women, persons of color and other underrepresented groups. In 2013, she coauthored *The Obamas and Mass Media: Race, Gender, Religion, and Politics* with Dr. Jannette Dates. She solo authored *Black and Mainstream Press' Framing of Racial Profiling: A Historical Perspective* in 2009. She has presented papers at numerous regional, national, and international conferences and has been published in publications such as *Public Relations Review, Journalism Educator, and the Journal of Magazine & New Media Research*.

About the Contributors

Candace P. Parrish, PhD, is currently the director and assistant professor of strategic communication and public relations mater's program in the School of Communication, Media and the Arts at Sacred Heart University. Having a background in social media research and practice, she is interested in social communication via digital platforms concerning topic areas from public relations to health. Candace has presented research regarding social media (and related topics) internationally and has won awards for her research regarding visual communication, public relations, social media, and health.

Lisa M. Paulin, PhD, is an associate professor in the Department of Mass Communication at North Carolina Central University. She earned her PhD in mass communication from the University of North Carolina, Chapel Hill. Her research focuses on Latinos in media, community journalism and issues of cultural citizenship.

Roslyn M. Satchel, PhD, is an award-winning media and culture scholar-activist. She serves as associate professor of communication and affiliate faculty with the Social Action and Justice Colloquium at Pepperdine University. Dr. Satchel's recent book, *What Movies Teach about Race: Exceptionalism, Erasure and Entitlement* brings her media, legal, and religious background together to examine cultural representations in the most influential films of all time. Dr. Satchel earned a PhD in media and public affairs at Louisiana State University, JD and MDiv degrees at Emory University, and a BA in communication at Howard University. She is an Itinerant Elder in the African Methodist Episcopal Church with more than twenty years in ministry.

Katie D. Scott is a second year PhD student on the accelerated PhD track in the University of Georgia's Department of Communication Studies. Katie holds a BAC from the University of Tennessee. Her research focus centers on women's health, with specific interest in communicating about chronic pain and critiquing the role of power in provider-patient interactions. Katie is also interested in intersectionality, feminist studies, and sexual communication.

Shavonne R. Shorter, PhD, is an assistant professor in the Department of Communication Studies at Bloomsburg University of Pennsylvania. Shorter investigates organizing processes in contexts such as education, politics, and within the media. Her scholarship has been published in *Health Communication, Developing Workforce Diversity Programs, Curriculum, and Degrees in Higher Education, Black Women's Portrayals on Reality Television: The New Sapphire, and The Problematic Tyler Perry*. She has presented at conferences sponsored by the International Communication Association, National Communication Association (Top Paper Recipient), Eastern Communication

Association, and Maryland Communication Association. In her spare time, she is committed to helping students take the steps to achieve their dreams.

Morgan W. Smalls, PhD, is a 2019 graduate of Howard University in the Department of Communication, Culture and Media Studies. She completed her Bachelor of Arts degree in communication and Spanish from Columbia College. She earned her Master of Arts degree in communication from The University of North Carolina at Charlotte. Her areas of research center at the intersection of Africana, women and gender, and media studies. Specifically, she uses popular culture as an entryway into larger conversations about race, class and gender. She is interested in the portrayal of Black women in media and social media and the counter narratives that are created to combat sexism, racism, and the lack of representation or misrepresentation in traditional media, such as television and film.

Shauntae Brown White, PhD, is an associate professor in the Department of Mass Communication at North Carolina Central University where she also serves as the coordinator of the women's and gender studies program. White's research focuses on media images of Black women, the politics of hair in the African American community and the negotiated roles of African American pastors' wives.